Got
What
It
Takes?

Got What It Takes?

Successful
People
Reveal
How They
Made It
to the Top

Bill Boggs

Collins
An Imprint of HarperCollins Publishers

HarperCollins books may be purchased for educational, business, or sales promotional use. For information, please write: Special Markets Department, HarperCollins Publishers, 10 East 53rd Street, New York, NY 10022.

FIRST EDITION

Designed by rlf design

Library of Congress Cataloging-in-Publication Data

Boggs, Bill.
    Got what it takes? : successful people reveal how they made it to the top / Bill Boggs.—1st ed.
        p.   cm.
    ISBN: 978-0-06-112292-7
        1. Success.   2. Celebrities—Interviews.   I. Title.
BF637.S8B575 2007
158.1—dc22

                                                                2006051696

07 08 09 10   10 9 8 7 6 5 4 3 2 1

For MUD

"Lives of great men all remind us we can make our lives sublime, and, departing, leave behind us, footprints on the sands of time."

—Henry Wadsworth Longfellow, 1838

Contents

One: The Path to Success

Two: The Mind-sets of Success

Three: The Practices of Success

Four: The Challenges of Success

Five: Advice for Success

Preface

During the thirty years I've spent in show business, I've had the privilege of interviewing thousands of famous and influential people, and I've always been fascinated by the enduring mystery of what makes one person more successful than another.

When you see a group of talented dancers in a music video, why do you suppose one goes on to become a star while the others fall by the wayside? Take any group of inexperienced interns at a major corporation: why does one aspiring mogul break away from the pack, soar past all competition, and end up running the whole company?

Is it merely a matter of a given individual being more talented than the rest? Is the person who succeeds simply just better at self-invention? Or luckier? What internal qualities or external resources does it take to triumph over obstacles? Is there some aspect of personality or character—optimism, perhaps, or stamina, or maybe just a stubborn refusal to accept defeat—that elevates certain contenders above countless rivals? Is it a question of passion, drive, hard work? Is it about who you know?

Of course, it's all of these things, and more. Determined to unlock the secrets of success, I set out on a mission to discover the hidden factors that have catapulted some of our era's most highly regarded leaders to the top in a wide range of fields. Over the course of a year, I interviewed forty-four different people, and—perhaps unsurprisingly—I heard forty-four different versions of "what it takes."

In the case of **Mark Burnett,** the groundbreaking producer who pioneered reality television with mega-hits like *Survivor* and *The Apprentice*, his instinct for choosing projects that resonated with his own personal passions infused his work with tremendous energy. **Diane von Furstenberg** is convinced that her fearlessless—a priceless gift bestowed upon her by her mother, a Holocaust survivor—is the quality that propelled her to become one of the most famous fashion designers in the world. **Bill O'Reilly,** host of the provocative FOX News show *The O'Reilly Factor* as well as a best-selling author, set out to conquer television and made every sacrifice necessary to reach that goal. Having turned himself into a household name, he credits his ability to persevere and keep his eye laser-focused on his objective. **Bill Bratton,** the only person to become police commissioner of the NYPD and also chief of the LAPD, believes that his achievements are the result of his relentless hunger for new challenges—a deep-seated drive that motivates him to seek ever-more-demanding assignments.

In tracking down such nuggets of self-knowledge, my quest took me from the Yankees' spring training camp in Tampa, where I interviewed the team's legendary manager **Joe Torre,** to the Embarcadero district of San Francisco, where I met with **Tom Perkins,** the venture-capital lion of Silicon Valley. I sat backstage at NBC's *Today* show with co-host **Matt Lauer,** walked the hallowed halls of the *New York Times* with Op-Ed columnist **Frank Rich,** and visited songwriter **Diane Warren**'s platinum-record-lined offices in Hollywood. Throughout my travels, my objective was to elicit the crucial insights that could guide and galvanize others.

You'll hear from **Sir Richard Branson,** the billionaire who set out to change the world by revolutionizing one industry at a time, and who has since become a leader in fields that range from music to aerospace. You'll learn what I was told by former New York governor **Mario Cuomo,** who invoked the immigrant legacy of his Italian parents in explaining his compulsion to out-work anyone. I'll share what I heard from **Anna Quindlen,** the Pulitzer Prize–winning journalist and novelist who, despite countless accolades, confesses that even now she sometimes secretly feels like a fraud.

You'll discover the early beginnings of celebrities like **Joy Behar,** who only found the courage to get up onstage when she was so broke that she had no choice. You'll peek inside the heart and mind of Academy Award-winning actress **Renée Zellweger,** whose fierce commitment to creative fulfillment trumps any amount of fame or fortune. And—speaking of Trump—I'll share with you what that indefatigable icon of success himself, **Donald Trump,** had to say about how he became the multi-industry powerhouse he is today.

My goal in writing this book is to share their insights and others' in order to help you when you find yourself temporarily stymied, or simply unsure of how to proceed in pursuing your own dreams. The book is organized around the most consistent themes that emerged from dozens of in-depth conversations, so you can zero in on the topics that most interest you. Interwoven throughout are additional smart tips and fascinating tales, along with some personal stories about my own career and the lessons I've learned.

For those of you who are just starting out in the work world, there is valuable advice on getting hired, making decisions, seizing opportunity, sustaining the will to prevail, and more. For those who are already on their way, stories about hard work, taking risks, and collecting wisdom abound. Those facing challenges along the road to success will be heartened by the inspirational examples of champions who learned how to triumph over fear, insecurity, adversity—and their own mistakes.

All of the industry leaders I interviewed were willing to share their hard-won wisdom and insights into the personal qualities they developed that enabled them to succeed in their particular realm. Since each individual's path and personality is unique, what one person swears is essential for success might be the polar opposite of what another equally illustrious person says. Taken together, however, their insights provide an invaluable primer on success—and how to achieve it. I hope that you will glean whatever is particularly relevant to your own quest.

We all know people who are disappointed when success proves elusive, often for reasons they don't fully understand. In sharing the secrets of some of today's greatest achievers, my goal is to instruct and inspire everyone who would like to follow in their footsteps.

My own life has long been enhanced by the amazing lessons I've learned from some of the most impressive people in the country, who have succeeded in fields ranging from the entertainment industry to sports to business and beyond. I hope you'll be able to use the practical wisdom, animating values, and inspiring examples provided in these pages to enrich your own life, and put you on the path toward accomplishing your highest goals.

Bon Voyage!

—Bill Boggs
  July 2006
  New York City

Biographies in Brief

Before we get started, I thought it would be helpful to illuminate the accomplishments of the "guests" in this book, so you can understand the unique reasons each is eminently qualified to discuss what it takes to achieve great success.

Joseph Abboud is an internationally acclaimed fashion designer, whose menswear line epitomizes earthy elegance. Joseph began his career as a salesperson, while still in high school, at the illustrious store Louis of Boston and worked his way up to become one of Polo Ralph Lauren's top designers. He launched his own label in 1987, which has since grown into a $150 million worldwide business and earned him the Council of Fashion Designers of America award as Best Menswear Designer two years in a row. Joseph sold the company in 2005 and is currently pursuing television-related interests.

Preston Bailey is the party/event planner the crème de la crème turn to when they want lavish, over-the-top glamour. He has created events for celebrities such as Donald Trump, Liza Minnelli, Matt Lauer, and many others. A native of Panama, Preston is the classic American success story, having arrived in the United States in 1970 with little more than a few dollars in his pocket. His early foray into event planning began with flower arranging, from which he amassed a following of high-end clients.

Maria Bartiromo has it all: brains, beauty, and bravery. In 1995, she made history as the first woman ever to report live from the New York Stock Exchange trading room floor. Today she is considered one of the leading financial journalists in the country. Maria is the host and managing editor of CNBC's nationally syndicated *The Wall Street Journal Report with Maria Bartiromo,* as well as the anchor of *Closing Bell with Maria Bartiromo.* She also regularly appears on NBC's *Today* show and writes a column for *Reader's Digest.*

Joy Behar is a co-host of ABC-TV's long-running hit show *The View.* She's a straight shooter who is blessed with natural comedic talents. Joy honed her skills in small comedy clubs in New York City, eventually going on to win a CableACE Award. The multitalented Joy has starred in her own HBO special, hosted a popular political radio show on WABC, appeared in several films, including Woody Allen's *Manhattan Murder Mystery,* and written a book, *Joy Shtick: Or What Is the Existential Vacuum and Does It Come with Attachments?*

Cathie Black has been one of the leading figures in American publishing for the past two decades, earning her the title "The First Lady of American Magazines." She began as a sales rep, and now as the CEO of Hearst Publications, she manages the financial performance and development of some of the industry's best-known titles: *Cosmopolitan, Esquire, Good Housekeeping, Harper's Bazaar, O, The Oprah Magazine, Redbook*—nineteen magazines in all.

James Blake is a professional tennis player whose star is steadily rising. After being named Rookie of the Year for the 2000 World Team Tennis season, he went on to become the third African American man to play the Davis Cup for the United States, and twice won the Hopman Cup. He surprised the world by returning to the court after overcoming three concurrent, horrific events:

breaking his neck, contracting shingles, and losing his father to cancer. Millions watched him during the 2005 US Open, where he played a stunning five-set match against Andre Agassi. Agassi won that match, but James won the adoration of the world with his sportsmanship.

Daniel Boulud is one of the premier French chefs in the United States. Since his early days growing up on a farm in Lyon, Daniel has created an empire in his name. He was the executive chef at Le Cirque for six years, guiding the restaurant to become *Gault Millau's* choice for best restaurant in the United States. Daniel now has restaurant outposts in New York, Palm Beach, and Las Vegas. He has amassed a stunning array of commendations, including Outstanding Chef of the Year at the James Beard Awards and Chef of the Year by *Bon Appétit* magazine. He has authored numerous books, including *Daniel's Dish: Entertaining at Home with a Four-Star Chef* and *Daniel Boulud's Café Boulud Cookbook*.

Sir Richard Branson is the swashbuckling entrepreneur behind the powerful Virgin brand that encompasses an airline, record stores, and many other businesses. As well known for his maverick sporting endeavors as his business acumen (he successfully flew in the first hot-air balloon to cross the Atlantic), Sir Richard has an inherent taste for trailblazing. Beginning at the age of fifteen with the outspoken publication *Student Magazine,* he has revolutionized a multitude of industries and is today one of the most successful and influential industrialists in the world. His newest endeavor is Virgin Galactic, which aims to take paying civilians into suborbital space.

Bill Bratton is one of the nation's premier law enforcement officers. He is the chief of police for the LAPD and is the only person ever to have commanded both the LAPD and the NYPD. With supreme confidence and a hunger for new challenges, Bill is steadily reengineering the department. In only three years, he dramatically lowered the crime rate and increased responsiveness, much as he did in New York City during his term. Bill began his career as a beat cop in a tough Boston neighborhood, where a superior noted about the self-assured young officer, "That kid's gonna be police commissioner one day."

Bobbi Brown personifies the natural, easy-going elegance of her popular Bobbi Brown cosmetics line. Bobbi studied theatrical makeup at Emerson College and began her career as a freelance makeup artist in New York City. Frustrated by the inadequate, boring makeup colors available, she created the products she most wanted to use, and what eventually became a million-dollar company was born. Today Bobbi serves as the CEO of Bobbi Brown Worldwide, which sells cosmetics in more than four hundred stores and twenty countries. She is the author of three books, *Bobbi Brown Beauty: The Ultimate Beauty Resource, Bobbi Brown Teenage Beauty,* and *Bobbi Brown Evolution: A Guide to a Lifetime of Beauty.*

Mark Burnett is the Emmy Award–winning creator and producer of breakthrough reality television series including *Survivor, The Apprentice,* and *Eco-Challenge.* With his out-of-the-box thinking and precise vision, he literally changed the landscape of American television. He is repeatedly named among the Top 101 Most Powerful People in Entertainment by *Entertainment Weekly,* and was featured as one of the most influential people in the world in *Time* magazine's Time 100 list. Mark came to the United States from England; his first job here was selling T-shirts on Venice Beach.

Peter Cincotti, twenty-three, is one of the leading musical voices of his generation. The singer, pianist, composer, and arranger—who began composing at age nine—became one of the hottest pop and jazz sensations to hit the scene in 2003 when his self-titled critically acclaimed CD hit the top of the charts. His second CD for Concord Records achieved similiar success. In 2007, Peter will release his debut CD for Warner Brothers, a major work of his own compositions that will be the prelude to his third world tour.

Jim Cramer is the dynamic host of CNBC-TVs popular show *Mad Money with Jim Cramer,* director of the stock-picking website TheStreet.com, host of the radio show *Real Money with Jim Cramer,* and the author of four nonfiction books. Best known for his wild antics on television and brilliant stock analysis, Jim originally made a name for himself on Wall Street as a hedge-fund manager, earning record returns. A true self-made man, Jim has valuable insights to share on what it takes to succeed.

Mario Cuomo is the former three-term governor of New York State. As the son of two Italian immigrants who worked day and night to support their family, Mario is known for his unsurpassed work ethic. Early in his life, he played minor league baseball, before an unfortunate knock on the head took him out of the game and changed the course of his life. His early foray into politics was representing residents of Queens when they opposed a construction project. He was appointed New York secretary of state in 1975, then became governor in 1983. Today, Mario practices law at a prestigious New York City firm.

Clive Davis is the mastermind behind many of the most notable recording artists of the past four decades, including Janis Joplin, Bruce Springsteen, Barry Manilow, Whitney Houston, and Alicia

Keys. With a keen eye for spotting talent and an innate drive to be the best, Clive systematically turned Columbia Records, Arista, and then J Records into music industry powerhouses. He is the consummate mogul in appearance and manner, and his beloved status led to his being the only nonmusician ever to be inducted into the Rock and Roll Hall of Fame.

Frédéric Fekkai is an internationally acclaimed celebrity hairstylist who began his career cutting hair in Paris. Today his salons in New York and Palm Beach command hundreds of dollars a cut. His drive to succeed has led to a hugely profitable line of premium beauty products that are considered among the best on the market.

Bobby Flay is a celebrity chef, television personality, and restaurateur. Bobby is a master of southwestern-with-a-twist cuisine, with restaurants in New York, Atlantic City, Las Vegas, and the Atlantis Resort in the Bahamas. He is the author of several cookbooks, including *Boy Meets Grill* and *Bobby Flay's Bold American Food,* as well as the host of three Food Network shows. He is also an Iron Chef on Food Network's *Iron Chef America.*

Jane Friedman, president and CEO of HarperCollins Worldwide, is a confident leader and a true visionary. She is constantly seeking, or creating, the next frontier; in the early 1970s she popularized the author tour, in 1985 she pioneered the audiobook business for the publishing industry, and in 2006 HarperCollins became the first publisher to create a global digital warehouse. Under her guidance, HarperCollins has become one of the world's largest publishing houses. Jane worked her way up the old-fashioned way: she began as a dictaphone typist at Random House and moved up the ranks through hard work and the will to succeed. She has received countless awards, including being named one of the Top 101 Most Powerful People in Entertainment by

Entertainment Weekly and was included on *Vanity Fair*'s list of 200 Women Legends, Leaders, and Trailblazers.

Christie Hefner has been chairman and CEO of Playboy Enterprises since 1988. She is credited with turning the company around from its lowest point in history and shaping it into the global powerhouse it is today. She guided Playboy into electronic media, making *Playboy* the first national magazine on the Internet. Today, the distribution of digital content is the largest profit center for the company. Christie is an intellectual heavyweight with the grace of a ballerina—a unique but very useful combination of traits that has made her one of the most successful executives in the magazine industry.

Linda Huett joined Weight Watchers as a member in 1983 to shed post-pregnancy pounds; by the year 1999, she became the president of Weight Watchers International and was named CEO one year later. Determined, focused, and professional, Linda has much to offer on the subject of starting at the bottom and climbing the corporate ladder to success.

Senator Kay Bailey Hutchison was the first woman ever elected to represent Texas in the United States Senate. In her second reelection, she received more than four million votes—more than any other candidate in the state's history. Humble and hardworking, Senator Hutchison serves in the Senate's leadership as vice chairman of the Senate Republican Conference. Prior to her career in politics, she was also Houston's first female television reporter, and has much to say about overcoming the obstacles women face in their careers.

Richard Johnson edits the high-profile gossip column Page Six in the *New York Post*. In a field where many would burn out from the seven-day-a-week pressure of writing, researching, and producing two pages of information, Richard has flourished for more than twenty years. He appears frequently on television and radio as an expert witness to the celebrity news scene.

Rikki Klieman is a legal analyst for the *Today* show and Court TV. She was designated by *Time* magazine as one of the country's leading trial attorneys, and has also achieved success as an actor and as the author of the best-selling *Fairy Tales Can Come True: How a Driven Woman Changed Her Destiny.* Indomitable, brilliant, and driven, there is no challenge Rikki is not capable of tackling.

Matt Lauer is the longtime host of the number-one-rated morning program in America, NBC's *Today* show. Matt began his career like many others in television: working in small markets. He enjoyed early success, but then faced several serious career setbacks. He never gave up, and ultimately prevailed by landing one of the top jobs in all of television.

Norman Lear is one of the most influential forces in the history of American television. He wrote and produced landmark series including *All in the Family, Sanford and Son,* and *Maude.* A master of collaboration, Norman has partnered with some of the best in the business to continually introduce cutting-edge programming. The name of his production company in the 1970s says it all: T.A.T., which is an acronym for a Yiddish phrase meaning, "Putting one's butt on the line."

Phil Lombardo rose from poverty to achieve untold wealth in the television business. Starting as an actor in local TV, then a director and a producer, Phil went on to become the first Italian American to manage an American television station. He then became the CEO of Corinthian Broadcasting, but left to risk forming his own company, Citadel Communications. He soared to even greater heights by acquiring ownership of seven television stations. Phil has also served as joint board chairman of the National Association of Broadcasters.

Jeff Lurie purchased the Philadelphia Eagles in 1994 for a record $185 million—the most ever paid in this country for a professional football team. Some thought the purchase was a risky venture, but the visionary Jeff Lurie knew what he was doing. Under his steady hand, the Eagles have become hugely profitable on the balance sheets and have been more successful on the playing field than at any other period in the team's history. Jeff is a power player with the soul of a swami, and his levelheaded leadership style prompted *The Sporting News* and *Pro Football Insider* to name him NFL Owner of the Year in 1995 and 2000, respectively.

Sirio Maccioni was orphaned after World War II in his native Italy. He came to New York City as a young waiter determined to make his way in the world. Today he is one of the leading restaurateurs of the world as the force behind the long-running success of Le Cirque. He and his wife, Edgi, and their sons Mario, Marco, and Mauro operate Le Cirque and Circo in New York and Las Vegas and Le Cirque in Mexico City. The Maccionis epitomize an outstanding family success story.

Craig Newmark founded the Internet website Craigslist.com that has revolutionized the way millions of people post classified ads. A self-proclaimed uber-nerd on a mission, Craig has a simple yet meaningful objective: to help people do everyday things with more ease. Whether you are looking to sell a couch or find a job, Craigslist.com has become the go-to site in cities across the country. Craig is based in San Francisco, where Craigslist.com originated.

Bill O'Reilly is the host of Fox News Channel's most-watched show, *The O'Reilly Factor,* and the author of five books, four of which reached number one on the *New York Times* Best Sellers list. Bill is an Emmy Award–winning television journalist who is famous for his provocative views and no-nonsense approach. Prior to *The O'Reilly Factor,* he was a correspondent for ABC's *World News Tonight.* Bold, confident, and commanding, Bill is a straight shooter who aimed for the top and definitely hit his target.

Mehmet Oz, M.D., is one of the country's most renowned heart surgeons. His schedule is a busy one: he is a professor and vice chairman of surgery at Columbia University, the director of the Cardiovascular Institute, a best-selling author (coauthor of *You: The Owner's Manual* and *You: The Smart Patient*), and a regular contributor to *The Oprah Winfrey Show.* Dr. Oz is a gifted communicator on a mission to educate people on how to protect their health.

Tom Perkins is a lion of the venture-capital world. As one of the original pioneers of Silicon Valley, he and his company funded some of the greats: Google, Genentech, and many others. Prior to launching his company in 1972, Tom was the first general manager of Hewlett-Packard's computer division and is credited with steering that company toward the enormous success it enjoys today. A classic mogul with a taste for the finer things in life, Tom built himself the world's largest yacht.

Bob Pittman has been instrumental in the success of several major consumer brands, including MTV, America Online, and Six Flags, by recognizing their common thread: their potential for mass-market adoption. First recognized for his success in turning around failing radio stations, Pittman moved into television and took advantage of the emerging cable-television industry to develop a channel combining two great consumer loves—music and television. He is widely credited as the founding father of MTV and is the former CEO of MTV Networks. Later, as CEO, he transformed both Six Flags theme parks and then Century 21 Real Estate before joining America Online, where he transformed the Internet into a mass-market consumer product, changing how we live, work, communicate, organize, and entertain ourselves. Pittman is a true visionary with vast business experience and insight into the crucial role risk plays in anyone's path to success.

Anna Quindlen has been capturing the minds and hearts of readers for more than thirty years. This Pulitzer Prize–winning journalist has written for some of America's most influential newspapers, including the *New York Times*, for which she wrote a regular column from 1981 to 1994; she has had a biweekly column in *Newsweek* magazine since 2000. Anna is also a novelist and has published four best-selling novels, one of which, *One True Thing*, was made into a major motion picture starring Meryl Streep. The best way to describe Anna is to say that she reminds one of the smartest and nicest girl in the senior class.

Frank Rich is another *New York Times* writer of acclaim to generously donate his time and insights to this book. As the paper's former drama critic and current columnist, Frank writes eloquent and brilliant commentary that has made him a favorite of readers. He is also the author of a memoir, *Ghost Light*. Prior to joining the *New York Times*, Frank was a film and television critic at *Time* magazine.

David Rockwell is the gifted architect and designer behind such innovative spaces as the Kodak Theatre in Hollywood; the restaurant Mad in London; Nobu, Vong, and the Grand Central Terminal Dining Concourse in New York City; and Mesa Grill in

Las Vegas; as well as the Mohegan Sun Casino in Connecticut. He has also designed the sets for hit Broadway shows including *Hairspray, The Rocky Horror Show,* and *Dirty Rotten Scoundrels.* His unique vision and determination to break through any and all perceived limitations make his a truly cutting-edge career.

Judith Rodin, Ph.D., was the first woman ever to be named president of an Ivy League college (The University of Pennsylvania). After leading the university for more than a decade, she broke through yet another barrier when she became the first woman named as president of the Rockefeller Foundation. A clinically trained psychologist, Dr. Rodin has fascinating insights into the ways of the human mind. She knows not only what it takes to succeed, but what it takes to rebound when we *don't* succeed—perhaps the most important factor of all.

Brooke Shields has had three tremendously successful career phases: first as a child and teen model (appearing in a now-classic Calvin Klein ad), then as a motion picture and television actress (*The Blue Lagoon, Suddenly Susan*), and later as a star of the Broadway stage in *Cabaret, Chicago,* and *Wonderful Town.* Beneath the beauty and genuine niceness that are her trademarks lies an iron resolve; Brooke, very simply, never gives up. She is driven to achieve her personal best in every endeavor, and it shows.

Joe Torre somehow manages to remain cool and collected no matter how tense things might get. As the manager of the New York Yankees, Joe has to answer to a press corps equal in size to the one that covers the White House, yet he never seems to waver. Joe had his share of setbacks prior to joining the Yankees—he was fired from three other teams—yet his steadfast belief in his vision prevailed, and he has led the Yankees to four World Championships, six American League Championships, and nine American League East titles. He is, by all accounts, an inspirational leader and a true winner.

Donald Trump's name has become synonymous with success. As the chairman and president of the Trump Organization, he has revolutionized the world of real estate like no other mogul in recent history. He has myriad outstanding properties, ranging from his world-renowned Trump Tower in New York City to the Trump International Hotel and Tower in Chicago, to Mar-A-Lago golf resort in Palm Beach, and Donald Trump continually sets new standards of excellence. But Donald doesn't stop at real estate. He is the best-selling author of *The Art of the Deal* and *Surviving at the Top,* and the mastermind and star of NBC's runaway hit reality show *The Apprentice.* Donald Trump is unstoppable in his vision and will to prevail.

Diane von Furstenberg made her mark on the fashion world in the mid 1970s when she designed her legendary wrap dress, which has remained a classic to this day. Elegant, fluid, and self-assured, Diane is fearless in her pursuits. A native of Brussels, Belgium, and the daughter of a Holocaust survivor, Diane came to America with little more than a simple knowledge of how a garment factory works. In a short time, she capitalized on her contacts and turned her brand into a household name. Today, Diane's clothing line is sold worldwide.

Diane Warren is known as one of the most prolific and successful songwriters of our time. Her extraordinary work ethic and drive have also earned her a reputation as the hardest-working woman in the music business. Diane has written songs for legends such as Elton John, Tina Turner, Barbra Streisand, Celine Dion, Whitney Houston, Cher, and many more. Her songs have also been featured in more than ninety motion pictures. With a Grammy to her name and countless number one hits, she shows no sign of slowing down. Diane is a shining example of what one can accomplish through unstoppable determination and hard work.

Renée Zellweger is one of the most beloved young actresses on the scene today. Since her breakout role in *Jerry Maguire* in 1996, Renée has captured the hearts of moviegoers around the world. She won an Academy Award for her role in *Cold Mountain,* was nominated for her gutsy performance in the movie version of *Chicago,* and also received a nomination from the academy for her hilariously nuanced work in *Bridget Jones's Diary*. Renée is the rarest among Hollywood actresses: centered, down-to-earth, and wholly dedicated to bringing her best to every performance, regardless of the size of the paycheck. Her insights about how "it's the doing that matters" lend a refreshing perspective.

Jeff Zucker is the CEO of the NBC Universal Television Group. Jeff made broadcasting history at the age of twenty-six, when he was the youngest person ever appointed as executive producer of the *Today* show, and his rise has been steady ever since. Under his leadership, the show was the nation's most-watched morning news program. Later, as the president of NBC Entertainment, he made NBC into a top-ranked network with hits such as *Law and Order: Criminal Intent, Scrubs, Las Vegas,* and *The Apprentice*. He is credited for creating the network's original summer programming that spurred a now-common industry trend. Today, he oversees all the network, news, and cable outlets of NBC.

Introduction
The Reasons for Success

I began each interview with the same question:

"Many people start out in your profession as you did—be it selling in a clothing store, going to Wall Street, cutting hair, getting a job in law, working at a little TV station, and so on—but very few have risen to the heights you have and accomplished what you have done. So, with that in mind, if you were speaking to the person reading this book who is hoping to excel in their career, **Why do you think you've been successful?**"

I initially asked this because I thought it would be interesting to hear what each person believed was the reason for their success, and, of course, it was. But eventually, I realized that the replies to this one simple question cumulatively formed an unofficial blueprint for success. Here's some immediate insight into the fascinating minds and characters of those who will reveal themselves in this book.

• • •

"I think I've been successful because, first of all, I have great stamina and resilience. And that's one of the things that has taken me along. You can keep going, keep going, keep going, but you are always going to have down days, and down years, and down months. **You have to be able to have the stamina and resilience to rebound and keep going.**

"I have natural energy, but I also think that stamina is just coming back and coming back and doing it again and again. That is partly innate, and partly that I'm very competitive."

—**Maria Bartiromo,** host of *Wall Street Journal Report with Maria Bartiromo* and CNBC's *Closing Bell with Maria Bartiromo*

"I believe that from day number one, **I've loved the business. And I was good at the business, and was very ambitious— not tortured by ambition, but very ambitious.** I think a lot of us women were raised to have expectations, but they weren't huge expectations. Many of our mothers wanted us to be teachers, perhaps have a family. But my dad had a huge influence on my life. I mean, he thought I could be anything I wanted. So I had that DNA gene in me."

—**Cathie Black,** president of Hearst Magazines

"Well, obviously, in tennis, there is the element of athletic ability. That's something that I'm just lucky to be blessed with. But otherwise, what has set me apart from I think a lot of other people is the work to get there. **You have to have motivation on your own; you have to be pushed on your own.**"

—**James Blake,** professional tennis player

"First of all, there's a very thin dividing line between success and failure. And I've been fortunate to just have stayed on the right side of that dividing line. Most people who start with nothing and sort of set up in business do fail. So, in order to succeed, **you just have to throw yourself wholeheartedly into what you're doing**. You have to passionately believe in what you're doing. You have to make sure that all the people around you passionately believe in what they're doing, and what you're doing. You have to be good at motivating and bringing out the best in people, and make sure that you appreciate those people. And then at least you have a chance of staying on the right side of that dividing line."

—**Sir Richard Branson,** international entrepreneur

"**I'm always willing to make a change.** I've never been any place in my life that I'm so content that I'm not looking for the next opportunity. I have a degree of self-confidence that, if I want to make a change, I can. The world is full of opportunities to be taken advantage of."

—**Bill Bratton,** chief of the Los Angeles Police Department

"It's really just **about having something in your gut that you're not going to fail**. You know, I think my being naïve—very, very naïve in the business world, and just in the cosmetics industry—has really helped me. Because I just never thought I would fail."

—**Bobbi Brown,** CEO of Bobbi Brown Worldwide

"My success probably has come from **choosing to start projects that I had a lot of congruency with,** where my actions and thoughts were in sync. I really cared about the projects. I really liked *Eco-Challenge*. I really liked *Survivor*. In fact, I didn't know if I'd make a penny from *Survivor*, but I knew the work would be good. And I believed that it would, at the very least, be a great key to a door in Hollywood."

—**Mark Burnett,** television producer (*Survivor, The Apprentice, Eco-Challenge*)

"**Support from my family** and my mother in particular. I think the way in which music was presented to me was vital to why it's become so woven into my life. It was never forced on me, but it was encouraged. I've never considered another option."

—**Peter Cincotti,** singer, pianist, and composer

"I have well in excess of the regular amount of enthusiasm for things that other people are not enthusiastic about. I have tremendous passion for what I do. And I am one of those people who is indefatigable, in the true sense that I beg someone to find someone who can outwork me. **I have always prided myself that no one can outwork me.** No one."

> —**Jim Cramer,** host of CNBC's *Mad Money with Jim Cramer* and founder of TheStreet.com

"I think the **incredible education** that came out of the Brooklyn public school system was amazing. I was always a good student. I was always impelled to succeed. That was within me."

> —**Clive Davis,** music industry mogul

"It's an interesting question, because, first of all, the word 'successful' scares the hell out of me. I'm not trying to be humble, or anything like that. **Being successful is like being on a bicycle. Once you think you are successful, you may fall off, because you do not pedal anymore.**"

> —**Frédéric Fekkai,** celebrity hairstylist and owner of Beauté de Provence salon

"I think, first of all, **I was lucky enough to find something that I really wanted to do**. And I really think that's the most important thing for longevity. I hate to use the word 'passionate,' because it's such a cliché, but that's a word that obviously comes to mind. I'm passionate about cooking."

> —**Bobby Flay,** restaurateur, cookbook author, and host of Food Network's *FoodNation* and *Boy Meets Grill*

"I think it goes back to, probably, when I was born. I grew up in a household in which my father was an artist and my mother was a model, which is sort of a cultural environment. **I was told from the time I was born that I could be anything and do anything I wanted.** And that has remained with me all my life.

"I hope I have passed that on to my children, because the most important thing I feel that a young person can have is that first support. I have seen many young people who have no confidence, because they were not told that they could do and be, and that they were smart, and that they were fun, and that they were interesting. Those were all things that I heard about myself from the time I was, you know, six, ten years old."

—**Jane Friedman,** CEO of HarperCollins Worldwide

"**I actually don't think about it.** I truly don't stop and think about either being successful or, as a corollary, why I'm successful."

—**Christie Hefner,** chairman and chief executive
    of Playboy Enterprises, Inc.

"**I'm a hard worker. I don't call in sick too often, and I like the daily deadline.** I think a lot of people might burn out after doing this for two or three years. But that's how I've done it."

—**Richard Johnson,** editor of the *New York Post*'s Page Six

"**I think I'm successful because I grew up with this label from my parents, for better or worse, that I was called 'Miss Remarkable.'** I got that nickname at birth. My parents had not had children for seventeen years of marriage. They decided to go through adoption proceedings, and at that point, my mother got pregnant. So I was labeled 'Miss Remarkable' as I emerged from the womb. My scripting as a child was, 'You can be anything you want. You can do anything you want. If you want to be president of the United States, you can do that.'

"Extraordinary positive reinforcement from the time I was born made me fearless. I never thought about issues of failure. I never thought about the fact that I could not do something. It doesn't mean there weren't things I could not do. But I was fearless. So I think the reason I am successful came from the way my parents scripted me from the time I was born."

—**Rikki Klieman,** Court TV anchor and
    legal analyst for NBC's *Today* show

"I think a lot of it is great work ethic. There's no question about it. I mean, **you have to be willing to put the work in that's required**. I know a couple of people who've been successful by accident, but they usually don't stay successful by accident. Then they have to put the work in. But I think the story with most of the people I know—and in my case, it's something I've been very conscious about—has been: you've got to make a decision in your life that it is going to take a certain amount of work to get to this place and then maintain that place. And if you're not willing to do the amount of work, then you should settle for something less. So I think work ethic has probably been the most important thing."

—**Matt Lauer,** co-host of NBC's *Today* show

"**I am a great collaborator. Not just writing; I'm a great collaborator in life.** Not that I haven't been a good writer, and not that I haven't been very aggressive about finishing things, getting done on time. I have a great drive to get it right. But there's always been somebody there to push me, to collaborate with me, to argue with me—and cause me to find the next best idea."

—**Norman Lear,** television writer and producer
    (*All in the Family, Sanford and Son, Maude*)

"I think it's a combination of things. **I never got discouraged.** And because I was determined to make it in this business and somehow get a job, both my immediate family and my extended family always responded positively to that. And they always kept their eyes open for Phil."

—**Phil Lombardo,** joint board chairman of the National Association of Broadcasters, and owner of multiple television stations

"**I actually think one of the reasons I've been successful is that I recognize the fragility of life.** Having had a father die when I was nine years old, you kind of realize that the time you have is very, very precious. And so, whatever I've wanted to study, work at, do in terms of recreation, friendships, relationships of any type, I think I sort of select and conduct myself as if you can't be really sure that you're going to have it forever. And therefore, you want to make the best of it."

—**Jeff Lurie,** owner of the Philadelphia Eagles

"There's a bunch of factors. Part of it was **feeling committed from the beginning**. When people suggested more than a simple e-mail list for events, I responded to that, and solicited more feedback. Did that. And we do that to this day. We listen pretty seriously to people, doing what we can, what makes sense."

—**Craig Newmark,** founder of Craigslist.com

"I was willing to be very, very disciplined, and persevere. All right? So if I didn't like the situation, I got out of the situation. I didn't let people abuse me. I just got another job. Most people aren't like that. So, you have to be very motivated to be very ambitious, and you have to persevere. **When you have a setback,** the old cliché is you get up and you dust yourself off. But it's true."

—**Bill O'Reilly,** host of *The O'Reilly Factor*

"I guess the thing I'm most proud of is that the formula we set up in 1972 still works. We haven't changed anything. **We stumbled across a way of doing business that has paid off enormously, and we just keep doing it.** And we're still excited about it."

—**Tom Perkins,** Silicon Valley venture capitalist

"Oh, that's such a difficult question. But I'm frequently asked whether I had a plan. A five-year plan, a ten-year plan. At thirty years old, the idea that you would have said, 'Over the next twenty years, I'm going to do a succession of columns for the *New York Times,* win the Pulitzer Prize, do a bunch of best-selling novels, and have three kids,' would have been unthinkable to me. So **my approach to my work was always incremental**. What can I do that scares me a lot?"

—**Anna Quindlen,** Pulitzer Prize–winning columnist
    and best-selling author

"**You have to have a passion for something.** In my case, it was for writing and theater. But it could have been for playing chess, or tennis. If you have a passion, that's a huge motivating factor. And for whatever reason, from a very early age, really before I was in two digits, I fell in love with the theater and I got interested in writing and reading."

—**Frank Rich,** columnist for the *New York Times*

"**I really, really love what I do.** I love engaging people, and I think that buildings, architecture, design, are in some ways about creating emotional connections. I feel lucky that my personal interest is about creating places that engage people."

> —**David Rockwell,** architect and founder and
> CEO of Rockwell Group

"**I think I've learned many lessons about success along the way, and I have applied them over and over again.** I have learned the value of perseverance. I think I've learned hard work. I believe in myself. I kind of have an internal compass, acquired self-confidence through life experience. I don't think it starts that way, necessarily. I think in the beginning, it's probably bravado, if it starts too early. But I do think you learn something from your successes. And I think I'm a risk taker."

> —**Judith Rodin, Ph.D.,** president of the Rockefeller
> Foundation and first woman elected president of an
> Ivy League institution

"I think about that a lot, because it's hard to pinpoint what makes someone successful. **When I look back, there's a series of events that seem to have precipitated my being put out there. But whether you stay out there is what I associate with success.** I started when I was very young. I was in the right place at the right time. My mom knew the right people, and started me modeling. And then it sort of snowballed."

> —**Brooke Shields,** television, stage, and screen actress

"**I try to have everybody feel important.** When you play 162 games, there's a game, or an inning, or whatever, that everybody's going to make a contribution. And then, when you look at it at the end—say, you win the World Series—you realize that contribution had to do with the season. I think it's important as a manager, whether you're managing a baseball team or a company, to make your employees feel that they're important. That you don't just pay attention to the people that hit home runs, so to speak. Because in the course of a year, you need everybody."

—**Joe Torre,** manager, the New York Yankees

"**I was fortunate to have parents who stressed education and discipline and who set a good example.** I learned a lot from my father about real estate development and construction, and about running a business. I was also very motivated to do something on my own, and had ideas that I was determined to see accomplished."

—**Donald Trump,** real estate magnate and
    star of NBC's *The Apprentice*

"It always starts from when we're little, I think. I had the feeling of not belonging. **Any kind of thing that made you feel small is always the first drive to want to do something.**"

—**Diane von Furstenberg,** clothing designer

"I like to think I have talent. I have talent, yeah, but also, I work my ass off. I work really, really hard. I've been obsessed, and a workaholic and a driven songwriter since I've been fourteen years old. I mean, I'm forty-nine, and I have not stopped. **I have not mellowed out; I have not chilled out.** I have not calmed down and taken a vacation. I haven't had a vacation in years."

—**Diane Warren,** Grammy Award–winning songwriter

"It's a difficult question to answer. It's not something that I can sit inside of and tangibly experience. I don't look at myself and say, 'Yes, I am successful,' today. It's that boring old adage, that **it's a journey.**"

—**Renée Zellweger,** Academy Award–winning actress

"I think I'm incredibly driven. **I put a lot of pressure on myself to succeed.** Maybe that's sometimes not so healthy, but I have a definite desire to succeed."

—**Jeff Zucker,** CEO, NBC Universal Television Group

ONE

The Path
to Success

1

Find Your Path

**James Blake • Craig Newmark • Frank Rich • Jim
Cramer • Bill O'Reilly • Joseph Abboud • Joy Behar •
Mario Cuomo • Anna Quindlen • Frédéric Fekkai •
Bobbi Brown • Bob Pittman • Clive Davis • Donald
Trump • Preston Bailey • Bill Bratton • Bobby Flay •
Cathie Black**

LAO TZU ONCE SAID, "The journey of a thousand miles begins with a single step." But how exactly do we know which way to go when we're first starting out?

I consider myself one of the lucky people who knew exactly what he wanted to do with his life. When I was about five years old, my parents gave me a tiny white Bendix radio. I would lie in bed at night under the covers—my parents of course thinking I was asleep—listening to this radio. I was fortunate to be able to hear the last few years of the golden age of radio: captivating shows like *The Lone Ranger, Sergeant Preston of the Yukon,* Bob Hope's, and Jack Benny's. I was particularly fascinated by the men on the radio who were interviewing people—Arthur Godfrey, Don McNeil, and my all-time favorite, Art Linkletter. I knew then that this was what I wanted to do with my life.

So I set out to become a talk show host. After thirty years in the business, I've interviewed thousands of people—movie stars, presidents, great writers, sports heroes, business leaders, and cultural icons. I'm continually grateful that I had a passion I could build my life around.

The number one rule I would pass on to anyone about having a successful career and life is to **follow the path of your passion**. Many of the people I interviewed identified their passion early in life. They were blessed with a talent, gift, or a fascination that ignited something within them and pointed to an obvious path. Of course, they still needed to dedicate a great deal of hard work, hours, and strong will in order to parlay their talent into a successful career, but the entry point was identifying their unique talent. For tennis star **James Blake,** it was extraordinary athletic skill. A gift for computer programming came naturally to **Craig Newmark,** founder of the landmark website Craigslist.com. For **Frank Rich,** columnist and former lead drama critic for the *New York Times,* it was an early love affair with the theater and the written word. An amazing memory and a gift for numbers helped **Jim Cramer,** the dynamic host of CNBC's *Mad Money,* realize when he was in college that he had a genius for picking stocks.

Conversely, some people begin their careers without a clear sense of purpose. Not everyone is fortunate enough to have the kind of identifiable skill or talent that serves as a natural career foundation. Vince Lombardi once said that it is our obligation to develop the God-given talent within us—but what if we have no idea what it is?

Other people I interviewed were not consciously aware of the abilities that would lead them to wealth and renown. As their stories will reveal, **one needn't necessarily possess an obvious gift in order to achieve success**.

Either way—whether they innately knew the path they were meant to walk or discovered it through circumstances—the choice to follow a path that ignited genuine interest and passion allowed these people to live lives of achievement and prosperity. Here are some of their stories:

• • •

Bill O'Reilly's reputation is that of someone who pulls no punches. Best known as the forceful host of *The O'Reilly Factor,* currently the most-watched television show on cable, he stirs up controversy with his outspoken opinions and anti-spin frankness. His official website features shirts, tote bags, and other items bearing his motto, "The Spin Stops Here," a perfect representation of his approach to life.

On the day I went to meet with him, I was walking down Avenue of the Americas toward the Fox News headquarters, when I hear a voice boom on my left, "Going to see me?" There's Bill O'Reilly alongside me, in lockstep. The first thing I noticed is that he's very tall and walks very fast. We went up to his office, which is filled with framed photographs of his family and the original front pages of newspapers featuring historic headlines from another era, including the one from the *New York World Telegram and Sun* the day Kennedy was shot. There are piles everywhere. The phone starts ringing almost immediately. Bill's a busy person.

We got right down to it. I asked him what turned him on to journalism, after a brief stint teaching high school English and history in Miami:

"I always had a talent," he said with his signature bluntness. "Identify what you're good at, and then try to make a living doing it. It's as simple as that. I could always write. I never took a writing class; I just had the gift. Everybody on earth—this is why I believe in God—every human being has a gift. Something unique to them, that they can do better than other people. I could write. And I had the Irish blarney. I could just talk. So I said, "Ooh, okay. I can write. What do you do with writing?' You go into journalism. Or straight novelist, or something like that, but that didn't even occur to me.

So I went to J-school after I taught high school, because I knew I didn't want to be a teacher. So I said, 'Let's go back to school, let's get the J-degree, and let's see where it leads.'"

"That was always the primary deal: Do something fun. Do something interesting. Rather than sit in an office and just get a paycheck."

—Bill O'Reilly

That decision to develop what he knew to be his God-given talent and develop it led to a reporting job at the *Boston Phoenix,* then back to Miami as an entertainment writer and movie reviewer for the *Miami Herald*. He moved into broadcast journalism to capitalize on the second half of his gift—his "Irish blarney"—reporting at stations in Scranton, Dallas, Denver, Portland, Boston, and ultimately, New York. You'll hear more of Bill's story a little later when he talks about his number one rule for how to succeed. But on the subject of finding one's path, Bill O'Reilly's advice is clear: he believes we're all good at something. **Find what *you're* good at and do it.**

• • •

Clothing designer **Joseph Abboud** takes a somewhat more soulful approach.

"If you can make a living from what you love doing, I don't think there's any greater joy in life," he said. "My path was a very organic path. I didn't have the classic business school, 'I'll do this and I'll do that.' It was really sort of a very organic path as opposed to a highway. It's kind of a path through the grass, you know?"

I met Joseph Abboud in his offices in Bedford, New York, on a brilliant fall day. Elegant and amicable, he embodies the energy of an artist whose work flows straight from his heart. It is immediately evident that his passion for clothing design is all-encompassing, from the name of the office complex he built ("Herringbone") to the awe in his voice when he talks about fabrics and colors, and about how nature inspires him (he once had thread dyed to match the colors of rocks he found while beachcombing in Ireland).

Joseph's love for clothing started early, when he was in high school. He learned everything on the job, first at the age of eighteen at the famous men's clothing store Louis of Boston, where he honed what his then-boss and mentor Murray Pearlstein described as his "native talent."

"Those are the words he used," Joseph recalled. "'Joe has native talent.' And it's an interesting phrase, you know? *Native talent.* What does it really mean? I guess it was sort of something I loved, that was instinctive. And he trusted me at twenty-two, twenty-three years old with big budgets, and being the buyer. I knew that I loved it and I felt skilled from it."

Joseph stayed at Louis of Boston for eight years, learning the ins and outs of the fashion business from the retail side. Then he reached what my personal mentor, Phil Lombardo, describes as a plateau. Phil told me: "In your career, you go along on a plateau, you get a vantage point from that plateau, and then you make a quantum leap to the next plateau."

"That's exactly it," Joseph agreed. "I stayed there for eight years. And then I thought, 'Well, is that all there is? Is this going to define my life?' And it might be curiosity or fear or anxiety, but I knew at thirty that I could do the job I was doing until somebody didn't want me to do it. But it wasn't enough of a challenge. So then I need to, you know, get to a Ralph Lauren, to get a slightly higher vantage point and have a better view of the world that I lived in. So I have seen my growth come from organic stages, never having an A to Z point of view."

"If you had asked me at twenty-two was I going to be a designer who was well-known, the answer was probably no. But I think it was the next logical step along the way of feeling fulfilled—and that's what I mean about organic growth."

—Joseph Abboud

Joseph Abboud took a quantum leap, which eventually did land him at Ralph Lauren, working directly with the famous American designer. He eventually became the associate director of Menswear Design for Ralph, and then reached another plateau, when he realized his earthy sensibility was moving in a different direction than the crisp, preppy Polo image. The next quantum leap was to parlay his unique vision into his own clothing line, which today is sold worldwide. The organic "path through the grass" has led to tremendous financial success (in 2000 he gave up control of his company to RSC Media Group for $65 million; sales are at a projected $200 million for 2006). Still, he maintains that it is his passion for clothing that gives him a sense of fulfillment in his work.

The Joseph Abboud story reflects a classic but invaluable adage: **Do what you love and the money will follow.**

• • •

Sometimes the role we play in our family as a child shines a direct light on our destiny, though it may take us a few wrong turns before we realize that. Comedienne and co-host of ABC's *The View* **Joy Behar** was a performer from the very beginning. "I was a funny kid," she recalled. In person, Joy is warm, smiling, and vivacious, answering my questions gleefully with the pacing and flair of a natural comedienne. We were sitting in a small, unglamorous room backstage, right after the taping of the show. "I was the center of a big Italian family, and I was basically a TV set. Before Lucy, there was always me.

"I was funny my whole life," she said. "It was right in front of me, what I needed to do. It was staring me in the face. It's a little trickier when it's your personality than when you can play the piano, like Marvin Hamlisch. It's a little harder to find, sometimes. But whatever you are at ten years old is what you want to be."

Joy went in a few wrong directions before she finally broke through the fear and hesitation that were holding her back and tried being funny as a profession. She started her work life as a teacher but got fired, which in hindsight she knows happened because she wasn't committed to the vocation. Wrong path number one. She went to work at *Good Morning America* as a secretary, which didn't feel like her natural path, either. Wrong path number two. She even refused a promotion, because she knew it wasn't right for her. Somewhere inside she knew what she was supposed to be doing.

"I knew I had something to offer, but I was scared to fulfill it," she said. "I didn't really have a role model. I mean, as much as my family was supportive of everything I would want to do, nobody really had a road map."

Fate then stepped in. "I had a near-death experience with an ectopic pregnancy. That was like, 'Oh, my God, I could really die now, and I haven't done what I wanted to do.' Then I got divorced, and then I got fired from my job at *Good Morning America*. So then I had no money, no husband, no backup, nothing."

So, out of necessity, Joy finally put a comedy act together and forced herself onto the stage. "It was like, you know, freedom's just another word for nothing left to lose," she said with a boisterous throaty laugh.

This was it. No more wrong paths. The ten-year-old funny girl is now one of the most recognizable comic talents on television. **Who were *you* when you were ten years old?**

• • •

To be in a room with **Mario Cuomo,** as I was lucky enough to be one cold November afternoon in his corner office at law firm Willkie Farr and Gallgher LLP, feels like a privilege. He is charismatic with an intellect that is palpable; you can almost literally feel him thinking. Though it's been decades since Mario Cuomo earned a dime as a pro baseball player, he somehow still exudes the commanding energy of an athlete: brains and brawn and a touch of red sauce from the old country.

Cuomo has given a lot of thought over the years to the question of what it takes. He gave his five children an important piece of advice: "What you should do is pray for a passion. Just pray for a passion. Something you're really passionate about. And if you don't have a passion, try to figure out why you're alive, and what it's all about."

Despite this sage advice, Mario confesses that he himself was never struck with sudden inspiration. It's hard to imagine that this reputable and highly respected politician who served as the governor for New York State three times and was tapped as a candidate for nomination to the United States Supreme Court didn't possess a sense of destiny about his life in public office. But he candidly admitted that finding his calling was a struggle.

"I've always resented one thing about what God did," he said, I suspect only half-joking. "He struck Saul in the tush with lightning and told him, 'From now on, you're Paul.' And I always said to myself, 'Do that to me and watch what I can do. Send me a little lightning, you know? And tell me exactly what you want from me. You want me to be a politician? You want me to be a lawyer?' Et cetera, et cetera. That's the key to everything."

> ## "It's hard for me to imagine going all through your life and not know, really, what you're trying to achieve."
>
> **—Mario Cuomo**

So if you're a person who doesn't know what you're meant to do, how would he advise you figure it out? The same way he counseled a hugely successful forty-eight-year-old attorney in his firm who earns $1.5 million a year but confessed that he doesn't know what he is doing it for or what he wants out of life:

"Just sit there and say to yourself, 'I've got a limited number of years. What do I want to do with them? Do I want to change the world? Do I want to raise a family? Do I want to have fun? Do I see my life as a basket of appetites, which I'm going to fill up with both hands, until I get old and the baskets start coming apart, and I lose the ability to fill what's left of the basket?' Try thinking yourself into a commitment to some purpose. Just try it."

• • •

Anna Quindlen may have won a Pulitzer Prize, but she wasn't the one who recognized the talent that would feed her childhood longing to do big things.

"I don't remember having any specific dreams," she told me. We were sitting in the living room of her town house on the Upper West Side of Manhattan, on a well-worn couch that she and her husband had bought years ago before they were married. Above us in a frame on the wall is her grandmother's crib quilt. All around us are symbols of a harmonious and treasured family life, and at the center of it is this wonderfully down-to-earth but brilliant woman. I've known Anna for many years, and I've always liked her; she's warm and accessible, and you can see a real spark behind her eyes.

"I think I had a kind of formalist longing to be important," she clarified. "I wanted to be a star. I wanted people to pay attention, as a little girl. I was one of those indefatigable tap dancers when I was a kid. It was always, 'Pay attention to me!' I was a big personality. I was really out there, but I don't think I had anything to hang it on. I mean, a little girl today who wants to be something can look around at the world and think of many things—she can honestly say to herself, "I'm going to be president,' you know? 'I'm going to be a senator. I'm going to run a company.' I hear all those things from girls today. I couldn't say any of those things. Who would have believed me, in the 1950s? But there was just a sense of wanting to be important."

As a girl, Anna consumed biographies of women who despite all odds developed a life in public—Queen Elizabeth I, Marie Curie, Elizabeth Blackwell. Also in the mix were the works and stories of notable female writers like Louisa May Alcott, Jane Austen, and Edith Wharton.

"So you didn't see yourself as a writer?" I noted with some surprise. I mean, here's Anna Quindlen, one of the foremost writers of her generation, and she didn't know she had the gift that would lead to award-winning columns in the *New York Times* and *Newsweek,* four novels, and two best-selling nonfiction books?

"I think over time, I started to see myself as a writer because I got a lot of positive feedback from teachers about my abilities," she admitted frankly. "I'm not quite sure why, but I had a pretty identifiable voice, which was kind of a second cousin to my speaking voice. Even as a kid. I mean, if I look at some of the stuff that I did when I was in seventh or eighth or ninth grade, you know, there's all kinds of things wrong with it. But there is within it, always, a hint of the writing voice that I still have today."

"Where do you think that comes from?" I asked.

"I don't know about that," she said. "I mean, I do think there's part of being a fairly fluent writer that seems to me to be almost inbred—written on the DNA. You know, you discover when you're teaching writing that you can take people about 80 percent of the way. And then there's another 20 percent that's just like having perfect pitch, or being able to do backbends—things like that."

"If it's at all possible, I think you should try to find work that really floats your boat. Because you don't know how long you're going to be around. I understand the thirst for more money, and promotion, and so on and so forth. But I've just never found that it's worth it to do a job that you're miserable doing."

—Anna Quindlen

She thought about it a little more. "But I'm also from a large Irish family, which is really inclined toward raconteurism. And I think that that was part of it. The sense that, you know, you sit around and tell stories. And the stories get bigger and grander and funnier and quirkier. And there's a way to tell the stories that's highly idiosyncratic and specific. Not in a kind of generic, homogenized way. And all of that leads you to having the kind of voice that a good writer needs to have."

The lesson here: **If you don't know what you're good at, pay attention to what others are telling you, because they may spot your gift before you do.**

• • •

Talent doesn't always have to be innate. Celebrity hairstylist and lifestyle entrepreneur **Frédéric Fekkai** didn't come into the world wielding golden scissors. One might think he did, given the fact that his eponymous salons in New York City and Palm Beach are among the largest and most luxurious in the world. His line of hair and skin care products, accessories, and home fragrances are sold in stores all around the country, and he is frequently quoted as the voice of authority on all things beauty-related. Sitting in his office surrounded by hundreds of new products, I could understand why people might peg him as a natural, because he seems so utterly in his element.

Yet he credits none of this to any sort of natural gift.

"I don't believe people when they say, 'You are gifted.' I do not believe in that. I think it's baloney. I don't care who you are. I mean, obviously there are some geniuses, but for me, it was not such a thing," A handsome Frenchman, Frédéric is, I would imagine, every woman's ideal of the European star soccer player, but with no rough edges.

Frédéric Fekkai learned his craft at the foot of a master, Bruno Pittini, the head of Jacques Dessange in France, which owns hundreds of salons. He observed, and practiced, and absorbed everything he could from his famous mentor, because he knew he wanted to become the best. "Because I'm ambitious, I became talented," he said.

Because he was ambitious, he became talented. He wanted to do big things, so he trained himself to do big things. He literally *taught* himself to be talented.

• • •

Sometimes it takes someone asking us the right question at the right time for us to find our calling. **Bobbi Brown,** the cosmetics industry entrepreneur who broke the mold by being one of the first to introduce natural-looking makeup for women and whose products are now sold in more than four hundred stores and twenty countries around the world, had no clue what she wanted to be when she grew up. She got all the way to college without any particular interest presenting itself as a career option.

"The best thing that ever happened to me in my whole life is something my mother did," recalled Bobbi, who embodies perfectly the natural style she is so known for. Casual and classic in white button-down shirt, jeans, and ponytail, Bobbi possesses not a scrap of pretension. "After I went to my second college, I came home and said I wanted to drop out because I didn't know what I wanted to do in my life. And my mom said, 'I don't care what you do, but you have to get a degree.' "

"It's a humongous surprise, believe me. To myself,
to my family, to everyone that knows me, that
I'm a successful businesswoman."

—Bobbi Brown

"I said, 'But I don't know what I want to do.' "

" 'Forget about what you want to do with your life,' she said. 'Pretend it's your birthday. You can do whatever you want.' "

"I thought and thought. And out of the blue I said, 'I want to go to Marshall Field's and play with makeup.' "

A flash of understanding about what gave her pure joy was the first spark, and Bobbi Brown has been "playing with makeup" ever since. She went back to school, this time Emerson College, and studied theatrical makeup, the art form that would eventually launch her career as a makeup artist and the company that now rivals industry giants like Lancôme.

Pretend it's your birthday, and you could do anything. What would it be?

• • •

Media mogul **Bob Pittman**—the man who engineered an entirely new chapter in the history of television and is credited as "the father of MTV"—is another success story with an early twist. Growing up as the son of a minister in Jackson, Mississippi, Bob's dream had nothing to do with media; his goal was to get his pilot's license.

"I always had a dream to fly airplanes, since I was a little kid," said Bob. "You could get a student pilot's license at sixteen, so at about fifteen I started focusing on learning to fly. And my parents said, 'Well, you'd better get some money.' So I asked every relative I had to give me money for flying lessons for Christmas and birthday presents. And I set out to get a job. I mean, I'd had little jobs, you know, sweeping stores and all, but I needed something that was more money. I tried a men's clothing store, and they said no, I was too young. I tried the best-paying job in town, which was bagging groceries at the Piggly Wiggly, and they didn't have any jobs. So I went to work at a radio station and got a job as an announcer.

"And God bless Bill Jones, who was the old guy who owned the station who gave me the job," he went on. "My original ambition was learning to fly, which I did. But somewhere along the way I got caught up in radio and just got fascinated with what was going on in radio—the creativity of radio, and creating these radio stations. And the battles one radio station had with another, as to who would win, and that sort of took over as my passion."

Once bitten by the radio bug, Bob worked as a DJ at radio stations in Mississippi, Milwaukee, and Detroit, and then moved into programming. He engineered his first ratings win at an FM station in Pittsburgh at age nineteen. He soon brilliantly turned around an NBC-owned Chicago country music station in what is considered one of the major success stories in American radio history, followed by similar success revitalizing its FM sister station. At that point, at the age of twenty-three, he was sent to New York to do the same with WNBC. While at WNBC radio, he produced and hosted a television show, *Album Tracks,* that ran after *Saturday Night Live* on the NBC-owned TV stations. Eventually at age twenty-five he turned to television programming and made history launching MTV, Nick at Nite, and VH-1, and moving from programmer to CEO of MTV Networks. Later he created *The Morton Downey Jr. Show* and served as chairman of Court TV at its launch. Over the next few years he became CEO of Time-Warner Enterprises and Six Flags, CEO of Century 21 Real Estate, CEO of AOL Networks, and President and COO of America Online, Inc. Finally he served as co-COO and then COO of AOL Time Warner.

Bob Pittman's most recent venture is his own private investment firm, which he founded with some associates who have worked with him since his days at MTV and NBC. In a nod to the impulse that started it all, he named the company The Pilot Group.

• • •

Sometimes we discover a talent within that surprises us.

"I never knew I had it in me," says the legendary music industry icon **Clive Davis** about his fabled golden ear. Imagine that: here's a man who has single-handedly carved the landscape of the music scene over the past forty years, and he never knew he had it in him. He didn't know that music would be the great passion of his life, or that he would go on to discover three generations of superstars from Janis Joplin to Bruce Springsteen to Alicia Keys. He didn't sense that he had what it took to run Columbia Records and be perhaps the most powerful influence in bringing rock music into the mainstream culture, go on to launch two famed record labels—Arista and J Records—and have the vision to partner with a young Sean "Puffy" Combs to create Bad Boy Records, the most successful hip-hop and rap label of the '90s. He certainly didn't anticipate that he would become the only non-performer ever inducted into the Rock and Roll Hall of Fame.

In person, Clive Davis appears the consummate mogul, commanding from behind a massive desk in the corner of an office with a breathtaking view of Central Park. He looks like the guy with the Bentley at the curb waiting to take him to his private plane to Saint Bart's. But underneath the natty clothes and luxurious trappings of hard-earned success is a hardworking kid from Brooklyn, New York, who believed his lot in life was to work quietly and diligently—for someone else. As a lawyer.

"As a Jewish guy out of Brooklyn, if you did well, you were either a doctor or lawyer," Clive explained. "That was the only way you could rise above your station."

Clive's original goal was simply to establish himself in a financially stable profession, and because he was a good speaker and had a way with words, law was his chosen path. Through a series of coincidences and, he says, pure luck, he ended up working at a firm that led to a job at Columbia Records, where he eventually worked his way all the way up to president. He heard Janis Joplin singing onstage at the Monterey Pop Festival in 1967 and had an inkling that voices like hers were the future of music, but he didn't know for certain that his instinct was actually pure talent until the artists he signed in that first wave hit it big.

I think it's pretty encouraging to know that Clive Davis—*the* Clive Davis—wasn't one of those people who early on possessed a grand sense of destiny. There is a lot of hope in knowing that **there are gifts within us still waiting to be discovered,** and that we can surprise ourselves, much as this now-legend did when he was first starting out.

• • •

In the beginning, where your path will take you may not be clear, and there is likely to be fear associated with the unknown. Take comfort in knowing that, as a number of successful people in this book attest, your path may be revealed in increments. Hard as it may seem to believe, you won't be catapulted directly from where you start to where you dream to be. Remember—the journey is the reward, and the journey should be fun.

End Notes

"I learned in high school how to handle people, and to navigate around them when necessary. I found each person a puzzle to be figured out, which I think became instinctive later on. This helped my negotiation skills and may have been an instinct I had naturally, but I definitely honed those skills along the way."—**Donald Trump**

"I wish I could say I grew up loving flowers. But it wasn't that. It was a situation that, once I started doing it, I realized how much I really enjoyed it."—**Preston Bailey**

"As far as ambition as a kid, all I wanted to be was a cop."
—**Bill Bratton**

"I used to think you had to be born with a talent, period. That you could not really accrue the skills. And of course that's not true. You can be trained, as long as you want to do it."
—**Bobby Flay**

"I think I found a niche at a place where I knew I'd enjoy it. I liked the people who were a part of it. I loved the idea of being in print media. I love looking at a magazine. I've always been a great reader of magazines. So it kind of came together for me."—**Cathie Black**

2
Get Hired

Sir Richard Branson • Mark Burnett • Bobbi Brown •
Joe Torre • Mario Cuomo • Jeff Lurie • Christie
Hefner • Rikki Klieman • Tom Perkins • Frédéric
Fekkai • Jeff Zucker • Jane Friedman • Bill
Bratton • Daniel Boulud • David Rockwell • Bill
O'Reilly • Sirio and Marco Maccioni • Matt Lauer •

ONE QUESTION I asked practically all the
participants in this book is what they look
for when hiring someone. I thought it would
be helpful to see what qualities these industry leaders look for,
because at some point, all of us will likely find ourselves sitting
across the table or desk from someone interviewing for a job, or
assignment, or appointment that we really want. What does it
take to make one of these people say, in the words of Donald
Trump on *The Apprentice,* "You're hired"?

• • •

Sir Richard Branson employs more than fifty thousand people
throughout his two hundred companies around the world, including Virgin Megastore and Virgin Atlantic Airways. As one of the

most successful and wealthiest entrepreneurs of our time, you might assume he looks to hire sharks. Not so:

"I look for people who are good with people. I look for people who will make sure they know the switchboard operator's name, and the cleaner's name, and not just their fellow directors' names, and will find time for them. In fact, the only time I think we've ever asked directors to go is if we feel that they're not looking after their people in the way that they should. So it's very much looking for people skills.

"Apart from that, you want all sorts of different kinds of people. They're all equally valid. I mean, an entrepreneur kind of person is very, very useful for an entrepreneurial company. But equally, you want managers as well who are not entrepreneurial. And so, what you're looking for is just to bring out the best in people based on what their own particular skills are. And make sure that if they're not quite right in one particular area, you move them into an area where they are right. And not try to look for the same in everyone you take on."

• • •

Mark Burnett, the visionary producer who pioneered reality television with hits like *Survivor, The Apprentice,* and *Eco-Challenge,* once heard the saying "Generalists run companies, and generalists hire specialists." He thinks of himself as the generalist in his production company—the one with the big-picture vision—and believes that he is able to have several television shows running at once because of the specialists he has brought on board:

"They have to have some experience, but sometimes I'll hire people without experience if I just feel a self-starting energy— people who don't need to check with you every five seconds on, 'What should I do next?' I would rather give people a general direction. And it's easy in this company. We have a certain style to

Be Resourceful

Getting hired takes more than just applying for a job and hoping something will happen. Almost always, we have to make something happen.

When **Bobbi Brown** first moved to New York City right out of college, she didn't know anyone in the makeup world. "How did I do it? I took out the Yellow Pages. And I opened it up to makeup, saw what was there. I went to see the Makeup Artists Union, met some people there who helped me do some soap operas, et cetera. They explained to me what it would take to get into the union, which was that either you're born into it or it takes you twenty years, so I knew it was time to look elsewhere.

"Then I opened up the pages again, and went to modeling. I went to the modeling agencies and started offering my services for free. I looked up photographers—I studied the fashion magazines and I looked at people's names, and just started going to see them. I'd look in the front of the magazine for the model booker. And I went there, and one day someone hired me. And that's how I got my first break."

---

our television—to our upcoming movie that we're doing, and our music. We have a certain style, so people know how it's supposed to feel.

"I don't really particularly want to stand over an editor while they're trying for two weeks to edit something. I'd rather give direction, let them go ahead and do it and come back to me with a finished result."

• • •

Joe Torre, the manager of the New York Yankees, on what he looks for in members of his coaching staff:

"I want to see their ability come out. And I want to make sure they have the ability not to agree with me just because I'm the boss. I think it's important, and I tell them that. Eventually, I

Tough Bosses

Joe Torre has one of the most notoriously difficult bosses out there in George Steinbrenner. It takes a certain amount of self-confidence to hold your own against such a force of nature, but Joe Torre is nearly always the picture of composure. What would he say to somebody who is dealing with a boss who hovers over them, criticizes, or who is just a difficult person in general?

"Well, you asked the question the right way," he said. "Because you don't handle tough bosses. You deal with tough bosses.

"First off, he's the boss. I think you have to understand that you have to think enough of yourself to be able to take criticism. You can't let something he says chip away at what you know is something you need to do. You know, I've never made a decision in this game, even from the first day I managed it, in order to keep a job. I have made every decision to try to win games as opposed to try to keep a job.

"And you know, with George Steinbrenner, he's a tough boss; I acknowledge that. You can't pick and choose the piece of your boss that you want to keep and the other piece you don't want to keep. You have to understand that it's the package. If you're gonna take his money, you're gonna have to take the criticism. That's something you just have to know going in. This keeps you from overreacting."

have to make a decision on what we do, but if they have an idea, I want to hear it. I like to delegate authority. I feel it's important to have the players respect my coaches as coaches who, in their own right, have something to bring to the table. So I hire as many smart baseball people as I can."

• • •

Mario Cuomo, as ever, is all about passion. Given the thousands of law school graduates seeking positions, here is what he said makes the difference for him:

"It's motivation that I'm interested in. If they don't have a passion, then I'm inclined to discourage them. Because to achieve excellence in almost anything important, you have to work very, very hard. And if you're not passionate about it, it's difficult to work very, very hard."

• • •

Jeff Lurie, owner of the Philadelphia Eagles, who is as famous for his calm, perfection-driven leadership style as he is for his team's record, looks hard at character when it comes to hiring:

"There's a few things, but the number one thing I try to hone in on is, Are they a really good human being? I wouldn't hire them if I thought they were just a shark, or an animal of some sort, you know. I'll give you a little example. I was interviewing head coaches once. And it's a big decision, when an owner decides who the head coach is going to be. It's really your on-field CEO. And one of the coaches I interviewed was really kind of arrogant with one of my assistants. And so I just crossed him off the list. This was a really good indicator. Whether it's janitors, waitresses, assistants, executive vice presidents, you learn a lot, I think, about a person as a human being."

• • •

Christie Hefner, the charming and enterprising CEO of Playboy Enterprises who led the company's successful initiatives into television and the Internet that now generate more than $650 million in licensed consumer products, values individuals who mesh with Playboy's corporate culture:

"I put a premium on smarts. You know, ours is a company, as Henry Luce said about *Time* in its early days, in which our assets go home in the elevators at night. That's what makes us who we are. But we're also a family company, and therefore I look for people who are smart but not arrogant. Who have a sense of humor. And have a sense of life being more than just their job, and yet be willing to work really hard. People who are collaborative and not territorial or political. I think those are some of the qualities that I look for and that, frankly, the people who succeed here have."

Seek a Mentor

Best-selling author and legal analyst for the *Today* show and Court TV **Rikki Klieman,** who herself mentors young women, wholeheartedly advises finding a mentor to model yourself after early in your career.

"Let's say you really like landscaping," said this indomitable woman, who is so on-the-ball that she showed up for our interview with prepared notes. "You think you'd be pretty good at landscaping, something you know nothing about. So what I would do is I'd go to the bookstore and I'd find the books on landscaping. And I would probably spend hours sifting though the books. I would go find out who the leading landscape architects around were; I'd do it on the Internet. And I would contact them. I don't care how remote they are. I don't care if I'm in LA and they're in New York, or London. I would write them a letter. I would send them a FedEx, or e-mail. But I would tell them, 'I'm interested. I've thought about this career. I want

• • •

Tom Perkins, the billionaire lion of the Silicon Valley venture-capital world, is the cofounder of Kleiner Perkins Caufield and Byers, the investment firm that has funded giants like Yahoo, AOL, and Amazon.com. In his world, thinking fast on your feet is what counts:

"A sense of urgency is the single most important thing I would look for. Time and money will solve all problems. But you don't have time and money, you know? So therefore, you've got to do it quickly. So a sense of urgency is the most important."

---

to become a landscape architect. And I'd like to meet with you.' "

This approach worked brilliantly for Rikki, who doggedly pursued Joe Oteri, the leading trial lawyer at that time in the court system in Boston where she clerked. "I called him up and I said, 'I'm Rikki Klieman. I clerk for Judge Skinner. May I make an appointment with you to come over to your office? I'd just like to talk to you about your work.'

"That's where it began," she said. "Joe Oteri remains an active mentor, friend, and father to me, to this day." Joe took her under his wing and taught her nearly everything she knows about trying cases. Rikki watched him in court, read his transcripts, and asked for his critique of what went right and what went wrong in her own cases. He became a tremendous proponent of Rikki's, making phone calls to help her get a job. Largely due to what she learned from her mentor, she became one of the most influential female trial lawyers in the country.

• • •

Lifestyle guru **Frédéric Fekkai,** whose own success is deeply tied to his desire to improve, needs to see a hunger to learn:

"I like people who are somehow confident, but don't think too highly of themselves—who know their limitations. I like people who are honest, who are true. People who are not afraid of saying that they make mistakes. I don't like people who just come and brag to me, and try to tell me how great they are. I like people who tell me they're not that great, but they want to be great."

• • •

Jeff Zucker, the upbeat CEO of NBC Universal Television Group, who made a name for himself early on as the executive

A History-Making Interview

In 1957, when **Tom Perkins** was a young graduate of Harvard Business School, he interviewed at Hewlett-Packard, then a small company with revenue of $25 million a year. He was scheduled to meet with Dave Hewlett and Bill Packard at a trade show, where, to his surprise, he found them busily setting up the booth themselves.

"I went to the show before it opened," he recalled. "They said, 'Come on down, we'll talk to you there.' So I did. And there they were, I don't remember, but it was probably the day before the show, and it was taking them longer than they thought. And I just started to help them, and having the interview. And they offered me the job."

"That's a great story," I said. "I was going to ask you what that original interview was like."

" 'Hand me that hammer!' " Tom Perkins laughed.

producer of the *Today* show and later with successes such as *Scrubs, Fear Factor,* and *Law and Order,* seeks a maverick spirit in those he hires:

"I want to hire people who are willing to take chances and make mistakes. And are a little crazy. Not so they're gonna get us in any trouble. But that they are a little out there and are willing to break some plates. We're in the television business, where crazy's good. So I'm always looking for a little crazy."

• • •

Jane Friedman, the brainy CEO of HarperCollins Worldwide (who, I'll say in the spirit of full disclosure, is publishing this book), doesn't want anyone trying to impress her with their intellect. Instead, she wants to feel as though she can connect with potential future employees on a basic human level:

"It's more what I don't like to see. I don't like to see anybody who thinks he or she is too sharp, or too cool. I don't like edgy people. I don't think an edge is part of an interview. There are certain young people who think that that makes you look cool.

"I also don't think bragging in an interview is a very good thing. I mean, most of the generation below us is very smart. That's a broad generalization, but they are; they're so smart! So you don't have to tell me how smart you are. I sort of know how smart you are.

"But I like people who are human. I like people who are warm. I like people who have a sense of humor. And I think you see that almost immediately. I like people who don't take themselves too seriously and don't try to sell me too much."

• • •

Los Angeles Chief of Police **Bill Bratton,** the only person ever to command both the NYPD and the LAPD, personifies self-assurance, so it's no surprise that he looks for something similar in those he hires to his force:

"I'm looking for confidence, ambition. I want self-reliant people. I want people who are risk takers, and who aren't afraid to take criticism.

"I also want people who are not vertical. By vertical, I mean, you know, I kiss-ass those above, and step on those below. I want people who are kind of horizontal. They deal with people above the same way they deal with people below—from that point of confidence. Appropriate deference to those above, but appropriate deference for those below, also."

Be Willing to Work for Free

Working for free can be the best way to break into a business. I've always said that when you are first starting out, unpaid work can also be viewed as an extension of your education. Several months working for free can teach you just as much as an entire year of graduate school.

When I was hosting and producing *Southern Exposure with Bill Boggs,* I put up notices at my alma mater, the University of Pennsylvania, among other schools, saying I was seeking an intern. A young guy named Richard Baker wrote me a letter that opened with a line I'll never forget: "I felt the hand of fate on my shoulder today when I saw the flyer on the bulletin board looking for help on your show in North Carolina." He wanted to get into television and saw this as an opportunity to learn. I went up to Philadelphia and met Richard at the electronics store where he was working. Within a few minutes, I said, "Yeah, come on down."

He drove down, got an apartment, and worked with me for about two years, absorbing everything he could about how to produce a television show. At first he didn't earn a dime; eventually

• • •

Daniel Boulud, one of the greatest French chefs in America, owns magnificent four-star restaurants in New York, Palm Beach, and Las Vegas. When he interviews prospective employees, he is searching for a particular mentality:

"I really want the person to understand what this business means and to really understand that he can be an asset here, even if it's in a low position. He can still be a big asset. I try to scratch in order to see if the person has an ambition to grow greater after me."

---

the station manager Phil Lombardo paid him a small amount. Ultimately, we became friends, and several years later, when Richard was in New York, we formed a production company. Richard went on to form a comedy management company, and today he is one of the premier comedy managers in the country.

Here's Richard Baker's explanation of what he got from his High Point, North Carolina, years:

"My nearly two years of essentially indentured servitude at WGHP-TV taught me a lot of things. Pumping out one hour of TV programming per day with our mere three-person staff was like getting a Ph.D. in television program production. I got to help conceive show/guest ideas, conduct preinterviews with guests, did the 'floor producing,' and even had to drive the WGHP station wagon to the Greensboro airport to pick up out-of-town guests. This was in addition to my part-time job at the station on the studio crew doing camera, lighting, and sound work on such classic shows as *Dialing for Dollars*. In a nutshell, I really learned TV production on both sides of the camera, and I managed to save $15,000 to $20,000 by not having to go to Syracuse or Boston University for a master's degree in television production."

• • •

David Rockwell is the visionary architect best known for his cross-disciplinary approach to design in the hospitality, cultural, entertainment, and set design arenas (W Hotels, Nobu, Vong, Mesa Grill, Cirque du Soleil, Kodak Theatre, *Hairspray, Dirty Rotten Scoundrels*). In keeping with his out-of-the-box artistic way of thinking, here's what he looks for in a young architect:

Go Where the Opportunity Is

Bill O'Reilly's response to why he thinks he is successful is straightforward: perseverance. Early on, he made a decision to make it to the top, no matter what it took. In his case, what it took was being willing to move ten times in fifteen years for new jobs that would challenge him, teach him, and take him to the next level. One of his rules for career advancement is one I share: **Go where the opportunity is.**

In the early '70s, I was working as associate producer of a show called *McLean and Company,* on KYW-TV in Philadelphia. Part of the deal I made when I took the job was that I could appear on air at least once a week. I created a role for myself— "Mr. Weekend"—appearing on the show on Fridays to give viewers ideas on what to do for the weekend. The show was successful, and I was getting exposure, but often I'd get bumped or have my time cut. I was learning how to produce a TV talk show, which proved valuable experience later on, but I wasn't even close to hosting my own show, which was my primary objective.

On New Year's Eve, I made a resolution to go anywhere in the country to get my own talk show. Within two months, a contact came through and I auditioned for Phil Lombardo in High Point, North Carolina, for a job that would involve creating, producing, and hosting my own morning talk show. The audition was a one-hour interview with a former heroin addict about drugs and addiction. I read a big article in *Time* magazine about heroin and wrote down questions I figured people would want to know; then I just talked to the guy as if he were sitting next to me on a long airplane trip. I got the job in High Point. I packed up and headed south, leaving behind family and friends to pursue what I knew was the next stepping-stone in making my childhood dream come true.

Everyone in Philadelphia—co-workers, relatives, friends, neighbors—was shocked that I would leave a big TV market like Philadelphia for a tiny place like High Point, North Carolina. For me, it was simple: I'd rather play the game every day in High Point and grow through that experience than sit on the bench 90 percent of the time in Philadelphia. What difference did it make that it was a small market? It was an opportunity that would challenge me every day. I lived three of the happiest, most successful, and most creative years of my life hosting *Southern Exposure with Bill Boggs*.

Bill O'Reilly opted for career advancement over comfort many times while on the way up. "In order to get to this level, you really have to roll with it," he said. "Because it's not a straight line, you know? What happens is that people get tired of struggling in their career and they say, 'Well, it's fun in Cleveland,' or 'I like it in Boston, or Miami, or Cleveland, and that's where I'm going to stay. I'm going to start a family, I'm going to settle down. And this is fine with me.'

"If you want to make it in a huge way, then you have to go beyond that," he went on. "And so, all the people that I know that I started with in school, and in the first years of my career, including here in New York City at Channel 2, they made decisions. And their decisions were lifestyle decisions. Comfort decisions; not a lot of risk. 'I have a good deal here. Why take another risk?'

"I decided to try to get to the top, just for ego purposes. I wasn't in it for the money. So I said, 'Look, I'm gonna dedicate myself, almost like an athlete, to becoming the best at what I do. I'm going to take chances. I'm going to get new experiences. So I was willing to be very, very disciplined, and persevere. It wasn't enough for me to succeed in Scranton, or Dallas, or Denver, or Hartford, or Portland. I enjoyed my time there. But I was always saying, 'Okay, so what's next?' "

"One of the things that's highest on the criteria for me is someone who is interested in things other than architecture. Because I think being insular is not helpful, and just referring to your own work. I believe in looking out at everything that's going on in the world around us. That's why the questions I ask in interviews tend to in some ways not be traditional questions, to get someone to talk about what they're passionate about. What moves them outside of architecture? You want someone who is curious, who is willing to investigate. And someone who understands communication."

• • •

Sirio Maccioni, his wife, Edgi, and their three sons, Mario, Marco, and Mauro, own and operate the famed Le Cirque and Circo restaurants in New York City and in Las Vegas, as well as a Le Cirque in Mexico City. I've dined at their restaurants for the past twenty-five years and have found the hallmark of their operation—beyond exquisite food—to be extraordinarily gracious and personal service, from the maître d' all the way to the busboys and the coat check attendants. Whatever they do in the hiring of their team, they do it right. Here are the criteria **Marco Maccioni** said they hold:

"You see someone who stands tall, who knows what they're doing, and you know that you're going to get a good answer, a good dialogue. What I look for, more than anything, is someone who's interested in what they're doing—not just coming to apply for a job. Just because you're looking for a job doesn't make you a good candidate. You have to know a couple of things about the profession. But more than anything, I think it's the attitude. And you know what? A smile."

• • •

Here's a last thought to remember that might be helpful: In the minutes before you go into an interview, think about how fortunate

Interview Smarts

I believe the key to any successful interview, job or otherwise, is to try to bond with the person with whom you're speaking. It is essential to make them feel relaxed and comfortable with you if you are looking to have a meaningful and fruitful dialogue. The simplest way to do this is to just be yourself, and to take a genuine interest in them. A job interview is almost like an audition, to a certain extent, and I think you can't hide who you really are.

One of the most poignant stories I heard that relates to this was from **Matt Lauer,** co-host of NBC's *Today* show. Early in Matt's career, he experienced a good amount of success in local television, eventually landing in New York City at the age of twenty-six to co-host *PM Magazine*. All signs pointed to continued ascent.

But then he hit a major slump. Four shows he hosted were canceled, one right after the other, and though he found some cable television work, he couldn't land a new job at the same level. In an emotional and financial crisis, he gave up his New York City lifestyle and moved into a very small cabin upstate to reevaluate his career. He needed money but didn't want to wait tables, because he knew he had less of a shot at a resurrection if anyone recognized him and perceived him as down and out. So Matt applied for a job as a tree trimmer, because he knew his face would be obscured by a hard hat. The next day, the phone rang. Matt answered it, expecting it to be the tree trimming company responding to his query, but it was Bill Bolster, the general manager of WNBC-TV.

"He gets on the phone and he says, 'This guy just brought me a tape of yours a couple of days ago, and I'd seen you around, but this tape got my attention. I know you used to host this show . . . what are you doing for dinner tomorrow night?

" 'Let me look in my book,' " Matt recalled saying, laughing in retrospect. "I'm doing nothing. I'm eating Beefaroni in a can." So he jumped in his car the next day to have dinner at 21 in New York with Bill Bolster and his wife.

You'll hear more of the details of this story in the chapter about adversity, but for now, just know that this interview was essentially Matt Lauer's match point. He was looking at severe underemployment, as Matt called it, and the possibility of having to make money chopping away at tree branches while hiding from the viewing public, versus being back on television every morning in New York City. A crossroads, to say the least.

Matt did what he does best: he went to that dinner and in the same relaxed manner he displays on television, he bonded with his potential employer on a very human level, eye-to-eye, face-to-face. "I think what got me the job—and if you talk to him, what got me the job—was that dinner," Matt said. "And it wasn't based on me telling him my visions for his morning news show or anything like that, because I didn't have visions; I'd never anchored news before. We hit it off in a way—he was from the Midwest, from Waterloo, Iowa, his wife was from the Midwest, and they are just good, normal people. You know, if my years of growing up in New York City taught me one thing, and other jobs I've had in the past, it's how to somehow connect with people.

"Here was a guy who controlled my fate," he continued. "My bank account is almost zero. I know how badly I need this job; he probably doesn't. I sat at that dinner and we clicked in a way that I haven't clicked at too many other business dinners."

So, what would Matt Lauer say to somebody who is headed to an equally important meeting that could change their whole career, their whole life?

"Be yourself," he said with conviction. "The thing that worked for me that night is that I was myself. I didn't walk into that restaurant pretending to be a news anchor. I went in there and talked about me. He asked me questions; I answered them in a straightforward way; my likes, dislikes, my passions, my concerns, my family. We just talked."

He laughed a little and added, "You know, I didn't think I really had that big a chance . . . maybe that relaxed me a little bit. I went in there with no grand expectations."

they would be to hire you, and remember all that you have to offer them. Most people are saying to themselves, "Gee, I hope they approve of me, I hope they like this, I hope they like that." But reverse the thinking by imagining their luck in seeing your value. Believe that and you will convey a confident edge.

3
Capitalize on Luck and Timing

Diane von Furstenberg • Mario Cuomo • Dr. Mehmet Oz • Matt Lauer • Jeff Zucker • Rikki Klieman • Joy Behar • Bob Pittman • Clive Davis • Christie Hefner • Maria Bartiromo • Dr. Judith Rodin • Bobbi Brown • Joseph Abboud • Donald Trump • Renée Zellweger • Frédéric Fekkai • Sir Richard Branson • Peter Cincotti

I BELIEVE IN WHAT I call the "Blueberry Pie Theory of Life." None of the stories I'm telling you about my career—or even the interviews in this book—would have happened if my father hadn't sat on a piece of blueberry pie in a hotel restaurant in Ocean City, New Jersey, when I was twelve years old.

While on vacation in Ocean City, my mother, father, sister, and I loved eating at the restaurant at the Lincoln Hotel. One day after lunch, my father got up from the table and saw that his practically brand-new tan linen slacks were covered with a giant stain from part of a piece of blueberry pie that hadn't been cleaned off his chair. The pants were ruined. People swarmed around him, but

Dad, ever the gentleman, didn't want to make a big deal of it and get someone in trouble, so we left the restaurant quickly.

The next time we came in, we were greeted with apologies and especially warm hospitality from the owners, Mr. and Mrs. Cope, who had heard what had happened and how my dad hadn't made a fuss. From that day on, they gave us VIP treatment every time we returned—which always included free pie.

"I think luck is an important ingredient. I think timing is an extremely important ingredient. And the chemistry of putting all these ingredients together is mysterious. But at the end, you're the cook. So you should understand how much of each ingredient to use at the time. It's like making a chocolate cake. You forget the sugar, it doesn't taste the same. You bake it too long, it doesn't taste the same."

—Diane von Furstenberg

Several years later, when I was at the University of Pennsylvania and desperately needed a summer job, my father thought we should go to the Lincoln Hotel and see if any positions were open. We drove down, found Mr. Cope, and I asked for a job. "Bad luck," he said. "This morning we just sent away a letter of acceptance for the last job we had open. Sorry." But his wife said to hold on, because she realized the mail at the front desk hadn't yet been picked up. We rushed over, dumped it on the floor, found the letter, and tore it up. I got the job.

As a result of that job at the hotel, I met many people, including those with whom I would start my career in show business. I can trace a direct line of successive contacts from that summer in Ocean City all the way to my big break: coming to New York to host *Midday Live with Bill Boggs*. So when my father got up that day with the blueberry pie smeared all over his pants—he not only showed me how to act like a gentleman, but he changed the entire course of my life.

Luck can come from anywhere, and it can be a crucial ingredient for success. As **Mario Cuomo** said, "What does it take? Most of all, good luck. No matter what else you bring to it, no matter how good-looking you are, no matter how suave you are as an interviewer, a television personality, you have to be in the right place at the right time, with the right opportunity. It's as simple as that."

Luck constitutes only half of the formula, of course. There's a story about how Paul Newman would always credit his successes to luck. That's the way he preferred it. But George Roy Hill, who directed him in *Butch Cassidy and the Sundance Kid*, turned to him one day and said, "Paul, with you, luck is an art." Paul Newman equipped himself to make the most of fortunate circumstances.

Luck—and the ability to recognize and take advantage of it—makes an imprint on our destinies. Here are a few of the lucky stories I uncovered.

• • •

Many of the people I talked with agreed that luck is getting yourself into a situation where you're primed to take advantage of it. Best-selling author **Dr. Mehmet Oz** nailed it when said, "Luck favors the prepared mind."

You've already heard **Matt Lauer**'s stroke-of-luck story of the general manager seeing his tape and calling him at his most desperate hour. That opportunity seemed to drop out of the sky, but if Matt hadn't developed his craft and put it on display on the tape, he likely wouldn't be appearing on our television sets every morning. He was prepared when luck smiled at him.

"Luck is something very different than something happening by accident," Matt explained. "Luck is knowing how to take advantage of breaks; knowing how to take advantage of the kindness of strangers. Being fortunate enough to meet the right people at the right time, and then capitalizing on those opportunities."

Jeff Zucker, the CEO of NBC Universal Television Group, also believes you need to be ready for luck. Jeff is a dynamic television executive who was promoted from president to CEO the morning we were scheduled to meet, but he was kind enough not to cancel the interview, even though the press was practically beating down his door. A consummate multitasker (he was walking the perimeter of his vast corner office, taking quick calls here and there, and checking e-mail, while still staying completely focused on what he was telling me), Jeff comes across as someone who is fiercely competitive and driven. Knowing he is a devout tennis player, I could imagine him on the court torturing me with cross-court winning shots.

"I think that, you know, you do need some luck. You do need to be fortunate, but I am also a believer that you make your own luck," he said. "And that you put yourself in a position to be lucky. What I mean by that is that you have to work hard. You have to do a good job. You have to come through; you have to deliver. And I think if you do all those things, you put yourself in a position then to take advantage of the good fortune that from time to time will come your way."

Rikki Klieman said something similar: "You can't get luck, professionally, by walking on some cloud of your own. You have to have put yourself in a position that luck will come to you, you know?"

Reflecting on the moment when Steve Brill, the founder of Court TV, called to ask if she would be interested in moving from working as a prominent trial lawyer to becoming an on-camera personality (which, as you will learn later, was her original life dream), she said, "I didn't get a call from Steve Brill to come on Court TV because I was some lawyer in the hinterland. The call to come to Court TV was the most dramatic, fulfilling change of my career—leaving the law when I was totally burned out and coming into this theatrical world, which was my world! What could have been better, being a lawyer, and being an entertainer? But Steve Brill didn't pick my name out of a hat. I had worked, at that point, for nineteen years, like a dog, to be in a place where I was doing seventeen-hour days and traveling on weekends all around the country lecturing to bar associations, so I was well-known. When Court TV covered some of my cases, he knew who I was.

"Luck, serendipity, timing, flukes . . .

you know, your talent carries you through

about 40 percent in this business, and I

think the combination of those things carries

you the rest of the way."

—Matt Lauer

"You can only have 'luck,' and you can only have the best timing, because you've proved yourself there," she added.

Are *you* prepared for a lucky break?

• • •

Besides being prepared for luck, you also have to actually be present—and by present, I mean literally *in the room*—for it to cross your path. Over the years, I've heard people say how important it is to just show up and be seen. That's why I always advise people to get off the couch and get out there. If I hadn't gone to a party at the Four Seasons restaurant for Jack Welch's new book, *Winning,* I would not have met Joe Tessitore, the president of Collins, the HarperCollins imprint publishing my book. Our conversation that night led to this book.

In a way, that's how **Joy Behar** landed her role as a co-host on *The View.*

> "Things happen to people, but they don't
> take them and use them. If you have
> good luck in life, use it correctly."
>
> **—Joy Behar**

"The part in the movie, or in my case, the job on *The View,* has to do with—I'm in the industry, I'm in the game. And I happen to show up at the right time," she said. "Because I met Barbara Walters when I did a benefit for Milton Berle's eighty-ninth birthday party at the Waldorf-Astoria. Somebody asked me if I would perform there. You know, you do benefits for free; it's not for the money. You do it for the good of whatever, but also to be seen. And I was there, and she was there. And I actually impressed her. So that's called good timing, I think."

The lesson is clear: **Say yes. Get out there. Be seen and meet people, so luck can find you.**

• • •

Timing, obviously, plays a significant role. As **Rikki Klieman** neatly put it, "Timing is not something in life. Timing is everything in life."

There's the timing of being in the right room at the right time and meeting the right person, as with Joy Behar meeting Barbara Walters. And then there is the greater dimension of timing, in which you are able to catch a wave of change just as it is gaining momentum.

Bob Pittman always has seemed to be just ahead of the next big media curve. "I was there when AM radio began to die and FM came on," he said. "And I was there for the beginning of the cable networks, and the revolutions—these specialized, targeted networks like MTV and Nickelodeon. I was even lucky enough to be there when the Internet really went to mass market."

Clive Davis, too, was there when a cultural tide was turning. By the time he was named president of Columbia Records in 1967, there were signs that the music Columbia Records was recording was being eclipsed by the tastes of the younger generation.

"I was looking at A and R [artist and repertoire] men who grew up with Tony Bennett and Jerry Vale and Johnny Mathis and Streisand, and I said, 'You know, we've got to get into the rock business.' But people who grew up with pop music find it very difficult to make that move. I, by luck, found myself at the Monterey Pop Festival at a time when it was the revolutionary festival."

The artists he discovered at the festival, including Janis Joplin, ushered in the new era of rock-and-roll for Columbia Records. He hired a new A and R staff of young people to help him scout for the artists who reflected the new tastes. The rest is music industry history.

In 1994, when the Internet was still in its hazy early stages, **Christie Hefner,** the enterprising chairman and CEO of Playboy Enterprises, launched Playboy.com, the first national magazine on the Web. Obviously, the Internet turned out to be more than a passing fad, and today, the distribution of digital content is one of the company's largest profit sources. In subsequent years, practically every single national magazine would boast an online edition.

Christie was there at the right time with the right content, and most important, with the right instinct to act.

Best-selling author and Pulitzer Prize–winning journalist **Anna Quindlen**'s early career fortuitously dovetailed with the fight for gender equality rights.

"In terms of what was happening in the world for women, my timing was impeccable," Anna said. "My father said to me one day on the telephone, 'Do you know what would have been the greatest tragedy for you? If you'd been born fifty years earlier, because you would have been one of the most miserable people in the world.' What he meant, of course, was that there wouldn't have really been any venue for the kind of inchoate ambitions, dreams, and desires that I had.

"The truth is that in terms of my hiring and promotion, during the first fifteen years of my career, being a woman was an advantage rather than a disadvantage. For example, I was hired at the *New York Times* during a time when it was trying to settle a class-action suit. Part of the terms of that settlement was to hire and promote and pay women in parity with men. And that wound up pushing me along very, very quickly, in a way that might not have been true otherwise."

CNBC's **Maria Bartiromo,** the stunning and brilliant host of the nationally syndicated show *The Wall Street Journal Report with Maria Bartiromo,* also found herself at a critical juncture in her industry.

"Luck and timing have everything to do with my success," she affirmed. Maria and I were sitting in a back room next to the kitchen in the Regency Hotel in New York, to avoid the noise of the power breakfast crowd dining nearby. I remember taking one look at her on television years ago and saying to my agent, "This woman is going to be a big star." She comes through on camera with charisma, and she really knows her stuff. Yet despite her beauty, talent, and preparation, she's quick to assert that synchronicity played a major part in her career.

"First of all, when I got my job at CNN Business News, business television was in its infancy," she said. "It was 1987. The stock market had just crashed. We were about to embark on an enormous bull market. I mean, it was great timing. So, yes, you have to have a hard-work ethic, and you have to be smart, and know what to do with opportunities. But you also have to have some luck, in being there at the right time."

Then, in 1993, she joined CNBC, and two years later she became the first reporter to broadcast live daily from the floor of the New York Stock Exchange—which she again says was incredible timing. "We were able to bring the cameras down there, and try to demystify what was going on down there. It was a moment in time when the stars were coming together: you had a great bull market; you had the democratization of information; individuals were wanting to invest themselves. And Dick Grasso, the chairman of the NYSE at the time, was open to the idea of bringing the camera down there."

The alchemy of factors combined with Maria's skills to make magic, as she helped to pioneer a new era in financial journalism. She continued to report live from the NYSE for ten years, eventually launching not one but two national shows bearing her name and two regular columns—one in *Business Week* and one in *Reader's Digest*—and becoming a regular contributor to the *Today* show.

It's a good idea to keep a sharp eye on the horizon for the coming waves, because you never know when you might find yourself poised to ride the next big one.

• • •

Many people I interviewed discussed the role that lucky coincidence played in their success, but I really believe it's important to **look behind coincidences for opportunities**.

A couple of years into my job hosting and producing my talk

show *Southern Exposure with Bill Boggs,* in High Point, North Carolina, I made a weekend trip back home to Philadelphia to take my mother and her best friend to see Frank Sinatra at the Spectrum. (I'd become a giant fan of Sinatra's after I sneaked in dressed as a busboy to see him at the 500 Club, in Atlantic City, during that summer at the Lincoln Hotel). On the flight from Greensboro, I read a little item in a newspaper I found on the seat about how WNEW-TV in New York City had a noon talk show that was in a state of flux. The host had resigned, and all manner of guest hosts were filling in.

Later that afternoon, as I was walking across Chestnut Street to meet my mother at Wanamaker's department store, I bumped into WNEW-TV's Judy Licht. How's that for a coincidence? Judy knew my work and urged me to call the station for an audition for the noontime show. Seeing her—a New Yorker—in Philadelphia, just a couple of hours after I'd read what she was telling me about, felt like an omen.

If I had not wanted to see Sinatra and hadn't flown from North Carolina that day, and hadn't been crossing the street at that moment, I would not have run into Judy. I would not have called WNEW-TV, or auditioned and gotten the job hosting what became *Midday Live with Bill Boggs.*

If you're living your life the right way, there are many times events will align themselves in what could be described as a weird coincidence. But really, when you experience something like that—for example, you've been thinking about someone you need to talk to and you run into them in an elevator—I believe it is a sign to look deeper and view the "weird coincidence" as a potentially fortuitous opportunity.

Dr. Judith Rodin, the first woman to become president of an Ivy League school (the University of Pennsylvania), told a great story about coincidence. Dr. Rodin has had a long and distinguished career that includes a seat on President Clinton's Committee of Advisors on Science and Technology, a professorship of medicine and psychiatry at Yale University, a reputation as a pioneer of the women's health movement, and more than two hundred articles and chapters in academic publications to her credit. I met with this warm, intelligent, orderly woman in her office at the Rockefeller Institute, the nonprofit charitable organization of which she now is president. She offered a slightly different take on being in the right place at the right time: she believes you need to be the right *person* at the right time.

> ### "I've had a series of lucky episodes, but I got rewarded because of the hard work."
>
> **—Dr. Judith Rodin**

When Judith was a freshman at Penn, where she earned her undergraduate degree, she took an introductory psychology course with a professor named Henry Gleitman. "I had come to Penn to be a French major, but he totally turned me on to psychology. He was absolutely amazing," she recalled. "And what I then learned was that his adviser, Richard Solomon, who was a leading psychologist, was looking for an undergraduate to work in his lab. And he told the TA [teaching assistant] in this course, 'Pick the person who got the highest grade on the midterm, and offer him a position in the lab.' I turned out to be the 'him,' and so, I had a position in Solomon's lab all four years of my undergraduate career, which was truly amazing. I worked with several of his graduate students, and did seminal work on learned helplessness that sort of propelled me to my graduate career.

"Now fast-forward," she continued. "I have a different name—my married name—which all my publications are under. I'm invited to give a colloquium at Yale; I was already a faculty member at NYU. And that day, a faculty member at Yale told them he was leaving and going somewhere else.

"They thought that I gave a dazzling talk, and so they offered me the job on the spot. The next day the chairman called me sheepishly and said, 'I shouldn't have done that. You know, we've got to form a search committee, and have to interview a bunch of people. This was much to impetuous,' and so forth. 'And by the way, you have to meet this faculty member who's going to be on the search committee who enormously dislikes your area of research. Doesn't respect it, doesn't think it's hard enough science,' and the like. I come into the room, and [the doubter on the search committee] turns out to be the graduate student who selected me to be the TA those many years ago. The rest is history."

"And you got the job," I said. "Perfect!"

• • •

Bobbi Brown has a more spiritual take on luck.

"I believe in karma," she said. "It could be the same thing as luck. But I think that there are reasons we have to do certain things in life."

Bobbi inherited her belief that you attract luck through doing good deeds from her grandfather, who was a primary influence in her life. Arriving in the U.S. as a Jewish immigrant from Russia, "Poppa" moved from selling newspapers to selling purses and eventually graduated to cars. Bobbi explains that although he was the kind of guy her friends were petrified of, he was really an "old softie" under his rough exterior—a kind, decent man who always tried to instill the Golden Rule in his children and grandchildren.

"One of my favorites stories that my grandfather told me is that one day, some guy came in that looked like he was off the street," she said, smiling softly at the memory. "All the salesmen were kind of ignoring the guy, so Poppa goes up to the guy, who had, like, a big paper bag, and he says, 'Hey, boss, how you doing? What can I help you with?' and the guy says, 'I'm going to buy four cars,' and handed him a bag of cash. Whether that actually happened, I don't know, but that was the story Poppa told me. And you know what? I don't judge a book by its cover. It doesn't matter who people are, or what they do for a living. I expect the same thing of people: to just be nice and kind and tell the truth."

> "You never know what you're going to get out of something, you know? So sometimes you do things for free in this life. Sometimes you go to places you don't want to go. I also believe the more you give, the more you get back."
>
> **—Bobbi Brown**

This personal code is what led to a chance meeting that catapulted her career to another level. Years ago, at her makeup counter in Neiman Marcus, Bobbi met a nice older woman. She was, of course, kind to her. The woman turned out to be Jeff Zucker's grandmother (Jeff, at the time, was the executive producer of the *Today* show), who insisted her grandson meet with Bobbi. As a result, Bobbi became a regular on the show.

"I believe that certain things are right in front of you," she concluded. "And if you're just kind, and giving, and nice, and your eyes are open, you might really just find them."

I agree. **The better you are to people, the more good will come to you.**

• • •

Sometimes a lucky break teaches you a lifelong lesson.

Designer **Joseph Abboud** confessed that he sees the world through rose-colored glasses. "You know, in learning the craft

Get the Contract

Since you already know I often see meaning in coincidence, it won't come as any surprise that I've picked up advice and wisdom from all kinds of unlikely sources. If we're open to it, fate will deliver to us exactly the wisdom we are meant to have.

Years ago, I was riding around New York City in the back of someone's limousine with some friends, when suddenly the driver realized he was late for another pickup. Rather than have him take me back home, I decided to just jump out there and go for a walk.

I found myself in the Twenties on the East Side, and since I didn't have to be anywhere specific that day and was feeling kind of introspective, I ducked into a tavern to have a quiet drink by myself. As I sat down at the bar, I noticed a guy in a suit slumped over a glass of whiskey; it seemed he'd been there for a while. He looked up at me, eyes well on their way to bleary, and said, completely unsolicited, "I'm gonna tell you something, and I want you to remember this all your life, whatever situation you're in: *Always get the contract.*" He turned back and sipped his drink without another word.

I don't know the events in his life that led to his unexpected revelation, but the drama of it all had a great impact on me. So throughout my career, in any business situation, I've made sure to **get the contract**. This practice has become so fundamental to me, in fact, that when my twenty-one-year-old son Trevor put together a list he refers to as "The Wisdom of Bill Boggs as Told to Trevor Boggs," **Get the contract** was number seven on the list.

that I learned, I learned about colors and yarns and fabrics and shape," he said. "I didn't learn about contracts and lawyers. I had this passion to create, and make beautiful things. And I thought it was in everyone's best interest to go there. I was a product person my whole life. I wasn't a business person."

A few times in his career, Joseph got burned a little because of this admitted naïveté. He told one story of narrowly escaping disaster:

Joe was about to sign a three-page contract in which he would have unwittingly sold his name for $10. Luckily, he spotted a fourth page, which was actually a note from the other party's lawyer. It said, "Don't show this to Joe, but just have him sign."

"I mean, how lucky?" Joseph said, still incredulous at how narrowly he escaped a huge mistake. "Like I always say, God touched me on the shoulder. Because if that man had handed me just three pieces of paper, I would have signed my name over . . . How lucky was I that, by mistake, he handed me the wrong piece of paper?"

Lucky breaks can sometimes be wake-up calls. Joe saw he'd had a pattern of not dealing carefully with contracts. That lucky break forced him to change his cycle of behavior.

End Notes

> "It's hard to say what was luck and what was talent. I learned to be patient and wait for the right time to pursue certain things, and I know how to negotiate for what I want."
> **—Donald Trump**

"There's always timing. There are so many variables that you can't control, especially in this particular field. I think a big part of it is recognizing what you can and cannot control, and put your efforts into the things you can. There's no control over the timing of things, what's available—whether or not you're physically appropriate for something. You can control preparedness. You can control education, and your knowledge or understanding of what's required of you. And you can work on bettering those things, very specifically."—**Renée Zellweger**

"Very often I joke around and say, 'Oh, we're not that smart. We're just lucky.' But you know, at the end of the day, to leave the joke aside, luck is something that you attract. It's something you create. You create luck by creating opportunity."—**Frédéric Fekkai**

"You certainly need some good fortune along the way. I shouldn't have survived some of my boating activities. So I definitely have been born under a lucky star."
—**Sir Richard Branson**

"Luck can't be underestimated. Sometimes being in the right place at the right time, and having the stars align, is out of your control. And that leads to the question of fate, or whether things are meant to be, which is a whole other discussion."—**Peter Cincotti**

"Luck plays a part, and you've got to be there to make of it what you will."—**Clive Davis**

4

Make Good Decisions

Renée Zellweger • Jeff Lurie • Mark
Burnett • Norman Lear • James Blake • Mario
Cuomo • Matt Lauer • Peter Cincotti

THE PATH TO SUCCESS has many forks, and the
signs at those junctures are not always easy to
read, except, of course, in hindsight. Decisions need to be made: Accept the offer or pass? Take the risk,
or play it safe? Make people happy, or stick to your guns and
piss them off? Take the money or hold out for the job you
love?

Personally, I'm not terrific at making decisions. One of my
strengths is an active imagination, so when I'm weighing my options, I usually have a good grasp of how different scenarios could
play out. Unfortunately, this clarity leads to its own kind of "analysis paralysis," as I sort through the pros and cons of each option.
So, for help, I turn to those who know me very well—my mother,
my wife, lifelong friends—and I seek out their objectivity. The
only problem I have is when they all disagree!

I gathered some interesting insights on making decisions during the course of my many interviews. If you're at a crossroads, I
hope one of these stories will be helpful to you.

• • •

Academy Award–winning actress **Renée Zellweger** does not let fame, power, or money tempt her into making decisions that are not congruent with her core values and passions.

Renée has A-list status in Hollywood, but she is at heart a hugely centered, soulful, and smart young woman from Texas. Renée is a neighbor of mine, and every time we meet and I see the sparkle in her eyes and her wide-open smile, I'm impressed by how refreshingly down-to-earth and caring she is.

Renée is best known for her breakout role as Dorothy Boyd in *Jerry Maguire,* her appearances as the zany and lovable title character in two *Bridget Jones* movies, winning the Oscar for best supporting actress in *Cold Mountain,* and her show-stopping performance as Roxie Hart in the movie version of *Chicago.* But she also famously turned down big bucks for the lead role in the 1998 remake of *Godzilla.* It's interesting to hear her talk about that choice, because it epitomizes the personal code she adheres to—the one that says she needs to feel inspired by work in order to take it on.

"It all comes back to happiness, and personal integrity, or what your value system is," she said. "And what you find rewarding in terms of the day. It's motivated from something much broader, like 'what do I hope for in life?' In general, I'm a curious person, and I like to learn things. I am fed by challenges that require that I broaden my ability to understand things."

Is that why she turned down such a huge amount of money to be in *Godzilla*? I wanted to know.

"Oh. Well, that—it's inconsequential. It's not important," she said. I could tell she was being genuine; this was not a memory she viewed as burdensome.

"But you weren't making any money at the time," I observed.

"Yeah, but it wasn't about that. I looked at the script and I thought, "You know what? I don't have anything to give to this.

I could show up on the set and I could put on the clothes, and I could say the lines. But when I read it, it doesn't say, 'Wow, wouldn't that be a day at work, right there?' I didn't look at it and think, 'Wow. You know, that scares the crap out of me. Look at what would be required in order to achieve this. To bring this to life.' I didn't look at it and say, 'I cannot contain myself for excitement about the idea of being involved in this.' And if you're gonna *have* to do it, you probably ought not to do it."

"I don't look at anything that I've done as a mistake. Because I never compromised myself, morally, for any of the work I've done. I've never not been able to sleep at night because I knew that I was not doing the right thing by someone else, or by myself, or that I had taken something under circumstances that were questionable."

—Renée Zellweger

"So you don't compromise much," I said.

"No," she said. "I know I hadn't really earned the right to turn down a movie part that was as substantial and significant as that. But on a very small note, I was able to recognize what I value personally. I knew that the satisfaction that would come from being involved in that experience would not be worth how I might have felt compromised."

What is *your* personal code of what you will and won't do?

• • •

Nearly every decision Philadelphia Eagles owner **Jeff Lurie** makes is scrutinized by the press and the team's legion of rabid fans. One of the main reasons I wanted to interview Jeff is that I've seen firsthand how he has lifted the spirits of an entire city by instilling such a positive feeling about their beloved team. The way he has improved the Eagles since he bought the team has made a huge difference in the collective psyche of the people— during football season, at least!

"With the fans, their intentions are great. They want to win, and they want to win big. But I think with fans, sometimes they want to think in the short term of what might be good for the next three weeks, or one year, and make decisions that would really impact our ability to sustain anything good. So we've got to analytically recognize where everyone's coming from, and then just try to make the best decision."

—Jeff Lurie

As it happened, our interview was scheduled for exactly the same day that Jeff had made a controversial decision to suspend Terrell Owens, one of the Eagles' star players, who had become a divisive force by holding out for astonishingly high contract terms, disturbing the harmony of the team. Though there was a swarm of controversy swirling around him, Jeff didn't appear to be preoccupied by it. He was calm, poised, and completely focused on our interview—almost Zen-like in his composure. Dressed all in black with salt-and-pepper hair, Jeff Lurie is elegant both in speech and manner—definitely not a hyper-macho, fist-pounding football team owner straight out of central casting.

Given what was going on, it was the perfect moment to talk about how to make decisions under pressure. Like Joe Torre, another sports guru who stays calm in the clutch, Jeff remains focused on the dictates of his own inner compass:

"I think this is one of the real reasons for the success of this team," he said. "Both myself and the key people I have around me have a sense of the way things should be done, and the way things should be built and sustained, and can be critically analytical at the same time. We've never, ever made a decision based on popular opinion. Most of the best decisions for the franchise, over the years I've owned the team, have been very unpopular decisions."

He went on: "You've got to just say, 'Look, we're gonna do the very best we can with what we think can happen.' That doesn't mean you don't listen, you know? But you've got to have your policy and agendas, and plan. If you don't have that, then you just kind of waver. You kind of fly in the wind."

Jeff Lurie's big-picture decision making, popular or not, has led the Eagles to the Super Bowl and many dramatic playoff appearances.

● ● ●

One reason making decisions is so difficult is that choosing one thing frequently means closing the door on all the other options. As producer **Mark Burnett** explained, the Latin root of the word "decision" is *"decisus,"* which means *"cut off."* However, I've learned that once you commit fully to a decision, you become that much more powerful.

That theory has been a guiding force for pioneering writer-producer **Norman Lear,** the creator of groundbreaking television hits like *All in the Family, Maude, Sanford and Son,* and *The Jeffersons.* Lear's talent and vision brought controversy to the sitcom, and changed the direction of American television.

I was fortunate enough to be a guest on Norman Lear's yacht

when he was sailing around Italy's Amalfi coast in the summer of 1982. I got to know him quite well on that trip. He was a lively and intelligent conversationalist, a good listener, and someone who knew he was making an impact with his life. When I interviewed him twenty-four years later, in his big, comfortable office at his company, Act Three, in Beverly Hills, I was every bit as impressed. At eighty-three, he hasn't lost a step. He has the same quick wit and keen acumen I remembered from those sunny days at sea.

> "You think you're committed, but at the moment of *real* commitment, the whole fucking universe conspires to assure your success."
>
> **—Norman Lear**

Like any successful person, Norman faced pivotal decisions along the way. Most notably, there was a point in his career when he had an offer for a three-picture deal with United Artists. It was a sure thing, and well-timed, since his pilot for *All in The Family* had been rejected twice by ABC television. Norman was on the brink of signing with United Artists when CBS decided they wanted to take a shot with his sitcom about the grumpy bigot Archie Bunker and his daffy wife. It was a classic fork in the road.

"Everybody in my life said, 'You've got to take this three-picture deal,'" he remembered. "But everybody that had seen the pilot laughed at the pilot, even when it was at its shakiest. So there was no question in my mind. This was something I had to do, if I could get it done. I understood the brilliance of Carroll O'Connor, and that little ensemble. I got that. They made me laugh until I cried. I think I understood the gift from the gods there."

Norman Lear turned down the three-picture deal and got *All in the Family* on the air, which, as we know, became an unprecedented success. He forged ahead without looking back, and that decision led to his becoming a television king.

• • •

Professional tennis player **James Blake** is a star in the tennis world. With his dramatic, high-profile quarterfinals match against Andre Agassi in the 2005 US Open, in which he conducted himself beautifully, honoring his legendary opponent, he captured the enthusiastic attention of devoted fans hungry for a new idol in their beloved sport. James fell in love with the game at a young age, displaying tremendous potential. At around age thirteen, he was faced with a choice: in order to become truly great, he realized he would need to let go of all of his other pursuits and channel his efforts into developing his game. His focus had to be tennis, to the exclusion of everything else. He knew what he needed to do, even at age thirteen, if he wanted to be a superstar.

I met James at the Mondrian Hotel in Los Angeles, one day after he beat Lleyton Hewitt in the finals of the 2006 Tennis Channel Open in Las Vegas. Tall, strong-legged, wearing a backward baseball cap and a T-shirt, he moved with a slow grace—very relaxed in his skin. Underneath the casualness, though, is the drive and determination of a major winner.

"I remember actually saying this to one of my teachers," James said. "That when I think something's important, I go after it with intention. I'm gonna do the best I possibly can at that. And I think when you do that, you have to realize that there's going to be other things that are sacrificed. I mean, if something is that important to you, you have to treat it that way. Basically, I gave up a lot of other things, other sports, other musical interests . . . I gave them up when I decided to really commit to tennis."

"You sacrificed to be the best," I said.

"Yeah," he said. "I always wanted to be—instead of being a

jack-of-all-trades, and pretty good at tennis, and pretty good at baseball, and pretty good at football, or anything like that, I said, 'No, I want to excel at one thing. And I want to treat that as if that one thing is very important.'"

Greatness usually requires some degree of sacrifice, and recognizing that may be the key to making tough career decisions. As Vince Lombardi said, "Anything is possible if you are willing to pay the price."

• • •

Mario Cuomo is as famous for the opportunities he did not take as he is for those he did. He turned down two invitations from President Clinton to join the Supreme Court, pulled away from consideration as a vice presidential nominee, and even said no when some in his political party urged him to consider the presidency of the United States. He believes we shouldn't necessarily jump at every opportunity that comes our way unless we are certain that it is right for us, and we for it.

> ## "You've got to have the strength to make intelligent choices."
>
> ### —Mario Cuomo

"My own habit, I think, is to consider all sides of everything, sometimes to a point where it's tedious for others," he said. "I ask, 'Is this good for me? How is it good for me? What will it do for me?' And then, 'What bad things can result from this?' And I try very hard to see all aspects of the situation. I've never been the kind of bold person who sees an opening and says, 'That's it, I'm sure,' and then rushes into it.

"They call me Hamlet," he admitted with a hint of a smile. "For spending too much time thinking about the presidency, for example. But it was such an important issue that I did spend a lot of time going both ways."

"You have two voices speaking to you," he went on. "The one that whispers in one ear and says, 'Hey, look, if you make it, you're gonna be sitting on top of the world. You'll be the most powerful person in the world if you're the president of the United States of America. And wouldn't that be lover-ly?

"And then the other voice says, 'Yeah, think about that one, Mario. You would be the most powerful person in the world. Is it fair for you to think of yourself as competent enough to bear that responsibility? I mean, do you really think there is nobody out there better than you are to bear that great responsibility? So don't get dazzled by the voice in your other ear telling you you're gonna be a big person. How about your obligation to be sure you're the very best?'"

The Tempting Offer

The kind of deeply considered decision making Mario Cuomo talked about isn't something we as a culture are used to. The prevailing mandate is to seize every big opportunity, but sometimes that just isn't in our best long-term interest.

In **Matt Lauer**'s darkest hour, when he really needed money, he was offered game shows and lucrative infomercials. He turned those down because he knew that if he took those jobs, he would never be able to do the kind of serious interviewing he wanted to do.

It's almost dead-certain that if Matt had caved and taken one of those opportunities, he wouldn't be the superstar journalist and interviewer that he is now on the *Today* show.

Mario's method of making intelligent choices is to give each voice careful and deep consideration. In the end, Cuomo chose not to run because, as he humbly puts it, "When it came to the presidency, I never felt that Mario Cuomo from South Jamaica, Queens, is the best this country can do."

• • •

There's a lot to digest here about making decisions. I'll leave you with one last thing that I've personally figured out about making decisions: If you are really waffling, you likely already know the answer in your heart. In other words, **when you don't know, you know**.

End Notes

> "I've been fortunate enough to spend time with a lot of very driven business people—Martha Stewart, Donald Trump, Jeffrey Katzenberg, just to name three. The commonality is pretty fast decision making. Just get it done. Yes, no, yes, no . . . not to vacillate, and sit around and wonder, until it's too late."—**Mark Burnett**

> "Wait for the right opportunity. Don't jump at something because you'll be able to make your car payment and go out to nice restaurants. Wrong reason."—**Matt Lauer**

> "When it comes to decisions, I follow my gut and that's what I live by. And you know what? If I'm wrong, I'd rather it be my mistake than someone else's."—**Peter Cincotti**

TWO

The Mind-sets of Success

5

Seize Opportunity

Bill Bratton • Frank Rich • Richard Johnson • Diane von Furstenberg • Joseph Abboud • Jane Friedman • Linda Huett • Anna Quindlen • Maria Bartiromo • Diane Warren • Bobbi Brown • Renée Zellweger • Mario Cuomo • Bob Pittman • Donald Trump

ANY MOMENT of high inspiration is a gift, and I believe it is our responsibility to act forcefully on it. Because I seized a particular moment years ago, I got my start on the road to making my dreams come true.

When I finished graduate school (the Annenberg School for Communication at the University of Pennsylvania), I had no idea how to go about making my childhood dream of being an interviewer come true. So I took the first job offered to me, as a writer in the publicity department at the Armstrong Cork Company, in Lancaster, Pennsylvania. Writing, I rationalized, would be a little bit like show business. And to the extent that Armstrong made my life feel like a very bad movie, it was like show business. Because about an hour and half into the job, I was miserable, and things went downhill from there.

I'd had boring jobs to make money while I was in school—bagging groceries, washing dishes, or selling vacuum cleaner bags door-to-door—but working at Armstrong was torture. It was incomprehensible to me how my co-workers—grown men, who were well educated—could get so wildly excited about things like floor polish, bottle caps, or ceiling tile. My basement office, which was the size of a garden shed, had a single window high on the wall. One afternoon I stood on top of my desk, looked up at the sky, and wondered, "How do I get out of this place and stop writing about vinyl Corlon tile?" The answer, as it turned out, was not far away.

One day, on my way to the men's room, I saw a couple of co-workers, Tom Patchett and Jay Tarses, standing in the hall with a few secretaries looking on, performing a very funny comedy routine they had written. (By the way, Jay was one of the people I'd met that fateful summer working at the Lincoln Hotel in Ocean City; he'd come to Armstrong at my suggestion because he needed to make money.) I'd been a lifelong fan of comedy duos like Abbott and Costello, Martin and Lewis, and Nichols and May, so I instinctively recognized Tom and Jay's comedic originality. When I asked them what they were up to, they said they had been writing comedy sketches as an outlet from the monotony of their jobs. Not surprisingly, these two creative guys were as bored by the minutiae of Armstrong's blown plastic containers and linoleum as I was. I asked to see another skit, and that, too, was hilarious.

That's when I had an epiphany. Really, I remember it as a blinding revelation: Patchett, Tarses, and I would quit our jobs and go into show business, and I would be their agent. I instantly wanted to do this. Somehow I *knew* this was our future.

From that moment on, I poured all my energy into developing their careers. We honed their material in small clubs, and I made cold calls to get them auditions. Within six months they were on national TV, on *The Merv Griffin Show*. Our bland jobs at Armstrong soon became a distant memory. Patchett and Tarses went on to have enormously successful and lucrative careers. In the three years I worked with them, I learned the ropes of the entertainment business and made contacts that would eventually open the door for my first break on television.

Throughout the interviews I conducted for this book, I heard important stories about how seizing opportunities changed the trajectory of people's careers. These leaders didn't sit around wishing something would happen. They kept their eyes open for opportunities, and when providence handed them what looked like an opening, they moved swiftly and boldly in the direction of their dreams.

• • •

Bill Bratton is the epitome of one who capitalizes on opportunities. Constantly driving forward, he consciously seeks out new situations that will challenge him. This, he says, is the primary reason for his long history of distinguished success, beginning as a beat cop in Boston, through his jobs as Boston police commissioner and New York City police commissioner, up through his current position as the chief of Los Angeles Police Department.

Authoritative and self-possessed with an air of refined machismo, Bill Bratton knows exactly what makes him tick. "Professionally, I like creating change," he said. "I like challenge. I'm not a maintenance type person. It's interesting, especially since I don't like to see things change in my world. I don't want a favorite restaurant that I go to to change much. I don't want a neighborhood to change. But in my professional life, I'm always changing. I don't necessarily like change in my personal life—things I enjoy—but in my professional life, I'm continually seeking new challenges."

Chief Bratton has a fascinating history. At several points in his career, he was faced with a choice to stay where we was, which was comfortable and financially rewarding, or seize the next opportunity and move on—and up. In 1993, when he was the superintendent in chief of the Boston Police Department, he was presented with the chance to leave his job after nineteen years on the force—*one year shy of a pension*—and become the New York City police commissioner. Many would have stayed and cashed out, but the prospect was too compelling for him to pass up.

"I've always had that degree of confidence that the opportunities will be there. And that I have the requisite skills to take advantage of them. If I get into something that I'm not enjoying, I'm not going to spend a lot of time there. Life's too short. I'm going to seek to move on."

—Bill Bratton

"I left for the challenge," he said, not surprisingly. "It was a risk, but I had confidence that at some point in my life I'd be able to make up for that pension by being in the private sector, make a lot of money . . . you know. I responded to the challenge. When I went, nobody thought that was going to be a success. To take on what was arguably one of the toughest policing jobs in America was a great risk. It was a point in time where I could basically kind of sit back and say, 'I've arrived.' Make sure I get my pension. But the bugle sounded, and off I went to New York."

Bill Bratton performed a history-making turnaround in New York, achieving the largest decline in crime in the city's history. After two years, however, that job ended because of personal clashes between himself and Mayor Rudy Giuliani, and Bill moved into the private sector. Though he was earning far more money than he ever had before, he was unhappy and bored. The excitement of the challenge was missing for him. So when the chance came to become the chief of the Los Angeles Police Department, he didn't hesitate.

"In Los Angeles, the idea was, 'Here's the opportunity to get back into the game,'" he said. "The motivation was enhanced by the whole new issue of 9/11, in the sense that there was a new crisis now facing the country, and cities, and policing. The policing now had to expand its paradigm beyond the traditional crime that we had dealt with successfully in New York and Boston. Policing, for the first time, had to deal with terrorism. When did policing ever have to do with terrorism? So it wasn't the same old business I was getting back into. It was a totally new set of challenges."

"If you have confidence, you can rise to any challenge."
—Bill Bratton

Bill Bratton's strategy of keeping his eyes open for new opportunities and never resting on his laurels has served him—and the communities he led—extraordinarily well. Three major U.S. cities are safer because of his drive to meet new challenges. His mind-set of success is absolute: **Never stop seeking out opportunities that challenge and inspire you.**

• • •

I have a list of mantras I use every day, one of which is, "I am aggressive in pursuit of my career goals." A significant practice of success that came up repeatedly in these interviews is the ability to **get noticed,** which is a palpable way of being aggressive in pursuit of your goals.

I met with **Frank Rich,** the former drama critic and current weekly columnist for the *New York Times,* on a freezing Sunday afternoon in February. Without the usual weekday thrum, Midtown was quiet, and as I crossed Forty-third Street, the lyrics from an old song went through my mind, *"New York on Sunday . . . big city taking a nap . . ."* Of course, there were still people at the *New York Times* offices, and they sent me up to the editorial floor to the small, sparsely furnished, pin-drop-quiet corner room where Frank writes his weekly piece for the Op-Ed page. I've known Frank for several years, and he has always impressed me as one of those people who is so smart that he brings a better game out of those around him.

"My first job in New York was as the lowest, lowest, lowest assistant editor for a magazine that hasn't existed in years," he told me. "It was just starting up, called *New Times*. It was started by a guy named George Hirsch, who had been the original publisher of *New York* magazine. And the idea was to make it sort of a well-written, new-journalism alternative to *Time* and *Newsweek*."

"I always had a fantasy about the *New York Times*, because I read about the *New York Times*. I looked at Hirschfeld cartoons. And it was kind of amazing, at thirty-one, to end up doing something that was such a direct hit on what I wanted to do, at least as a child."

—Frank Rich

"Anyway, the job was a very menial job," he continued. "It was trying to line up possible writers, doing first reads of pieces, reading a slush pile. And one of the things *New Times* was going to do was hire a film critic. In fact, they were, if memory serves, about to hire David Denby, who was a little older than me, and who would later become the film critic of both *New York* magazine and *The New Yorker.* At the last minute, they decided they couldn't afford to pay a freelance film critic. So I sort of raised my hand and said, 'I wrote film reviews in college. Could I do it?' So I did it for free. I didn't get paid for it. I remember, my salary was $10,000 a year, and I did these long essays, every issue of *New Times.* But that really led to my career. Because then a year and half or two years later, the *New York Post* saw my reviews and offered me the job as film critic there."

Raising his hand was a pivotal moment in Frank Rich's career. It led to a successful stint at *New York Post,* after which he was hired as a film and television critic at *Time* magazine, which in turn led to his illustrious job at the *New York Times.*

If you're aiming high, try reminding yourself daily to be aggressive in pursuit of your career goals. Put yourself out there and vigilantly **watch for opportunities to get noticed**.

• • •

It's a good idea to **not dismiss an opportunity as too small,** because you never know where something may lead.

"It's very important to pay attention," said fashion designer **Diane von Furstenberg,** whose name is synonymous with her iconic wrap dress that has remained a coveted classic for more than thirty years. Diane exudes the sensual femininity for which her clothing is so well known. Though we were sitting at a table in the dining area of her offices in Chelsea, I could picture her as a beautiful cat curled on a high plush pillow, serenely observing the world below.

"Pay attention to the opportunities," she repeated. "Because there may be an opportunity that opens up, that you just go in, and you don't even know how important it is. And it will change your life."

When Diane was a young woman, a friend offered her an internship in his clothing factory in Italy. Seeking something that would give her the sense of independence she desperately craved, she jumped at the chance—one that a lot of other people might have dismissed as too insignificant to consider. She observed the operation closely for nearly a year, absorbing all she could about designing and manufacturing, until the day she found out she needed to move to America with her husband. Panicked at first because she did not want to lose her sense of independence, she then realized that she'd learned enough in the factory to invent herself as a designer in her new country.

"So I said, 'You know what? Let me make a few samples in the factory. And I'll try to go and see if I can sell them in America,' which is what I did. I made a few samples, and I came to America. Boom. So that's the lesson. Pay attention to opportunity. Look and learn, especially when you're young. Look and learn, and something may come up. And it did."

Diane von Furstenberg's tremendous career might never have taken shape if she had not accepted an innocuous job in a factory in Italy. When the next opportunity arose, which was to pursue

Show Up on Sunday

Richard Johnson is the debonair, quick-witted gossip columnist and editor for the *New York Post*'s influential Page Six. He made me laugh when he shared this funny story about getting noticed:

"I remember there was a guy who I used to work with, who wasn't on staff. He was just freelancing, you know, on those shifts once in a while when somebody would call in sick or something. And he would just show up on Sunday, even when nobody had told him to come in. And so, the assignment editor wouldn't realize that he hadn't been scheduled, and just gave him stories to do. So it worked like a charm."

her husband's connections in order to show her designs to Diana Vreeland, the influential editor-in-chief of *Vogue* magazine at the time, she seized it again. Ms. Vreeland liked the product, gave her huge exposure, and Diane von Furstenberg's dresses became a multigenerational social phenomenon.

• • •

Another clothing designer of international repute, **Joseph Abboud**, wisely seized an opportunity that others overlooked as unworthy of their efforts.

When he started as a part-time salesperson at the upscale clothing store Louis of Boston, he was at the bottom of the pecking order. The impeccably dressed veteran salesmen worked on commission, so they naturally recognized all the big customers. One day, a woman walked in whom they didn't recognize. She was a little loud, so they gave her to Joseph—in their eyes "the pischer kid," as he described himself (using the Yiddish description of a "little squirt"). Joseph didn't see a low-level customer; he saw a chance to shine.

"I ended up selling her about twenty-five dress shirt and tie combinations," he recalled, laughing. "I remember all the commission guys were dying, because they all passed her off. And here I was, nice to her. She had her husband's suit, and I was laying out shirt and tie combinations. I remember walking to the cash register with my arms wrapped around a $2,000 sale. This was 1968, so today that would be like a $15,000 sale. And I remember thinking, 'You know what? I can do this.'"

Besides the boost it gave to his confidence, that sale earned Joseph major points with his boss, who saw him walking toward the register to ring up that pile of clothing. Suddenly the "pischer kid" was taken a little more seriously, and thus began his eight-year rise within the ranks of that organization.

Sometimes the small-but-meaningful opportunity shows up as

a chance to do your absolute best, even if you are not assured of a payoff.

• • •

You can't have a sense of entitlement if you plan to get ahead. The two mind-sets are mutually exclusive. Time and again, these interviews revealed stories about people who made the most of every opportunity they could find in order to learn, no matter how menial the task.

"You have to be aggressive, absolutely. You can't just sit back."

—Jane Friedman

Be Willing to Start at the Bottom

No matter how far you've gone in your education, once you decide to take that plunge into the cold waters of the workforce, it's important to adjust your mind-set and understand there's a possibility that you'll start at the very bottom.

Linda Huett, today the president and CEO of Weight Watchers International, oversees a global business with more than forty-six thousand employees. However meteoric her rise, this corporate superstar still started at the very bottom of the organization (actually, below the bottom . . . she initially walked into a meeting as a paying member with sixty-five pounds to lose).

"I'm always prepared to start at the bottom," she said, referring not only to her initial job at Weight Watchers as a

Before she became CEO of HarperCollins, **Jane Friedman** worked her way up through the ranks of Random House, starting as Dictaphone typist and leaving nearly thirty years later as executive vice president. She scaled the corporate ladder deftly, viewing every task as an opportunity—even the dreaded errand of fetching coffee.

"One doesn't have to flip from place to place to place to achieve that kind of growth," she explained from her large, book-lined office. Jane is at once commanding and charming, with powerful eye contact that draws you in. "I did it by paying attention to every detail of everything that came into that company. The mail. I never minded opening the mail. I never minded answering the phone. I never minded getting coffee for someone. I never minded anything that would put me in the middle of the action."

What would she say to someone who feels they are above going to get the coffee?

---

meeting leader, but also her prior successful career as a retail manager, where she began as an entry-level saleswoman at Heals and Son home furnishings store in London.

"I actually enjoy starting at the bottom, because you learn so much about an organization. Education can give you the theory. Work gives you the experience. If you truly want to understand how an organization works, or what the product, or what anything is, getting that understanding by actually working at different levels in that organization is just a plus."

As both **Jane Friedman** and **Linda Huett** wisely pointed out, working your way up through an organization gives you invaluable insights into its inner machinations, much as the conductor of a symphony understands the individual contributions of the instruments in the orchestra.

"I tell them, 'Don't even go there. Everybody starts at a certain point. Accept it. I don't want to hear, you know, you don't want to get coffee. I don't want to hear that you don't want to type. I don't want to hear that you don't want to be a messenger. Do it. Learn. If you're going to get the coffee, make sure you have a conversation at that coffee machine, so that something good comes from getting the coffee. Use every experience.'"

• • •

Finally, I think it is important to remember what **Anna Quindlen** learned the hard way about opportunity: **If you don't ask, you don't get.**

"I was once given a piece of advice by one of my colleagues at the *Times*, which was invaluable," she said. "I was in a little bit of a snit, because I hadn't been given a job that I wanted. I was thinking of leaving the paper. And he said to me, 'If you don't ask, you don't get.' And I hadn't asked. I just sort of assumed that I

Introduce Yourself

When CNBC's **Maria Bartiromo** was first starting out, she worked as an intern at CNN. Whenever and with whomever she could, she made an effort to seek out new projects.

"I remember saying, 'You know what? I want to go say hello to the woman who runs the news desk in general news,'" she said. "And I would go in, and I'd say, 'Hi, I'm interning here, and I'm down in business news. I just wanted you to know, if I could ever help you, I'm there, ready to do whatever it takes.'"

Be proactive; let people know you're there and eager to do whatever is needed. Opportunities will follow.

was talented, and I was invaluable, and good things would follow from that. As opposed to thinking, 'I have to go in there and say, This is what I want. How can I get it?'"

Be demanding, commensurate with your talent, she advises. Otherwise an opportunity meant for you could very easily go to someone else.

End Notes

"I'm an opportunist. To me, being an opportunist is not negative. It's being somebody who recognizes and then takes advantage of an opportunity."

—Diane Warren

"If I stepped back and waited for everyone to do everything, it wouldn't happen. You see a little window or door, you go for it. And if it closes, you go to the back door."

—Bobbi Brown

"My parents didn't project their insecurities or fear of failure or embarrassment onto us as children. It was always the opposite. It was, 'Why not try?'"

—Renée Zellweger

"Fix your focus on something that you really desire. And then go after it."

—Mario Cuomo

"Any time you change your day-to-day, it's a risk. But you're
taking it because the reward is great, if you succeed."
—Bob Pittman

"I'm not a complacent person. I like to grow and move on
from each accomplishment. Each achievement creates the
opportunity for the next."**—Donald Trump**

6

Identify Your Drive, Mission, and Purpose

Sir Richard Branson • David Rockwell •
Craig Newmark • Dr. Mehmet Oz • Brooke
Shields • Senator Kay Bailey Hutchison •
Clive Davis • Renée Zellweger • Diane von
Furstenberg • Joy Behar • Bob Pittman • Jeff
Zucker • Diane Warren • Jim Cramer • Phil
Lombardo • Jeff Lurie • Joseph Abboud •
Anna Quindlen • Richard Johnson • Donald
Trump • Christie Hefner • Linda Huett •
Frédéric Fekkai

AN IMPORTANT MIND-SET of success is knowing *why* you want to be successful. Whether it is personal fulfillment, a mission, a desire to better your station in life, or very simply survival, it's essential to understand what you are working toward—or for.

The ambition of truly successful people may be powerful, but it is never blind. The people I interviewed all had clear reasons for why they work as hard as they do. Some are on an external mission, to change things in the world around them. Others are driven by more personal reasons. Either way, a sense of purpose helps fuel their drive.

What are *you* working for?

• • •

Ever since his counterculture days as a fifteen-year-old, when he started the controversial magazine *Student*, **Sir Richard Branson** has had the gleam of revolution in his eye. "The Rebel Billionaire," as his reality television show dubbed him, is on a mission to transform the world, one industry at a time. He also hopes to transform the world's environment, as evidenced by his 2006 pledge to contribute $3 billion from his companies' profits to fight global warming in the next decade.

"As a fifteen-year-old, when I was thinking of leaving school, I'd never had any interest or thoughts of becoming an entrepreneur or businessperson. I wanted to start a magazine and use the magazine as a vehicle to change the world. I saw a lot of things around the world that I didn't like. I didn't like the way we were being taught at school. I thought the teachers had contrived school lessons, to basically just occupy our time in the dullest way possible, not really to teach us anything. I wanted to try to make a difference. But in order to become an editor, I had to become an entrepreneur.

"And ever since, you know, I've created things where I felt there was—that would sort of upset the status quo. I mean, the airline industry was abysmally run twenty-one years ago; I created an airline because I wanted the kind of airline I'd like to fly on. I wanted to make the airline experience an enjoyable one, which it wasn't, in those days. And you know, that's been my principal purpose for going into it. I've had to become a businessman just to make sure that that airline survives.

"My principal reason for going into a business is, in a sense— like a painter painting a picture—to create something which I'm really proud of. And if I've created the best, hopefully, then, you know, people will like it. And the figures will fall into place."

• • •

In a similar vein, architect **David Rockwell,** who is noted for his unconventional innovations in design and is on a personal mission to break through perceived limitations and barriers, said:

"If I look at my career, it's all been about quantum leaps. It's all been about not believing limits. I think limits are about defining a problem—a creative problem, a design problem. What intrigues me is blowing away those limits, and not seeing the blinders."

• • •

Craig Newmark is the quirky and brilliant founder of Craigslist. com, the ingenious classifieds website that posts in more than thirty-four countries and has helped millions of people do everything from find an apartment to sell a bicycle. What is most telling about Craig is that he has famously turned down millions of dollars from potential investors and advertisers, preferring to keep the site's mission pure.

I met Craig in a San Francisco coffee shop on a sunny winter afternoon, near the Craigslist.com offices. He seems to enjoy the description that has been applied to him as an awkward, grown-up nerd. He's got a sly twinkle is his eye that lets you know he's up to something. Craig is a real power-to-the-people kind of guy who is determined to propagate an old-fashioned but highly admirable principle:

"Upon reflection, I realize that I've stuck with the values that we all, in theory, learn from our parents and religious institutions, for real. Not the fake stuff you hear a lot. But just that helping people out is a pretty high value. And just following through with that. A big chunk of that is obsessing about customer service. We've built, with our community, a culture of trust. And that matters.

"Intellectually, this is all very gratifying. I know that I'm—well, let's say our team is helping millions of people out with basics. Our site is about everyday needs, like finding a place to live, or a job. The statement I make is that what I want to do is find the small ways where I can help other people help other people help other people to change the world."

• • •

Best-selling author **Dr. Mehmet Oz** is on a slightly different kind of mission. I met the charismatic Mehmet, one of the most respected cardiothoracic surgeons in the country, early one morning in his office at Columbia University New York Presbyterian Hospital in New York City. He operates on four hundred patients each year, writes award-winning and best-selling books, contributes frequently to magazines like *Time* and *Newsweek,* and appears often on national television shows, including *Oprah, Good Morning America, NBC Nightly News,* and *Dateline.*

Mehmet doesn't do these things in a quest for fame or wealth. Though national exposure has undoubtedly given him both of those things, he remains laser-focused on his goal to change the way Americans view and treat their bodies:

"At a certain point, you begin to understand you have insights into issues that most people around you don't—laymen, who don't know medicine. You have those 'eureka' moments, when a patient's eyes light up when they finally understand what you just said. You think to yourself, 'My goodness. There are millions and millions of people who don't get it, the way this person didn't get it. How do I get all of them to have these eureka moments?'

"I realized that I could stay in my office like this and have one-on-one conversations and change people's lives profoundly, but one at a time. And I thought, you know, if I do four hundred operations a year, for twenty-five years, that's ten thousand heart operations. Ten-thousand people whose lives I've changed. And I'm happy for that. You don't always change them positively, by the way. You just change them.

"But do one *Oprah* show, and you get eight, nine million viewers. And so, if I wanted to get out broad messages, I realized I should scale it, and deliver that same message to a few million people at once, in a way that people can grasp."

• • •

The talented actress **Brooke Shields** is propelled by a hunger for self-improvement.

I've known Brooke ever since she was eleven years old. Enchanting as a child, she has grown into a kind, gracious, beautiful woman. I met with her backstage between her matinee and evening performances as Roxie Hart in *Chicago*. Even in full stage makeup, her natural appeal shines through.

Brooke has reinvented herself several times in her career, transitioning gracefully from child model to screen actress, to television star, to the Broadway stage. Despite her career longevity, she still pushes herself in order to grow:

"I have an incredible sense of drive," she said. "I'm ambitious. Because I'm a perfectionist, my ambition is a very personal one. So, for instance, when I'm doing a show like this . . . when we're finished with our interview here, I'm working on a certain sixteen counts of a song. I've got three more weeks, and I could get away with just doing it the way I do it, until the end of the run. But it's not enough for me.

"So there's something about what I believe is my drive and my ambition to constantly be better, and get better. When I was younger, I wanted to be liked. So that meant I was on time, I was early, and I knew everything. I said please and thank you, and I did everything that was expected of me. That was my version of it.

Maybe that was a child's ambition. Now I understand it's based on improving my talent.

"I'm more competitive with myself than I am with anybody else. Because I'm never good enough for myself. I'm constantly looking at myself and saying, 'It's not good enough. I have to get better.' I'm always trying to make myself better."

• • •

Senator Kay Bailey Hutchison made history as the first woman elected to represent Texas in the Senate, receiving more than four million votes—more than any candidate in the state's past. Despite her role as the fifth-highest-ranking Republican in the Senate, Senator Hutchinson harbors a surprising belief that propels her:

"I think one of the motivations that I have had is that I don't consider myself successful. I still don't; I never have. And I think it's part of the drive."

• • •

After more than five decades in the music industry, mogul **Clive Davis** is still fueled by a childhood desire to ace every test and earn straight A's.

As a young boy going through the Brooklyn public school system, Clive was the consummate A-student. He was always impelled to study and work hard, and had an innate desire to excel. Later, in college and then at Harvard Law School, he was faced with a do-or-die scenario that forced him to couple A-student work habits with a powerful survivalist instinct, which ultimately propelled Clive Davis to achieve all that he has.

"I had a scholarship to NYU, and I had no money," he explained. "My parents were not in the position to offer me any economic help. And they died when I was eighteen and nineteen. After the death of both parents, as a freshman in college, I had a total sum of $4,000 to my name. That was my total asset, living with my sister and family in Queens, as I prepared for college and ultimately law school. If I didn't get close to an A-average, I would lose my scholarship. So, that definitely hones that drive to exceed, to excel.

"To me, it was survival," he said. "It was the idea of, 'What do I need to keep my scholarship?'"

In each new endeavor and level of success that peppers Clive Davis's bio, there is evidence of this survivor instinct and the aspiration of the A-student to succeed. He continually set sky-high standards for himself, whether he was building Columbia Records

Self-reliance

Achieving a sense of autonomy is a huge accomplishment when you're starting out. When you're able to stand on your own two feet, you establish deep-seated roots that allow you to fly high.

Renée Zellweger's goal when she set out on her own at age eighteen was to know that she could take care of herself. "As soon as I established that, I knew everything else would be fine," she said. "I recognized that as long as I'm able-bodied, I will be able to take care of myself."

In her young life as the daughter of a Holocaust survivor, **Diane von Furstenberg** was deeply influenced by her mother's message about the value of personal sovereignty. "The fact that I wanted to be independent, and I wanted to do something with my life . . . that was the absolute key to things. Freedom is a huge part of my drive."

Renée summed it up beautifully:

"Be independent and self-sufficient in the world. And then everything else is possible."

into a legendary institution or, years later, launching J Records at a time when many—himself included—wondered if he could make the same magic again (he did, many times over).

• • •

Desperation can often propel us like nothing else. It was only when comedienne **Joy Behar** was flat broke—with no job and no

Money, Money, Money

Is making money important? Here's what a few people had to say:

"No one should take a job for money. Life isn't about how much money you have. It's about how content you are, and how satisfied you feel. Money doesn't give you contentment. You may do something that makes you a lot of money, or you may do something that doesn't. You need enough money to live, and to have what you need to provide for you and your family. But what you really need is a sense of satisfaction from what you do."—**Bob Pittman**

"Yes. Absolutely. I mean, if you want to be independent. You can't be independent if you're not financially independent. Beyond that, I'm not greedy."—**Diane von Furstenberg**

"I've never been driven by money. I think that's a bad motivating force. I think that if you're in it for money, you'll make the wrong decisions."—**Jeff Zucker**

"These songs, they really earn a lot of money. But money has never been my motivator. You know, fifteen, twenty years ago, I had enough money to never work another day and live a very nice life. I don't care about money."—**Diane Warren**

prospects—that she was able to mobilize in the direction of her dreams:

"To get up in front of a bunch of people at night and try to make them laugh, you've got to be confident. And I never had the confidence to do it, really. So now, I needed the money. And the money was the motivating factor to get me to do it."

• • •

"After you make some money, then you can do what's in your heart."—**Jim Cramer**

"Making a comfortable living has been motivation, but not that much. I mean, until recently, the only thing I lacked in my life was a parking space. So that's about it. I was able to afford to recently buy a bigger TV than my CEO has. And that's good. But, you know, how many things do you need?"—**Craig Newmark**

"Never worry about what you're being paid. If the job and the opportunity are going to make you better, make you smarter, the money will come. And it's never failed me. I never took a job for money; I took it for the opportunity to learn, contribute; I took it for the opportunity to contribute; I took it for the opportunity to grow."—**Phil Lombardo**

"Making money's never been a goal. It's never been a reason for our existence. The reason that one has to make money is so that things that we're creating can survive. For instance, if you create beautiful things, things you can be proud of, you still have to pay the bills. You have to make sure that people have jobs. And therefore, making money is, in a sense, a necessary evil."—**Sir Richard Branson**

Making Mom Proud

Philadelphia Eagles owner **Jeff Lurie**'s father died when he was a young boy, and his mother raised him, his brother, and his sister on her own. If he were to look deep into his psyche, he admitted, he would have to say that his success stems from a desire to make his wonderful mother proud.

"I have a drive, in a sense, to prove my mother right," he said. "Right about how she brought me up. She had to be the mother and the father, starting [when I was] nine. And she had an autistic son as well, my brother. You know, people in our society assume that success goes with business, or with being a doctor, or whatever. I wanted her to be successful as a mother—to prove how wonderful she's been with me."

I completely understand this. I'm still motivated to please my own amazing ninety-two-year-old mother, who believes I can do and be anything.

Having something to prove can be incredibly motivating. When an embittered former business associate claimed **Joseph Abboud**'s plan to create an independent label would fail, he was determined to prove himself:

"He said to me, 'This is the best job you're ever gonna get. If you leave here, you're never going to get anywhere.' Well, at that moment, that was the best motivating force in my life. To say, 'You know what? I don't care if I sweep floors for the rest of my life. But if you think you're going to define what I'm going to be able to achieve . . .' It struck a chord that someone else was going to define who I was, and what I was going to be."

• • •

Full creative expression is **Renée Zellweger**'s guiding force. In each role, she strives to achieve her personal best. Here's how she eloquently puts it:

"Part of the satisfaction, in a strange sort of way, is making a challenge maybe more difficult than it has to be. Or seeing how much further you can take something in a positive direction. As long as there's still a window of opportunity to better something, then I don't want to stop. It's all very selfish, when you think about it. Because whatever someone else might experience on the flip side of it is residual, to some degree.

"It's a feeling. You know when you're writing something, for example, when you are fully expressing an idea and when you haven't. It's so satisfying, at the end, when you know it worked. I mean, it's not like I need to go and have a flag made and walk around with the 'Look What Happened' flag. It's just very quiet, personal satisfaction."

• • •

Anna Quindlen wastes no time in pursuing what she wants to accomplish, out of keen appreciation for the fragility of life:

"I think I have a very hyperactive sense of mortality that grows out of having lost my mother when I was so young, when she was so young. So I think that while there's a tendency on the part of some of my peers to think, 'Oh, someday I'd like to do X or Y,' I don't really believe in someday. I believe in today, and maybe on a good day, tomorrow. So my sense is always that if there's something I want to do, some role that I want to fit into my life, I'd just better do it right away. And I think that that has really enabled me to kick myself out of my comfort zone with some regularity."

• • •

The *New York Post*'s **Richard Johnson,** who started working at its legendary gossip chronicle, Page Six, in 1984 and quickly became the column's editor one year later, works to maintain the high expectations he has for himself and his life:

"I think I always wanted to achieve something, and be extraordinary. I didn't want to settle for some sort of mediocre life. So I think I pushed myself."

• • •

Ask yourself: What is the goal—the mission—the fuel behind your ambition? Finding the answer will galvanize your efforts and dramatically increase the power of your determination.

End Notes

> "I think something bigger is in charge, be it destiny or whatever. My personal mission is to enjoy my life and family and continue in my work, all of which I love."
>
> **—Donald Trump**

> "My role and my passion is to make women feel confident and attractive. I know how to do that."
>
> **—Diane von Furstenberg**

> "You have to believe in what you're doing. I couldn't be somewhere and simply mouth a point of view, or philosophy, or argument to support the position of the company I worked for. I would have to be somewhere where I believed in the values of the company. It starts with that."
>
> **—Christie Hefner**

"I'm ambitious to make a difference. That has always been the
driver for me."—**Linda Huett**

>"I believe that everybody has a beauty. Many people do not
>use it; they have no idea how to enhance their beauty. I
>enjoy tremendously helping people to understand how easy
>it is for them to look better, and feel better. So I'm educating
>people to be more 'them,' and that's what I think is the most
>beautiful thing ever."—**Frédéric Fekkai**

"Anyone who's worked with me at this hospital—who gets up
and works the hours that you work to be here—is ambitious.
But you have to temper that ambition with a more profound
love for humanity."—**Dr. Mehmet Oz**

7

Cultivate Self-Confidence

Bill O'Reilly • Joe Torre • Diane Warren • Matt Lauer • Bill Bratton • Christie Hefner • Diane von Furstenberg • Linda Huett

IF THERE IS ONE CORE BELIEF that was instilled in me early on, it came from my mother. She told me over and over: "You can do anything you want if you really put your mind to it." That message is part of the foundation of my life. She helped to teach me to believe in myself, and so I understand that self-confidence can be learned and practiced.

There's no one formula for its growth; it is a very personal process. My confidence developed in many ways. I've always had a measure of faith in my gifts and in my ability to work hard, but that core confidence has been nurtured by the work I've done, the confirmation of others, and the daily practice of self-affirmation. In the beginning of my television career, I had doubts about competing with others who were far more experienced. But my confidence grew by remembering I had talent as a public speaker that would help me develop the skills I needed to succeed.

The successful people who contributed to this book seemed to have an intrinsic sense of their inner power. Believing in yourself is *vital* for success. It is so important, in fact, that I don't think you are capable of scaling the great peaks in life without it. (I've come to believe that **you are very powerful provided you know how powerful you are**.) If you take nothing else from this book, I hope that you will try to incorporate this one insight into your inner matrix. It will arm you to deal with life and help you achieve enormous satisfaction.

• • •

A singular example of someone who believes in himself is **Bill O'Reilly**. Bill radiates confidence. He has a rock-solid inner core, which he credits in part to his days playing college baseball and football.

"I never doubted my ability to be able to do my job well," he said matter-of-factly. "I always had that confidence. It's like an athlete. Because I did play college sports, I understand the athletic mentality. I always knew on the athletic field that I had the ability to win most of the games, and I took that into my career. When they'd give me an assignment, I never said, 'Gee, maybe I can do this.' I said, 'I'm gonna do a great job.' So, I always had that kind of an attitude, which a lot of people think is an ego thing. I think it's self-confidence, based on past performance. So I brought that in. And I was cocky, and had a swagger. But it helped me. It worked for me."

As the years go by and as you accomplish more, you will feel more secure in your abilities and your personal power will grow. Even though a little part of you may always feel unsure—I believe everyone feels that way at times—you can reason with that uncertainty, because you have empirical evidence that you can succeed.

What past experience can *you* draw upon to affirm your ability to succeed?

• • •

It's difficult to believe in yourself when no one else does. Yankees manager **Joe Torre** was able to do this, despite the evidence that seemed to indicate he did not have what it took to successfully lead a winning team.

"At first, I didn't have the confidence I have now, because confidence comes from accomplishment. I think when you accomplish, all of a sudden people sort of listen to you, because you have a little bit of a track record."

—Joe Torre

Before his illustrious run with the Yankees, Joe had a past checkered with what many regarded as failures. He was fired from the Mets in 1981, which was his first managing job, and then again from the Braves in 1982, and then the Cardinals in 1995.

In 1996, Joe was presented with the opportunity to interview with the top brass of the Yankees. A few days before that meeting—which he refers to as one of the most important days of his life—he came upon a passage in a book that validated his faith in his management style despite his record.

"I remember I was in the weight room, and I was thumbing through one of Bill Parcells's managing books," he recalled. "I wasn't really reading page for page; I was just thumbing through it. And I just came upon this one little sentence, where he said, 'If you believe in what you're doing, stay with it.'

"A light went on," he continued. "Because, you know, I'd been managing three different places. I was fired from three different places. And you know, the thing that follows you is, 'You don't have what it takes. You're a players' manager.' You know, a players' manager when you lose is bad; a players' manager when you win is good. So I decided—and it was more comfortable for me—to approach the managing job here the same way I'd approached the other ones."

He went into that interview and promised to execute nothing but his own vision. Obviously, he got the job, and since that day in 1996, the Yankees have won the most World Series titles of any team in the past decade.

Joe's valuable lesson: **If you know something to be true in your heart, stay with it. Trust your instincts and believe in what you know; there's a good chance it will prove correct.**

• • •

When I told songwriter **Diane Warren** that I use mantras and aphorisms to reinforce my confidence when it wavers, she told me that she relies on something she calls her "Inner Winner."

You may not immediately know who Diane Warren is, but I'm sure you've heard one of her songs. She has written hits for a stunning array of stars, including Celine Dion ("Because You Loved Me"), Cher ("If I Could Turn Back Time"), Whitney Houston ("You Were Loved"), Aerosmith ("I Don't Want to Miss a Thing"), and Trisha Yearwood ("How Do I Live"), to name a few. Diane is best known for her ballads, and her songs have landed on the *Billboard* chart more than one hundred times, been featured in more than ninety major motion pictures, and been nominated for four Golden Globes, nine Grammys, and six Academy Awards. Considered one of the most prolific and successful songwriters of her time, she has a star on the Hollywood Walk of Fame bearing her name, as tribute to her big-time contribution to the music world.

Diane and I met at her offices in Hollywood, the walls of which are plastered with gold records. In person, she looks nothing at all like you would expect someone who writes soft, flowing love songs to look. She has a music-biz edge, with short, punky black hair and rocker chick clothes. She composes her work on the piano, but I could just picture her with an electric guitar jamming on stage.

"I would say, when they would invariably turn me down, 'You're gonna be sorry someday. I'm going to be the biggest writer of my generation, of my time.'"

—Diane Warren

From the age of fourteen, Diane has been fiercely determined to make it as a songwriter. Her stories of attempting to get noticed are the stuff of legend. No matter how many producers slammed the door in her face, she kept knocking. She threw her tapes into the car windows of music executives, and once literally got on her knees and begged Cher to record her song (which, by the way, was "If I Could Turn Back Time").

Like the rest of us, though, Diane needs a confidence boost from time to time.

"I can have those—you know, like, 'eh, you're nothing' moments," she admitted. "I think everybody has that. And then I have this part of me that's positive. I call it my Inner Winner. And that's what keeps me going. You know? That's that positive light.

"It's the part of me that knows I'm gonna do it, I'm gonna make it," she continued. "It's that little thing that was in there when I was starting out. That kept me going when doors shut in my face. It's still there. Because there's times when, you know, things aren't going great, or this thing isn't working out, you know? So my Inner Winner always keeps me going."

• • •

You can also **find confidence by identifying the qualities within you that are similar to those of others who have succeeded**.

When I became the associate producer on a new local talk show in Philadelphia, one of first duties was to screen fifty to sixty tapes submitted for job of host. Eventually we singled out a Canadian journalist named Bob McLean. The whole time, as I was looking at the personalities on those tapes, though, I kept saying to myself, "I could do this. They don't have anything I don't have." I confirmed my belief that I had the ability to do what they were doing.

It was the same for **Matt Lauer,** who set his sights on the *Today* show and didn't give up. He never quit, because deep down he believed he possessed the same qualities that some of the TV greats displayed.

"I was a student of the business early on," he said. "You know, I grew up in the business with some pretty strong role models—people that I really respected—Bryant Gumbel, Ted Koppel, some other people."

"Watching them, not necessarily being friends with them?" I asked.

"At the time I wasn't. Early in my career, I wasn't," he confirmed. "But I watched them. And you know, as immodest as this sounds, some part of me thought that I had some of their qualities. It comes back to this people thing . . . I always knew that when I sat down with people face-to-face—if you would give me a meeting—I was usually going to get somebody to give me a job."

If you have a specific aspiration, seek out those who have succeeded at it. Watch what they do. Can you recognize yourself there?

End Notes

"Self-confidence is a more subtle way of saying 'ambitious.' If you have confidence, though, you can rise to any challenge."—**Bill Bratton**

"My mother gave me incredible gifts, not the least of which was that kind of unconditional love that a good parent gives a child, that makes you feel you can do anything. That gives you the confidence to pursue what you want."
—**Christie Hefner**

"I'm a major, major, major influence on myself. I have a huge relationship with myself. Huge. I am my best friend. I rely on myself. I like myself. I see totally my faults, but I just enjoy me. I love being alone."—**Diane von Furstenberg**

"It never enters my mind that I can't do anything I put my mind to. I know I can't be a brain surgeon, and I know I can't be president of the United States. So I just don't put my mind to things that I don't think I could do, anyway."—**Linda Huett**

8

Strengthen Your Will to Prevail

Maria Bartiromo • Joseph Abboud • Diane Warren • Preston Bailey • Mark Burnett • Frédéric Fekkai • Dr. Mehmet Oz • Mario Cuomo • Tom Perkins • Rikki Klieman • Jeff Lurie • Donald Trump • Brooke Shields • Bill O'Reilly • Jane Friedman • Jeff Zucker

I ONCE HAD the privilege of interviewing Joe Frazier, shortly after he had defeated Muhammad Ali in the 1971 Heavyweight Championship:

"Joe," I said, "you had to win the last couple of rounds to win the fight. You were exhausted, but you came back and did it. What did you draw on?"

"I went all the way back to the plantation, and sharecropping, and I could feel my ancestors in my fists," he replied.

I remember looking at those big fists and thinking that I had no idea when I first started listening to that little radio when I was five years old that I've ever be so lucky to meet people like Joe, and all these other incredibly successful people. Or that I'd be able to observe firsthand how each of them seemed to possess a will to prevail because they believed in their God-given talent. They had a force within them, because they knew just how powerful that faith in themselves could be—whether times were good or bad.

The road to success requires many things, but above all, it demands determination and an undaunted tenacity. Throughout the interviews, I asked people what they did to fortify what I have come to call their **emotional endurance**—the internal and intellectual fortitude needed to continue on an upward trajectory. Interestingly, each knew exactly what I was talking about, because deep down, they connect to an inner resolve that aims to triumph no matter what circumstances might throw their way.

• • •

"It's called being mentally tough," said CNBC's **Maria Bartiromo**. "You have to be mentally tough. When you have certain goals that you're looking to achieve, you must keep the finish line in focus. You call it emotional endurance, I call it being mentally tough."

And tough she is. It took real courage and grit to pierce through the old boys' club and be accepted as the first woman to report live on a daily basis from the floor of the New York Stock Exchange. Not everyone was willing to allow the winds of change to blow through.

"I did have a lot of pushback," she admitted. "Luckily, Dick Grasso was the head of the exchange, and he allowed it, and I felt that he was ally of mine. But I remember this one guy who hated the whole idea of a reporter—and a woman who didn't know what he knew—being on the floor. At one point, he turned to me—yelled at me—and said something like, 'Get out of here, now! This is not your business. You will not go on television with this. You don't know anything about this. Go run along.' At that moment, I was shocked. I stopped for a moment, and I said very calmly, 'Do not speak to me that way.' I turned around and walked away, and went about my business.

> ## "Stamina, for me, is just coming back and coming back and doing it again and again."
> ### —Maria Bartiromo

"So I did face pushback," she continued. "But every time, I kept coming back. And what I also kept doing was study, study, study. I knew that if I knew my stuff, and I made sure to understand the content and speak intelligently, and make sure that I was on the air with the right stuff, they couldn't touch me."

• • •

What Maria Bartiromo calls being "mentally tough," **Joseph Abboud** calls having a "move-the-mountain mentality."

"I think for any really successful person, that's one of the intangibles that sort of separates them from the rest," he said. "I really believe that. Ask any of us: life isn't just this wonderful launchpad. There are obstacles, and there are problems; there are battles. You know, my wife will say I'm obsessive. If I want to move a sign within the state, I'll call the state every day until we get a sign moved. People say, 'We can't get the state to do anything.' But I don't accept that."

At the time we met, Joe was in the process of trying to launch a television show about men's fashion. His energy was focused on seeing it succeed.

He went on: "I think that's a true test—how far you're willing to go, how much you're willing to give. And I think you need a lot of that. A discipline, for me, has always been that if I think it's logical and intelligent, and I think it's a good idea, I'll keep going after it. Like this television thing. I think it's so real. It's a zone nobody filled. Nobody thought of it, and you know what I say? Why not me? Maybe I'll never get there. But you know what? Why not keep trying?

"Sometimes that takes a toll on you. I mean, it's a lot of work. It can affect your family, and the hours you work. But at the same time, without it, I don't think I would have gotten this far. And I think without it, I won't get to the next level. It's like playing a game of squash, or tennis or something. You physically may not be able to do it, but you always try."

There it is, in a nutshell: **Keep trying.** Never give up.

• • •

Songwriter **Diane Warren** is a prime example of someone who never gives up. Her boldness, as I said, is legendary. When she was starting out, Diane chased producers down the street, and threw her tapes to performers on stage. She snagged a job at a music industry delivery service called Music Express, and while making deliveries, Diane would track down the A and R people to slip them samples of her music. One day, when delivering a bottle of champagne to David Foster of Earth, Wind and Fire, she asked for his phone number so she could send him some of her songs (she got fired from that job after two weeks).

It all started when Diane was young, when her passion for music was ignited. Music was her solace and her sanctuary, and she knew even then what she wanted to become. At age fourteen, she convinced her dad to get her a subscription to *Billboard* magazine. She meticulously combed those pages to see who wrote and produced every song mentioned. At fifteen, she was banging on publishers' doors to get her music heard, refusing to be daunted by rejection.

"I was not gonna not make it," she said with a laugh. "I was so determined. I listened to my soul, I listened to my ear. And that was telling me to keep going, no matter what. If the door slams in my face, I'm gonna kick it down. That's the kind of person I am."

Diane wears two necklaces around her neck, which she leaned forward to show me. One says, "Believe in your passion, believe in your power, believe in being stubborn." The other says, "Fuck you."

"If I believe in something, you can't stop me, you know?"

—Diane Warren

"So I have a little edge about me, you know?" she said. "But for me, it's like, 'Yeah, I'll show you. You say I'm not gonna make it? I'm not good enough; you don't want to sign me? I'll show you.' I just roll my sleeves up and work harder."

• • •

When I asked Diane Warren where she believes her ferocious determination came from, she said, "I have relatives that came over from Russia, and sometimes I feel almost like there's an **immigrant gene** in my body. You know, when they came to America, they wanted to make something of themselves."

Others I interviewed also seemed to possess that immigrant gene. Celebrity event planner **Preston Bailey,** for instance. Preston has engineered huge, fanciful parties for people like Donald Trump, Donna Karan, Liza Minnelli, and Matt Lauer. I found Preston to have a commanding presence: tall, handsome, in incredible shape, and with a big, warm smile. When he first came to America from his native Panama at age nineteen, he had $50 in his pocket, no job, and no specific dreams. He arrived in New York City—his sister's place in Brooklyn, to be exact—took one look at the lights and verve of Manhattan, and realized very quickly he would have to hustle if he wanted to make it here.

Preston soon got a job as a teller in a bank during the day and as a part-time salesman at Bloomingdale's in the evening. Then he modeled a bit, but that didn't pan out as he'd hoped. So he went to work for an interior designer friend, arranging fresh flowers in Park Avenue homes. He made a lot of mistakes, but the desire to prevail drove him onward.

"I didn't know what the hell I was doing," he remembers with a deep laugh. "What I did do, however, is do a lot of research. Every magazine that I opened, I looked at floral designs. I read floral books. And then I was fortunate enough to land Christie's galleries as one of my clients. While there, I started looking at some of the great master paintings of floral designs that they have for the sales. And somehow, that even interested me more—the idea of creating

The Immigrant Gene

"The chance for an immigrant is far greater than for a person born into an American family, because in the American family, you have a safety net. An immigrant has no safety net."—**Mark Burnett**

"I come from a very humble middle-class family in the south of France. And I always wanted to make money. This was not a secret. I mean, from the day I started, I only wanted to do better, and get better, and earn a lot of money, and be wealthy. And I came to this country for that great reason. To learn about how to be wealthy, and to have the ability and opportunity to do so."
—**Frédéric Fekkai**

floral design as art started forming. That experience was really the foundation for what developed later, and where I am today."

Eventually, the opportunity to plan his first wedding came along. Then another, and another. With his own two hands, the immigrant who had arrived with no skills or money fashioned himself into one of the premier event planners in the country.

Those who come to the United States from elsewhere have a keen sense of the opportunities this country offers. **Work like you *have* to make it, and watch what happens**.

• • •

Optimism plays a huge role in perseverance. When you *believe* things can work out, there is a greater chance that they will.

I once saw a PBS documentary on President Ronald Reagan, in which people who knew him said that he had the capacity to

---

"My parents came, like most immigrants to this country, trying to find a better system. Both are Turkish. They wanted a system that allowed them to reach their full potential. They had left their entire world to seek a better life, where if you worked harder, you excelled. That was a tremendous motivation, to have the paradigm that if you work harder, you will win."—**Dr. Mehmet Oz**

"My mother and father were immigrants. They were uneducated, from Italy. I watched them every day, working themselves to the bone. Never going to a theater, never going to a movie. The example they set is something I've never gotten past. Any time I kind of lagged in my own effort, as I did a couple of times in the campaign, I was embarrassed by remembering what my mother and father went through."—**Mario Cuomo**

---

will himself to be optimistic. He literally *chose* to see things in a positive light, even if it didn't come naturally to him. Cultivating that quality has true merit. **"I am developing willful optimism"** is now one of my daily affirmations.

Tom Perkins's line of work—venture capitalism—consists almost entirely of challenging situations. Whether his company is helping to create an unproven search engine like Google or Yahoo, or biotechnology corporations like Genentech, Tom refuses to focus on the possibility of failure.

"I guess I've always had a pretty positive attitude that there's always a solution," he said. Not unlike Clive Davis, Tom Perkins is the very portrait of a tycoon. We were sitting in his office in the Embarcadero district of San Francisco, but I could completely envision him on the deck of a yacht, wearing a blue blazer and white pants.

"I mean, it's so easy to encounter people who will tell you why it can't be done, and how it won't be done, and why everybody else has failed at doing it, and just don't even try, and go in a different direction . . . blah, blah, blah. And I guess, I don't know if it's arrogance or ignorance, or some of both, but I've just ignored that. I've always figured, 'I will figure out some way to get this thing done.' And almost always, there is a way."

One Foot in Front of the Other

"I still use this physical activity as a metaphor," offered Court TV's **Rikki Klieman**. "I've been to two health spas where you began each day by walking up a mountain. And I hated walking those mountains. I really had trouble waking up. I was always in the back; they were going to have to wait for me. I mean, I really had trouble. And I really learned to just say, 'I can. I will.' All the way up the mountain. And suddenly, I was at the top of the mountain."

Philadelphia Eagles owner **Jeff Lurie** also consciously chooses a positive attitude.

"That's been very important to my success," he said. "In every way. First of all, it attracts people to want to work with you, if you see the best in people. If you can see what wonderful things can happen, then you all can work toward them. As opposed to someone who thinks the glass is always half empty. That doesn't mean I can't be analytically critical, and analyze where things are bad. But the optimistic view of life, I think, gives you a more energized sense of everything, whether you play tennis or operate a sports team."

Remember, **Attitude is a choice**.

Playboy founder Hugh Hefner once told me that if he'd known in advance how difficult it would be to launch a magazine, he likely wouldn't have done it. Like Hugh Hefner and so many others in this book did, keep your sights focused on success—not on the obstacles—and you're halfway there.

End Notes

"I think my determination gave me the mental toughness I needed. I am a tenacious person and not easily discouraged. After a while, you learn to expect certain things—such as problems—as part of the deal. You can't achieve great things without some obstacles. That's just a fact of life and I didn't fight it; I just worked along and through whatever faced me."**—Donald Trump**

"The will to prevail is constant, because the alternative is nothing."**—Brooke Shields**

"I wouldn't say I'm particularly optimistic. I'd say I'm realistic. You know, I don't get up every day clicking my heels. I get up going, 'I've got to go to war here. And I've got to win the ratings war, and I've got to beat the competition, and I've got to do a good job, and I've got to be tough in what I do.' I'm basically steady, with my eye on the ball. And the ball is to win in what I do."—**Bill O'Reilly**

"I'm called the Pollyanna of the business. I am totally optimistic about the fate of book publishing. I get furious at some of my other comrades who are doom and gloom. When I entered this business in the late '60s, I was told the novel was dead. That's one of those great generalizations, and, of course, it's not true. I think we have a healthy business that is constantly evolving. I think the only doom and gloom is the limitation of the boss."—**Jane Friedman**

"Because I had been in the theater from the time I was a child, I was unafraid of rejection. I mean, totally unafraid. The word 'no' to me was irrelevant."—**Rikki Klieman**

"I don't accept defeat easily. And I never give up. The game's never over until it's over. I've never accepted defeat until the last whistle blows, or the last ace has been served against you."—**Jeff Zucker**

9
Defy Category

Jim Cramer • Bobbi Brown • Peter Cincotti • David Rockwell • Anna Quindlen • Norman Lear • Craig Newmark • Brooke Shields • Cathie Black • Joseph Abboud • Preston Bailey • Jane Friedman

NO HUMAN BEING is one-dimensional—so why should our careers be? People want to put you in a box so they can understand how to categorize you. Resist it.

At the dawn of my career—in my early twenties after escaping from that dead-end writing job at Armstrong—an inner voice told me that I didn't want to be labeled. I really don't know where that drive came from, but I just instinctively knew I did not want anything to prevent me from expressing myself the way I wanted to express myself. "Defy category" was what I was pledging for my life in the years ahead. As time rolled on, I've found it gratifying to surprise people by going beyond the labels of what conventional thinking wants us to be.

Once I accomplished my initial desire to be an interviewer on television, I used that as a base to try a wide array of activities in show business. I've hosted talk shows, public affairs shows, and demo-oriented TV shows. I had a game show on CBS-TV and anchored the news for WNBC-TV. I co-executive produced and hosted a syndicated comedy show for Fox-TV, had a steamy late-night talk show, a long-running interview food series on Food Network, and hosted two series on the Travel Channel. I even covered boxing for Showtime. I've produced rock and roll, ballet, and jazz programming for television; published a novel; written essays for the *New York Times*; created an Off-Broadway show about my career titled *Talk Show Confidential*; executive produced both the controversial *Morton Downey Jr. Show* and Court TV; acted in movies, television, and on stage; and even appeared in musical cabaret.

Believe me, others have been far more successful than I in each of those categories. But I've done all of that stuff, and all of that's who I am.

Many of those interviewed for this book are category-defying pioneers. None would have had lasting impact if they had done what was expected of them.

• • •

With his trademark *"BOOYAH!,"* **Jim Cramer** exploded onto the media scene as the host of CNBC's *Mad Money,* much in the same way he did as a tornado-like trader and hedge-fund manager on Wall Street in the '80s and '90s. Jim blasts through the screen with his energy—bold, brash, and completely in your face. He rants, gestures wildly as he defiantly proclaims his opinions, and even throws chairs. Some worship him (there are entire websites dedicated to tracking Jim Cramer's stock picks); others quickly switch channels. He is *definitely* not the conventional image of a television host.

Jim had a "madman" quality when he ran his astonishingly profitable hedge fund in the late '90s. He was infamous for tossing watercoolers and generally unleashing his roaring energy. Nonetheless, he established a reputation as a brilliant stock analyst and was phenomenally successful (his fund yielded groundbreaking returns, and his net worth is estimated at around $50 million). At a certain point, however, Jim Cramer realized he was severely burned out and needed to make a life change.

Jim turned to his professed original love of broadcast journalism, appearing on two moderately successful shows, *America Now* and *Kudlow and Cramer*. In hindsight, Jim explains that the shows' appeal was hampered by one very simple fact: Jim Cramer wasn't being his natural self. Trying to fit into the classic mold of a television host, he suppressed his characteristic combative, fiery antics, and came across as stiff and uncomfortable on screen.

Being with Jim in person is a different experience from watching the man who is screaming at you on television. He is less intense, much more subdued and thoughtful—even reflective. He and I met on the set of his show at the end of one of his typically long (thirteen hours or more), jam-packed days, and the mellowed timbre of his voice and casual posture, with feet up on a chair, gave him a relaxed air. Ruminating about his new career on television, he stated very precisely what he believes it takes to make it in that arena:

"You must be yourself," he stressed. "There'll be people all over who will tell you, don't. I mean, for three years, I was told don't be yourself, that 'yourself' is no good. And it was just unbelievable how bad that advice was! And I was no good. I had no numbers. It was not interesting; I found myself bored. And that's the cardinal sin."

On *Mad Money*, Jim Cramer's current show, he is entirely himself, no holds barred. The climbing ratings and cultlike viewership prove he was right.

"If I were at my hedge fund, I would pace, I would run around, I'd throw things. I'm doing everything now that comes naturally to me. You know, if you want to see the difference between this and before, just roll the tape when I was on *Kudlow and Cramer*. I was unbearable. I was chafing, and horrible. And I'd go home

An Unconventional Pact

"Here's the bargain I made people," said **Jim Cramer,** regarding his reputation when he ran his hedge fund as an unapologetically intense boss. "There was a bargain. It's such a misunderstood bargain that I cringe when I hear people say I was mean. Because I don't want to be a mean boss. I try to be as polite as I can, but when I was there, if you came in, and you were twenty-four years old, and you say, 'What do you expect of me, Mr. Cramer?' I expect everything. I expect six days. You can pick which day off, for religious purposes. I need you in here by six AM every single day. I will fire you if you came later. If you cry, or I get to you with any of the things I do, you must leave. And this is to every secretary, not just traders. In return, I promise to make you rich."

and just say, 'God, I'm playing this guy on TV. It's awful.'"

It can be very tempting to conform to standard parameters for how you look, speak, dress, or act, especially if others are assuring you it's the golden road to success. But if that's not in sync with who you are, it is never a good way to go. **Be yourself, even if others are telling you otherwise.**

• • •

Cosmetics maven **Bobbi Brown,** who pioneered "the natural look," originally made a name for herself as a freelance makeup artist by blatantly ignoring the fashionable makeup style of the times.

"When I started out as a makeup artist, the look was very white skin, red lips, very cutout features," recalled this fresh-faced, utterly natural woman. "It was not my style. I couldn't do makeup that way. I always did makeup on a model to make the look healthy and natural. That's how I always did makeup on myself. And people said to me, 'You're never gonna make it in this business if you do makeup like that.' I had a successful photographer and a successful makeup artist tell me I needed to change if I wanted to make it."

"It's really just about doing things differently, and doing something you believe in."

—Bobbi Brown

"In other words, you had a vision of how makeup should be done," I said.

"I didn't even know if it was a vision," she said laughing. "But it's all I knew how to do. I knew how to make people look good and fresh and tan and healthy. And people weren't doing that at the time. Even hairdressers—a hairdresser said to me, 'You really should cut your hair and get a style if you want to work in this business.' I remember that, because my hair was probably exactly the same as it is now, one length, in a ponytail. But I only knew how to be me."

Bobbi eventually realized that if she wanted to have makeup in her kit to accomplish her vision, she would have to create it herself. She found a chemist to help her make a lipstick that "looked like lips," as she described it. First she sold the lipstick to her friends. Then she figured since her friends liked it so much, other women would, too. So she gave one to a friend who was an editor at *Glamour* magazine, who wrote a tiny column about it and listed Bobbi's home phone number as the order line. In response to growing demand, Bobbi created another color, and another—all natural in tone—shipping everything out of her house. Eventually, she met a woman at a party who was the cosmetics buyer at Bergdorf Goodman, told her about the product, and the line took off from there.

Someone **has to be first with any new trend. Why not you?**

• • •

I first met the brilliant singer, songwriter, and composer **Peter Cincotti** in 2001, when we starred together in the Off-Broadway show *Our Sinatra*. He was only seventeen years old at the time, and it was his first time singing on stage. A one-time child prodigy on the piano, Peter was a master of many styles; at that point, he particularly loved jazz and had won numerous international jazz piano competitions. Since then, I've watched Peter progress from a young, charming high school student to being a performer with a bestselling CD on Concord Records and a second one two years later.

When Peter released his debut album in 2003 to fantastic critical acclaim and chart-topping success, he unwittingly created golden handcuffs for himself. When it came time to release his next album two years later, all expectations were that it would have a similar feel to the first one. However, like other forms of artistry, musical talent evolves, and Peter's creativity took him in a different direction. The new album defied the niche he had carved for himself.

"Some people looked at my second record as a risk, because it's a big departure from my first," Peter said.

"In what way?" I asked.

"In the fact that it wasn't pure jazz. That there are elements of pop; elements of different styles of music. Because my first record succeeded and was at the top of the charts, the fact that I didn't follow that formula that many people wanted me to was a big risk. But, like I said, it wasn't what I was feeling. I wanted my

Group, which feels more like a giant cabin in the mountains than an office space in downtown Manhattan. Filled with more than two hundred architects and designers—many of whom glanced up just to say "hi" as I walked by—working in cluttered, woodsy cubicles, the place has a very warm and familial feeling. Indeed, David revealed that his primary inspiration is creating spaces that foster a sense of community. Whether it is the Kodak Theatre, where the Academy Awards are held, or a free-standing building for Cirque du Soleil in Walt Disney World, he builds spaces that radiate a feeling of what he calls "communal celebration."

Growing up with a mother who was involved in community theater, David was inspired at an early age by the spirit of creative collaboration in the theater. On a trip to New York City at the age of eleven, he went to see *Fiddler on the Roof* and ate lunch with his brothers at Schrafft's, the legendary Broadway hangout. Both of those experiences made a deep impression on the young David. He fell in love with New York that day, and with dining out. David told me that restaurants and theater became his "core passions," which he eventually combined with his formidable talent for design.

"Early on in my career, I had certain people say to me, 'That's not architecture,'" he said. "'Restaurants aren't architecture, theater isn't architecture. Architecture is museums. Casinos aren't architecture. What interests me is finding design where other people aren't looking for it. If you look at casinos, for instance, there is a huge constellation of star architects who are now going after these casinos in Singapore. So apparently it was architecture. But people need to wait until it's been proven as architecture."

David never waits until something is proven before acting. He broke through the barrier of what is considered "true architecture" and designed grand yet welcoming dining establishments such as Vong, Nobu, and the Grand Central Terminal Dining Concourse in New York City. Then, in a move that shocked some in more snobbish architectural circles, David designed the imaginative sets for *Hairspray, The Rocky Horror Show,* and *Dirty Rotten Scoundrels.*

"What do you say to somebody who likes the idea of defying category?" I asked. "How can they do it successfully?"

"I think you have to be willing to risk failure," he responded immediately. "Because there's no other way to do it. No one actually *wants* to have something that doesn't work. But I think you've got to be willing to really take a risk. I think, creatively, if you're risk-adverse, you repeat what you've done. And ultimately, that wears out."

> "I am extremely intolerant of things like 'reasonable.'
> I don't find 'reasonable' interesting at all."
>
> **—David Rockwell**

You may find yourself in an industry that seeks to keep things "pure," like architecture. But nearly every innovation was once considered renegade—or was thought to compromise some imagined ideal—or was even declared dangerous (rock and roll in its infancy was called "the devil's music"). But at the epicenter of each change were visionaries who *just didn't care.* **Moving ahead of the pack requires defying convention and following your own unique vision.**

• • •

Writer **Anna Quindlen** was well-established as a journalist when she wrote her first novel. She knew before she penned a single word of fiction that she would meet resistance.

"After years of being a journalist, how many times did people say to me, 'You're gonna make it up?' Just, incredulously. People would say, 'Well, you know, God bless you, Anna; nobody's really going to take you seriously as a novelist, because you've always been a journalist.' And one of the biggest charges I get now is that sometimes I'll be at a bookstore signing, and a woman will say to me, 'You write a column? You do journalism, too? I only know you as a novelist.' And I think, *'Yes!'* "

"So often the things we do out of fearlessness—
saying, 'You know what? I don't care. I'm gonna take
that leap.' Those are the great successes."

—Anna Quindlen

Anna's advice for anyone who might be a little nervous about breaking genre, so to speak, is simple but profound:

"I think that if you can get rid of the fear—if you can acknowledge it, confront it, fold it up, put it in your pocket, and go on with what you're doing, it can make a huge difference in what you can accomplish."

• • •

There are so many leaders who ignored convention and dared to defy category: **Norman Lear,** who was the first to introduce controversial topics in sitcoms in the 1970s; **Craig Newmark,** who astonishes and confounds the world by refusing to "sell out" and accept millions of dollars for advertising on his site, Craigslist.com; and **Brooke Shields,** who refused to be pigeonholed into one medium (modeling) and achieved fame in movies, then television, and now on the Broadway stage. The mind-set of "defy category" has allowed these people to break barriers and achieve things that some might once have perceived impossible.

End Notes

"The status quo was never something that was very appealing to me."—**Cathie Black**

"I thought there was a huge void. That somewhere between Georgio Armani and Ralph Lauren—right in the middle of the Atlantic—was a great place for American style. Whether it was the shape, the silhouette, the colors—all of that—it didn't exist in the market."—**Joseph Abboud**

"I laugh, I think it's funny, I really do, that certain people think my work is vulgar."—**Preston Bailey**

"Everything is changing. I think change keeps one young and on one's toes. I don't ever want to say, 'That's the way we have to do it, because that's the way I've always done it.' I don't believe in that. I believe in growth."—**Jane Friedman**

THREE

The Practices of Success

10
Work Hard

Jim Cramer • Diane Warren • Craig Newmark •
Dr. Mehmet Oz • Frank Rich • Tom Perkins • James
Blake • Maria Bartiromo • Bill O'Reilly • Mario
Cuomo • Donald Trump • Marco Maccioni • Jeff
Zucker • Diane von Furstenberg • Bob Pittman • Phil
Lombardo • Dr. Judith Rodin

MY FATHER USED TO SAY to me, **"You're only going to get out of something what you put into it."** He was 100 percent correct. Whether you're developing your muscles, refining your skills as a television host, or publishing a magazine, I believe the effort-success ratio is almost mathematically measurable.

The work ethic of the people in this book is among the most extraordinary I've ever seen. They put in as much sweat, brainpower, and hours as it took to achieve their goals. If hard work scares you, skip this chapter and just chill out, because you're about to hear stories from people who worked as if their life depended on it. Why? They had faith that they would succeed through the sheer force of their efforts.

Of course, there is a difference between working joyfully and slogging away. This brings us back to the link between work and fun.

From the day I left my awful job at Armstrong Cork Company, I've been in show business. Yeah, it's work sometimes, like when I racked up nine straight seven-day weeks on camera hosting *Midday with Bill Boggs* and *Comedy Tonight* simultaneously. But it was still fun.

There's no question that sometimes you'll feel you're toiling away. That's why it's crucial that what you're doing be aligned with what you care about. As Confucius said, "Find a job that you love and you will never work a day in your life." So, yes, these people worked hard, but they did it happily in the spirit of passion.

Not all of these stories are pretty. But the fact that so many people, when faced with challenges, didn't hesitate to roll up their sleeves, jump in, and do whatever it took reminds us yet again that **success doesn't come easy**. Sometimes it takes everything you've got. And then maybe even a little bit more.

• • •

Jim Cramer is a machine. He rises at 3:45 AM to work out and start voraciously searching for stories to feed his multiple media outlets. By the time the day ends, he will have written several columns for his website, TheStreet.com, bellowed his way through the taping of *Mad Money with Jim Cramer* on CNBC, hosted his nationally syndicated radio show *Jim Cramer's Real Money*, checked hundreds of e-mails, and made a powerful impact on the way millions of people invest their money.

"I am one of those people who is indefatigable, in the true sense that I beg someone to find someone who can outwork me," said Jim. "I have always prided myself that no one can outwork me. No one. If I need to be ready tomorrow, I don't think anyone getting the material starting now will be as prepared as I will be by tomorrow at 8:00 AM."

Jim's resolute work ethic and absolute drive to be the best has yielded a huge list of accomplishments throughout his life, including graduating magna cum laude from Harvard College and earning a law degree from Harvard Law School, founding Cramer Berkowitz, his $450 million hedge fund, and authoring three books. He drives himself relentlessly, fueled by an obsessive need to be the best.

> "I'm one of those guys who gets up in the morning and is like, 'Today's the day. Today's the day I'm gonna be unstoppable."
>
> **—Jim Cramer**

As of this writing, it remains to be seen whether Jim's television success will rival his incredible accomplishments on Wall Street. If his past examples of work ethic are any indication, I would say it's a pretty good bet that it will.

• • •

It was once said about **Diane Warren** that despite her commercial success and massive financial worth, she still works as if she needs to pay the rent.

"Tell me about your work ethic," I asked Diane.

"It's insane," she said, laughing.

"I read a quote saying you were the hardest-working songwriter in the business," I said.

"Yeah," she said nodding. "I don't know anybody who works harder than I work. All I do is work. I'm not one of those people who stays up all night and all day. I mean, I get a good night's sleep. But I get here at 8:30 in the morning and I don't go home until about 9:30, ten at night."

Diane Warren is the epitome of a singularly focused artist. She doesn't cook. She doesn't take time off. She admits she doesn't do anything much, really, other than work. It's a formula that might not suit everyone, but it's what got Diane Warren where she is today. Diane told me she recently drove past a woman sitting on the side of the road with a guitar strapped around her. She reflected that she could have just as easily been that woman were it not for her obsessive work ethic.

"It just really hit me, 'There but for the grace of God go I,'" she said. "I mean, that could have been me. The question you asked, what made me make it? I like to think I have talent. I have talent, yeah. But also, I work my ass off. I work really, really hard. I've been obsessed, and a workaholic, and a driven songwriter since I've been fourteen years old. I'm forty-nine, and I have not stopped. I have not mellowed out. I have not chilled out. I have not calmed down and taken a vacation. I haven't had a vacation in years."

"It's weird. Because every day, I feel like I'm starting.
I look at the wall, the star on the Hollywood Walk
of Fame, one Grammy, but it's like it doesn't
mean anything. It's the rearview mirror. I don't look
in the rearview mirror; I look straight ahead.
I'm always like, 'What's next?'"

—Diane Warren

Diane just keeps moving, much like a great white shark. She receives nominations, awards, and all kinds of accolades, but she just keeps working. Her deep-seated passion and need for songwriting drives her continually forward in search of the next big creative hit.

"I have to do it," she said. "I have to do it. If I don't do it, I'll die."

• • •

Craig Newmark is so deeply committed to his cause that he didn't bat an eye at the vast amounts of time and energy he puts into maintaining his site:

"I don't think of it as discipline. I just do what I need to do, like pretty much anyone else who has to plug away."

—Craig Newmark

"I haven't had a day off in . . . probably since '99, or something like that," he said. He shrugged casually, like that was no big deal. "Maybe from before that, but I don't recall. That's not a complaint. And that's not a big problem."

Working Smart

It isn't always about the quantity of time, but the quality of time you put in.

"I never, ever go to lunch," said **Dr. Mehmet Oz**. "My entire career, unless there's some huge event I'm speaking at, I won't go to lunch. The reason for that is that it's right in the middle of the day, and it breaks my focus completely. I'll do a seven AM breakfast if I have to. I'll go to dinners all the time, and I do. But when I'm in my work mode, I don't want to be distracted. Focusing is really my key to success. It's not just that I work. I think I work smart, not necessarily hard."

• • •

Though you'd never know it from reading **Frank Rich**'s weekly columns on the Op-Ed page in the *New York Times* or the reviews he used to write as the paper's drama critic, the words don't just flow effortlessly from his fingertips when he sits down in front of the keyboard. He must dedicate long hours and considerable effort to his craft, just like everyone else. For one *Times* column, Frank spends nearly a week gathering ideas and research, making notes, writing drafts, and editing.

"I always want to do better," he said. "I always want to improve. I never want to slough anything off. And it's extremely labor-intensive to write fifteen-hundred-word essays each week that are heavily reported, for an audience that is so demanding. You make one mistake, and it can take months to live down.

"It's so daunting," he continued. "It's not like, 'Oh, I come back and write what I think, and that's it.' For instance, take a theater reviewer. That, too, is very hard work. Reviewing theater and movies seems extremely glamorous if you're on the outside: 'Oh, my god, you get all these free tickets,' and so forth. But the reality is different. It is exciting, but it also involves tremendous amounts of concentration and preparation. Anybody can have an opinion. It's easy to say, 'I loved this play,' or 'I hated it.' But to me, really good criticism—of the quality you want to see at places like the *Times* or *The New Yorker* or the *Washington Post*—has to explain why and what happened, and how it all works. The opinion is the easy part.

"You have to put in the hours. You have to. I guess there are people who are in this line of work for other reasons, but for me, the goal has always been to be the best writer and journalist I can be. I've learned a lot through the years about writing. But it's never like a slam dunk for me. Each piece is a challenge, and each one takes me just about as long as the one before."

• • •

Venture-capitalist **Tom Perkins** is another industry leader who knows the misperceptions one might have about his profession.

"You can't be in the venture-capital business if you don't want to work very much," he said. "I mean, the idea that you just sort of place a few bets, and then go play golf, and come back and see what happens is just so incredibly wrong it's ludicrous. In my case, at the height of the madness—I would say in the late '70s through the mid '80s—at one time, I was chairman of the board of twelve or fourteen companies at the same time. Three of them were on the New York Stock Exchange at the same time. That's kind of a record.

"I just worked all the time. Weekends, nights. All day long.

The Discipline of a Winner

James Blake knows he was blessed with athletic ability. But that isn't what makes him a champion.

"What has set me apart from a lot of other people, I think, is the work to get there," he said. "With tennis, you have a coach, but you kind of need to be pushed on your own. Because there are a lot of times when you can make decisions on your own, on whether or not you're gonna get up and do the extra work. Whether or not after a match you're going to do extra work, or after practice, you're going to do more. Especially once you make it to the pro level. Because your coach is then employed by you. And so if you don't feel like working, you can tell your coach pretty much that you don't want to."

Always something going on. I never got a phone call that was good news. It was always some crisis that I had to get involved with. Part of the approach at Kleiner and Perkins was, 'Call us when the problem is small. Don't try to put the fire out yourself; call the fire department. We're the fire department. It'll work out better for everybody in the end if that's what you do.' So that means when they call, you've got to respond."

"What did it feel like during those times?" I asked. "Did it feel like work?"

"I would get tired," he admitted. "But the exhilaration would keep me going. At one time I told somebody, which I think is true, that stress successfully overcome is triumph. You know? There was a lot of stress, but a lot of success, and the feeling of accomplishment is huge."

Over and over, I heard stories from people whose families instilled in them at a young age the practical value of hard work. And so, they worked for every single dollar and achievement they earned, rarely complaining about what it took. They did not develop a sense of "entitlement"—a trait that can greatly hamper your drive.

• • •

Maria Bartiromo grew up in a tightly knit Italian family who owned a restaurant. Here's how that experience influenced her work ethic:

"One of the most important themes I have, which I've gotten from my parents, is to work hard. Really hard. I mean, my father owned the Rex Manor, in Brooklyn. It was a catering hall on Sixteenth Street and Eleventh Avenue. We had a restaurant area, a big bar area, and two big catering halls, where we did weddings and stuff. I was the coat-check girl on the weekends. I grew up walking into the kitchen, seeing my father sweating, with a bandanna around his head, and watching my brother as the waiter, my sister as the hostess, and my mother. We spent every weekend, every holiday at the Rex. Because that's the way we would be together.

"So it was definitely this theme of work really hard, always. I mean, they have instilled in me this tremendous work ethic. And I do believe that this is why, today, I've achieved some success. Because there aren't any shortcuts, I believe firmly."

"How did that influence you in your career?" I asked.

"When I began my career, I would do anything that they asked me to do," she said. "I started at a radio station—WMCA—with Barry Farber. I was sort of his assistant. Whatever he wanted me to do, I would do. In fact, one day he wanted me to drive him, because he had a problem with the refrigerator, and he had all this barbecue. And I had to drive somewhere. I mean, that's crazy.

"Then I went to CNN," she continued. "And I worked the overnight shift three times. Once it was 2:00 AM to 11:00 AM Another time it was from 4:00 AM to 1:00 PM And after I finished one at 1:00 PM, I would stay there and do pieces and try to write, so that I could get ahead. And, you know, be there."

Maria's willingness to do whatever it took continued in each stage of her career. She climbed the ladder at CNN by volunteering for every opportunity she could find.

"At CNN, I was able to do everything," she said. "I started as a production assistant on the overnight shift, then was promoted to a regular shift on *Moneyline*. Then I was promoted to writer, overnight shift. Then promoted to writer, regular shift. I got hooked. When I was finished at noon with my job as a production assistant, I would go to the assignment-desk head and say, 'What are we working on?' Maybe there were economic numbers that were coming in, and they needed sound bites from economists. I would say, 'Oh, I'll go.' And I would go with the crew and interview economists."

"You could have gone home," I observed.

> ## "I've had so much love in my family. That helps you feel confident, and helps you be driven. It gave me confidence that I'm not alone, that I have support."
>
> ### —Maria Bartiromo

"Oh, I was sleepy," she admitted, smiling. "I could have gone home, but I actually didn't want to. I wanted to be there, and I wanted to do everything. That's how I gained so much experience, in order to have a chance to go on air. And then I was hired at CNBC in 1993, as an on-air reporter."

Next time you see Maria Bartiromo looking cool, polished, and glamorous on television, remember, she started out checking coats at the Rex Manor in Brooklyn—something she never forgets.

• • •

The point here isn't that you need to sacrifice everything in your life in order to succeed. Everyone's path is unique and will demand different things from them at various times. Ultimately, it will be up to you to determine how much of yourself *you* need to invest to yield whatever level of success you are aiming to achieve.

End Notes

"I've always worked hard, since I was twelve years old. I've painted houses, and I'm a working-class guy. You know? I've never not been that. Didn't have any creature comforts growing up. Work ethic was instilled very early on. My parents basically said, 'We don't have money to give you. So if you want something, you work for it.' "**—Bill O'Reilly**

"If I really want it, I'm capable of a very, very strong work ethic. Physically, I've always been very strong. Pure blessing. There's no accounting for it. Just, God was good to me. I could work you to death. I mean, you'd be smarter than I was, taller than I was, stronger, better-looking. But I could beat you just by outworking you."**—Mario Cuomo**

"I very often work twelve to fourteen hours a day, and I also work on weekends, but you have to take into consideration that I own four golf courses, and I will be golfing when I can on weekends. I have a lot of properties and business interests, and I take an active interest in each of them, which requires the amount of time I spend working. But it's not a hardship to me. I enjoy myself very much, or I wouldn't be doing it."**—Donald Trump**

"My father's always been the most diligent of all workers. He's the kind of guy who would work sixteen-, eighteen-hour days for months and months, and not worry about anything else except dedicating himself 100 percent to work. He started as an orphan, and having to do the American success story. So everything that he has, literally, he's achieved on his own, through hard work."—**Marco Maccioni,** referring to his father, **Sirio Maccioni**

"I always say sleep is overrated. If you can get by on less sleep, there's more hours for you to get things done. Personally, I need very little sleep; I think that's a fortunate thing. I've probably averaged, over the course of my career, fourteen-to-sixteen-hour days, regularly. And I sleep four to five hours a night."—**Jeff Zucker**

"I work for myself. When you work for yourself, on one side, it's easier, because you don't take any orders. But you do a lot more. If you want to do things, you have to work. But as you get used to it, you get to enjoy it. It's like exercising, or eating well. It's all the same, really."
—**Diane von Furstenberg**

"If I'm going to work, I'm going to take it seriously. Everything I've ever done, I've been willing to work like a dog. No one's ever questioned my work ethic. That's what it takes. It takes getting on the plane in the morning, and flying to California to have a meeting, and flying back that night on the red-eye.

And going home to take a shower, putting on a fresh set of clothes, and going to work the next day."—**Bob Pittman**

"I've always said, 'Somebody may be smarter. But nobody'll work harder than I will.' And ultimately, I will succeed. And I will succeed far more than the other person who says, 'I'm gifted.' Well, I'm gifted, too. But I'm willing to work hard to make my gift be even better."—**Phil Lombardo**

"The question is, what do you ask and expect of yourself? And what gives you satisfaction? I never want to give a B-plus talk. I never want to write a B-plus paper. I just don't."
—**Dr. Judith Rodin**

11

Collect Wisdom

Phil Lombardo • Brooke Shields • Sir Richard Branson • Renée Zellweger • Diane Warren • Mark Burnett • Bobbi Brown • Joseph Abboud • Rikki Klieman • Cathie Black • Norman Lear • James Blake • Craig Newmark • Jane Friedman • Diane von Furstenberg • Dr. Judith Rodin • Jim Cramer • Matt Lauer • Donald Trump • Preston Bailey • Anna Quindlen • Joy Behar

WHEN I WENT DOWN to High Point, North Carolina, to host *Southern Exposure with Bill Boggs*, I met the man who would be not only my greatest champion, but also my mentor: **Phil Lombardo,** the station manager at WGHP-TV. Phil gave me one of the most important gifts I've ever received—complete freedom to promote, create, and host my show according to my vision. He trusted a rookie like me, handing me the reins and letting me run. After only three months on the air, we beat the *Today* show in the ratings.

Phil was an inspiring figure; no one at the place worked harder than he did. He was the first Italian American to be general manager of a television station. He'd grown up poor, in a tough part of

Chicago, and was the only one of his friends who'd made it out of the neighborhood. He exuded raw masculine power—imagine a taller, stronger, more handsome version of Michael Corleone and you've got a picture of Phil. It was clear that he was going places. Since leaving High Point, Phil has had extraordinary success and amassed a personal fortune, first as president of Corinthian Broadcasting and then as head of his own station group under the ownership of Citadel Communications Corporation.

Much of what I know about hosting and producing television, I learned at WGHP under Phil's guidance. Beyond the example he set, Phil taught me some valuable lessons. I'd like to share one that might help you. It's Phil's "plateau theory" of career evolution, which he recalled in our interview for this book:

"I look at life this way. It's a series of plateaus. What you try to do is to realize where you are now, and where you would like to be next. And that's the plateau. Once you get to that plateau, all of a sudden a different vision exposes itself, and now you can see where the next plateau is. Okay? But if you think you can see from the first to the last, I think you are being very naïve and foolish. At each plateau—think of yourself going up a hill—new vistas open up. And you see things you couldn't see before. Each one requires a quantum leap. It's a risk, and you can't be afraid to take the risk."

I hope you are fortunate enough in your life to encounter a Phil Lombardo of your own. Nearly everyone I interviewed for this book had tucked away some adage, advice, or pearl of wisdom passed along to them, whether from their parents, a boss, or even an unexpected and unlikely source.

• • •

Brooke Shields, on what she learned from her mother, who was her first manager:

"My mom taught me to love what I do, first of all. Because she had such a passion for movies, and theater, and everything that surrounded it. She taught me that if I didn't love something, it made no sense to keep doing it. I was regarded as a commodity in the modeling world, but if I didn't want to work that week, we would go on vacation. Or we would go to my dad's, or we wouldn't answer the phone. And so it wasn't the most important thing in the world.

"She also taught me that there's always going to be someone else. There's always someone coming on the scene that's new, and you can't get too comfortable in any one space. But there's enough to go around, and you have to believe that. We're not taught that in the industry I'm in. You know, it's, 'This is what's hot now.' And she always said, 'You know what? There's enough work out there to go around. Work generates work.'"

• • •

Sir Richard Branson is fortunate enough to have befriended and worked closely with the inspiring human rights activist Nelson Mandela, who famously forgave his captors and united with them for the good of South Africa. From his mentor, Richard learned much about how we should behave in business and in life:

"There was somebody who once stole records from our company. Everybody assumed that we would automatically sack him. But by actually calling him into my office, and having him apologize . . . fifteen years later, he's still working at the company. And he's given his all, because we were willing to give him another chance. We've all messed up. I mean, I messed up when I was a teenager with the tax man. It taught me that running a company 100 percent right, and sleeping well at night, is absolutely critical. And being given a second chance.

"What else has Mandela taught me? We spend quite a lot of time on using the fact that Virgin is financially strong, and that we've got a lot of expertise in the entrepreneurial world, to tackle social issues. Whether it's building businesses that will make a difference and pledging the profits to good causes, or looking at how AIDS is being tackled in Africa, or how malaria's being tackled, and trying to find better ways in which these problems can be dealt with. Mandela's been very good at looking at these issues himself, as well."

• • •

Much of the down-to-earth quality that keeps **Renée Zellweger** grounded in the swirling tempest of Hollywood stems from her immigrant Swiss parents:

"It was a very interesting upbringing to be the child of people who experienced war firsthand. Because their value system is much more pure. When every day you're not quite sure if you're going to see the sun come out, you develop as a person in a much different way than someone who takes things for granted. And so, you know, I lived in a house where it wasn't so much about aesthetics. It wasn't about acquisition. It wasn't about new stuff. It was about time shared, and being present. It was about making a difference, because you could.

"There was never a subtle suggestion that we might like to try to manipulate ourselves in a way that wasn't natural in order to appease in some way. It was about seeing something within, and developing it. My mother was constantly saying in my ear when I was growing up, 'Oh, you can do it. You can do anything you want to.' And I believed her."

Don't Give Up

Said **Diane Warren,** when asked what success rules she learned from her father: "Don't give up. Don't give up. Don't give up."

• • •

Producer **Mark Burnett** also received a message from his parents while growing up that gave him the confidence to pursue his dreams:

"The thing that I carried from my parents, even though we came from a very working-class, poor neighborhood—factory worker parents—was that anything's possible. My mother used to tell me stories about the guy who started Woolworth's. Started with a shopping cart, and sold door-to-door. And of course, you know, made a profit on his wares. And eventually that company had thousands of stores.

"That gave me a lot of inspiration. Just because you're born into a poor family and don't have a chance at a private school or great university, it doesn't mean you can't really make it. In fact, it's your own choice. Abraham Lincoln said, 'You're as happy as you make up your mind to be.' I think it's the same for success: You'll be as successful as you make your mind up to be. The benefit that my mother in particular gave me was to not limit my thinking to believe that where I am now is where I will stay."

• • •

Bobbi Brown reflects on what she learned from her mentor, Leonard Lauder, chairman of Estée Lauder Companies Inc., who purchased Bobbi's company in 1995:

"He's a big believer in the written word. He always tells me that I should always write a proper note. He says, 'People will savor notes.' Please save his notes. You don't realize how important your notes are until you see someone who says, 'You wrote me a note four years ago.' He's right. You have to do the right thing.

"As far as products and just doing what I believe in, he was the first one of any of those corporate bulls up there that just always believed in me. He said, 'You have to do what's right for you. And you've just got to come up with more ideas.' He really taught me to be true to myself."

• • •

Joseph Abboud spent several years working directly for Ralph Lauren, whom he describes as brilliant role model:

"There is nobody who is more steadfast in his beliefs than Ralph. He's a very good guy. He's very quiet, but, man, when he believes in something, he makes you believe in it. He's got the power of conviction like I've never seen in anyone.

"He so much knows what Polo Ralph Lauren is. But more important, he knows what he isn't. And that's what I learned from

Model Yourself

Rikki Klieman advises young people to closely watch others who have achieved success in their chosen field.

"You need to watch people who are older and better. If you're in my world, television, you ought to be watching television. You should be watching Diane Sawyer, Barbara Walters, Katie Couric, and others. Watch what they're doing, and why it works and why it doesn't. You need to watch someone who does what you do, and has done it longer, and really model your conduct and your path after them. Modeling is different than mentoring, because you're not in contact with that person. It's just a model for you.

"The second thing I believe is that you ought to read a lot of what people do that you do. Meaning, read biographies about these people. Read articles about these people, to understand what helped them that might help you."

him—that you can't be all things to all people. You know, be true. And he is."

• • •

Cathie Black, the president of Hearst Magazines, has been dubbed "The First Lady of American Magazines." She was president and then publisher of *USA Today* when it launched. From Al Neuhart, who was the chairman of Gannett and founder of *USA Today*, she gleaned valuable insight about leadership:

"We were on a mission; the stakes at *USA Today* were really big. Neuhart put together a team of people that just—I mean, we couldn't take no for an answer. It wasn't acceptable or good enough. This was his baby, this was his dream. And he was not going to let us screw it up.

"I think people love to hear that from somebody. They love to hear what your dream is, and what your vision for something is. If it makes sense, and if you can lay out what their contribution is going to be—if you can let people feel a part of something, no matter whether their job is small or really big, they're with you. And they're going to help you achieve that goal."

• • •

Producer **Norman Lear** often turns to a brilliant piece of advice on writing that he attributes to George S. Kaufman, the playwright, director, producer, and critic known for his contribution to 20th-century American comedy:

"If you have a hole in the plot that you must live with, don't sweep it under a rug. Hang a lantern on it. Life is full of those kinds of holes in the plot, that you must live with, you know? Don't sweep them under the rug. And it's been true in business. This is where I've been valuable in my business relationships, because I've understood those kinds of things. Not the business end of it, but the common-sense essence of that."

• • •

Rikki Klieman's optimism stems from a practice her mother taught her years ago:

"I wake up consciously now understanding and literally giving voice to the blessing of life every morning. When I was a child, my mother would come to my bed every night and say to me, 'What are you thankful for today?' And I had to have some answer, whether it was the sun, the moon, a tulip, a lollipop. That lesson gave me an ability to be optimistic about life, because there's always something to be thankful for."

• • •

James Blake has had the same coach since he was eleven years old. Beyond the technical elements of his formidable game, James absorbed from him some valuable life wisdom that allows him to keep the game in perspective:

"Brian Barker is someone who's filled just about every role in terms of mentor, big brother, coach, and just friend, really. Since I was eleven, obviously, the roles kind of changed. When I was that age, I was kind of bratty, and had a temper, because I was so competitive. I'd always want to win. And he calmed me down and really put things in perspective. He helped me realize that the end goal should be to put your racket down at the end and be happy."

• • •

Craig Newmark credits his Sunday school teachers as the primary influence behind his do-good mission:

"I realize in retrospect that I absorbed a lot of what they taught, and it's with me now. I just remember a sense of trying to do what's right, whatever that means. And as saccharine as it sounds, this Golden Rule thing seems to work."

• • •

HarperCollins CEO **Jane Friedman** picked up a piece of advice from her former boss years ago that has served her enormously well:

"Bob Gottlieb, who was the boss of Knopf in those days, once said, 'The most important thing I can say to you, Jane, is have ideas. Doesn't matter if they're good or bad. Have ideas.' And that has stayed with me forever. I always had ideas. I always wanted to do something more. I was never just satisfied. I wasn't unsatisfied, or dissatisfied. I just wanted more. So I invented jobs. I created

Tough Lessons

Several people shared stories of learning significant lessons from their parents the hard way:

"My mother was a survivor of a concentration camp. So my mother wanted me to be free. She gave me the best gift in the world: she never allowed me to be afraid. Fear was not an option. So if I said I was afraid of the dark, she would lock me in the closet. I wasn't allowed to be afraid. And I thank her so much for it."—**Diane von Furstenberg**

"There's a famous story in my life, from when I was about six. I was traveling to my grandmother's, and about five miles before we got to the house, my mother opened the door and told me to make my own way there. And I got lost in the depths of the English countryside. But that was my mother's attempt to make sure we stood on our own two feet. I think it did help me stand on my own two feet and gave me confidence that I could deal with difficult situations."—**Sir Richard Branson** the audiobook business for the publishing industry, and it's now a billion-dollar business."

* * *

Dr. Judith Rodin was the first woman to become president of an Ivy League university. It was her father who taught this education pioneer to set high expectations for herself:

"My father was amazing. He was the early drive behind me. If I got a 97, he asked me what happened to the other three points, always. And I didn't resent that. I actually found it very motivating.

"When I got out of college, I was having the time of my life, working as a newspaper reporter. My bank gave me this credit card. One day, in Mobile, Alabama, I used that credit card, and the guy said, 'It's not working.' So I called my father and said there was a problem with the credit card. He said, 'Oh, no, there's no problem at all. I don't think you understand how hard it is to work in this country. The credit card's no longer yours.'

"I said, 'Pop, I have no way to make enough money to live.'

"And he said, 'Maybe you should have thought about that when you took that job.'

"That was my father's driving lesson. I despised him for it, for a long time, and now I love him for it so much. It was so right. I didn't know. I thought my mom was right, that you've got to do what's in your heart. But I think my mother was right *after* my father was right. After you have some money, then you can do what's in your heart."

—Jim Cramer

Even when I was young. He made me know in ways large and small how much he expected of me.

"I did feel pressure, to be honest, but it was actually not anxiety-producing. It was motivating. And I think parents have to calibrate, knowing the personality of their child. I think my father recognized that I was very driven, so he helped sort of up it a

A Father's Imprint

I take my role as Trevor's father very seriously. One of the highest honors I have ever received was in 2000, when I was named Father of the Year by the National Father's Day Committee. I stood up and said I accepted the award on behalf of all the fathers who are wearing themselves out working three jobs to ensure their children are provided for and have all the opportunities in life they may never have had.

It was gratifying to learn how many of the people I interviewed credited their father's work ethic as a major influence in their lives:

"In order to sustain our family, my father would get up in the middle of the night. He was a combination engineer and janitor for an industrial building. In the middle of winter, when it was cold, he had to get in there and make sure that the building was warm before the people came to work in the morning. And nobody had to tell him. He would watch the news, determine what needed to be done. He would get up in the middle of the night and get there, and then come home at his normal hour. But he would increase his day by two, three hours because of his commitment."

—Phil Lombardo

"At one point in his career, my father was an insurance
salesman, and he did well at it. Then he went into kind of a
fringe family business, and did well at that. No matter what
he was going through in his particular career path, he always
got out of bed, and he always put in the time. He always did
his job, and everybody could always count on him. I think
that's been enormously helpful in my life. It's set me off on the
path of knowing how to be dependable."
—**Matt Lauer**

"My father told me to 'know everything you can about what
you're doing,' and I listened to him. He also set the
example, which is a powerful example to young children.
He was disciplined and very professional in his work, and
dealt with people fairly. We also saw that our parents had a
strong bond, and our home life was solid."
—**Donald Trump**

"My father had an amazing work ethic, and integrity. I mean,
this is a man who got up every morning in Panama at
midnight and worked until seven that evening, then came
home. I think my work ethic came from him, greatly. We
came from a very, very poor background—I mean, we ate,
but there was always that desire to better themselves. And
the only way that you can do that is by hard work, always
trying to see where you could move forward."
—**Preston Bailey**

"I felt very strongly that I needed to conform to what my
father expected of me And I would say that probably until I
was thirty-five or so, I was at some sub-rosa level very angry
at him for expecting too much. But in a fairly short period of

time, I went from feeling that way to realizing that what he had asked of me had wound up working for me, and making me into a person I quite liked being. And that it therefore only made sense for me to stop being pissed off. And I did."—**Anna Quindlen**

"My father fell in love with tennis, and then he and my mom passed that on to me, and I kind of fell in love with it as well. I think I picked up that same trait that he has—when he did something he liked or that he felt he needed to improve at, he went at it 100 percent. And so that's the way I do it."—**James Blake**

notch, whenever he thought it was appropriate to do that. I think if you have a highly anxious child, you wouldn't want to do that. It would be seen as too much pressure. But I loved doing well; I loved being recognized."

• • •

Sometimes inspiration can come from the least likely source. **Joy Behar,** who for three years hosted a political radio show on WABC (and who made me swear I would say that she disagrees vehemently with the views of her inspirer in this story), received some advice from radio personality Rush Limbaugh that has always stayed with her:

"When I left the radio, he said to me, 'Whatever you do in life, Joy, be bold.' I took that very seriously. Because I learned when I was on the radio to take the slings and arrows of hideous people calling sometimes, and being so mean. And writing hate letters, and all sorts of things. After a while, you just take it in stride, and you don't worry about what people think of you."

12

Don't Take Anything for Granted

Jim Cramer • Clive Davis • Craig Newmark • Maria Bartiromo • James Blake • Matt Lauer • Frédéric Fekkai • Donald Trump • Diane Warren • Bobby Flay • Diane von Furstenberg • Bob Pittman • Jeff Lurie

• • •

EVERYTHING MUST BE EARNED. It's that simple. Just because you've accomplished A, B, and C does not mean that D, E, and F will easily fall into place. A false assumption people sometimes make is to believe that because they've achieved a certain level of success, they are guaranteed future triumphs.

A good reputation or record is wonderful, but it will not generate the energy required to achieve new goals. Success mandates a constant drive forward, and that means never resting on your laurels.

• • •

At the crescendo of his Wall Street days, **Jim Cramer** had been on a multiyear hot streak. Repeated winning picks and massive financial success seduced him into believing he had an infallible golden touch.

"I had tremendous hubris going into 1998," he admitted. "I'd had year after year of great stock picking. Beginning of '98, I bought a stock, Cascade. And the stock immediately goes down six. I remember saying to myself, 'That's ridiculous. Stocks that Jim Cramer buys don't go down six.' You know? So you get into that mentality that suddenly you're really good. And you don't run scared. And then you can get killed."

"Don't pretend you know something. Because you'll always go wrong. Precision, integrity, not faking it, are really important."

—Jim Cramer

Jim refers to that period in his life as his "omnipotent phase," when he literally felt that if he liked it, it had to be good. That stock, however, cost him a lot, both in dollars and ego. Jim recognized that arrogance wasn't serving him well. Being the battering ram that he is, Jim of course rebounded and went on to have his biggest year ever in 2000, when he was making $400,000 a day trading. As a result of that Cascade experience, though, Jim retained a very basic lesson:

"Recognize humility. You know, be humble."

• • •

To look at music mogul **Clive Davis** today, you'd never suspect his modest beginnings. But underneath the natty clothes and luxurious trappings is a hardworking A-student from Brooklyn who rates himself as only as successful as his last report card.

"I would say that pessimism has played a bigger role than optimism, in that I never assume a record is gonna be a hit," Clive

Don't Buy the Hype

"Where do you place yourself in the pantheon of tech pioneers?" I asked Craigslist.com founder **Craig Newmark,** whose website is considered one of the most groundbreaking and wildly popular in recent history.

"I don't," he replied.

How's *that* for humble?

---

said. "I never assume that something is gonna be a success. I come from a philosophy, 'You've got to earn it at every level.' And you've got to do everything possible to give it a chance to soar, and be a success. I don't, because I sign an artist, believe, 'Oh, he or she is going to be the next biggest artist in the world.' I don't at all. That's rule number one."

> "I assume nothing. I know everything has got to be earned and won. And there are no shortcuts."
>
> **—Clive Davis**

From Aretha Franklin to Bruce Springsteen to Whitney Houston, Clive Davis launched each artist with the same determination and energy. He didn't presume that just because a song was emerging from his label, Arista Records—or later J Records—that it would succeed. In fact, the prospect of failure is so real to him that he goes that extra mile to ensure it doesn't happen. Just as he did growing up, Clive does whatever it takes to get to the top of his class.

Granted, his report cards are now Billboard charts and gold records, but Clive Davis is still acing them.

• • •

Maria Bartiromo and I discovered during our interview that we have an unexpected thing in common. We both love—and live by—the tenets in Rudyard Kipling's immortal poem *If*. I've had a copy of that poem up on my wall nearly all my life. One of Maria's favorite lines is, "If you can talk with crowds and keep your virtue; Or walk with kings, nor lose your common touch," which illustrates beautifully her commitment to staying grounded no matter what heights of success she reaches.

"You can never forget where you came from, or who you are—or lose your humility," Maria said. "I do think some people get this sense of entitlement, this sense of 'It's not like I've had any luck; I'm just great.' You know? It's a wonder. As soon as you lose your humility, I think it's the beginning of the end. I never do. I never will."

• • •

Nothing will make you appreciate good fortune more than the bracing jolt of adversity.

Tennis professional **James Blake**'s career was thriving until a series of horrifying events collided all within a very short period of time: he broke his neck, his father died of stomach cancer, and he contracted shingles, which attacked his facial nerve. It took time, patience, and hard work to recover and come back, but James did it with grace. In the aftermath of that terrible life phase, he developed a profound sense of appreciation for how fleeting success can be.

"Our careers are finite," he said. "And it made me realize there's gonna be a long part of my life without tennis. I really do want to make the most out of the time I have, and kind of treat this career like a sprint. I want to do the absolute best I can, work as hard as I possibly can, and treat everything now as if it was kind of icing.

Because none of it should really be expected. I can't ever wake up and expect to be top twenty in the world, and expect to win tournaments, or anything like that. I've got to work hard to do that every single day. And then, when I'm all done, it might seem like it was a long time. But it will just have been one part of my life."

It's easy to get lured into a false sense of security. But as any professional athlete knows, all it takes is one popped knee or one shattered vertebra to put you out of the game. No matter what

Being in the Zone

"Every athlete talks about how great it is to be feeling that way," said **James Blake,** when I asked him about getting into the zone. "And tennis is no different. You can feel like every shot's going to go in. You're almost cautious at that point. You're swinging freely, but you're cautious. You don't want it to ever end. And when it does, I think it's actually tougher to win a match. You play that well for maybe half of it, and then you're kind of back down to reality. A lot of people just assume it's going to continue. And when it doesn't, they still expect everything to go right. They kind of panic, and it ends up hurting them.

"But you learn from that," he continued. "When you're in the zone and playing that well, and maybe kill someone who's around your same level, and you get out of the zone, you need to remain focused. And think, 'Okay, I still need to work hard to win this match. I need to figure out ways to win.'

"The zone is really just something where you are focused on one point at a time. You're focused on winning that point, and not thinking about the situation a lot. Not thinking about your opponent. Not thinking about who's in the crowd. Thinking about winning one point at a time, and playing your best."

field you are in, success is something to appreciate and savor on a daily basis, because you never know what life can bring.

• • •

Matt Lauer will never take fame for granted. He, like James Blake, knows how tenuous it can be. When four of his television shows were consecutively canceled and he was purged from the A-list, he realized very quickly what matters in the long run.

"There was something that Horace Greeley said, of all corny things, and I've used it in graduation speeches and other speeches I've given; actually Jim Wright said it as he was leaving the floor of Congress when he was ousted years ago. The quote is something to the effect of, **'Fame is a vapor; popularity is an accident. Those who cheer you today will curse you tomorrow. The only thing that remains constant is character.'**

"All the hype and hoopla of what we do—the good seats at restaurants, and the autographs, and the people who tune in and write you letters—that's one thing, but you know what? It evaporates quickly when you're not there. So, what do you have, what's your calling card after that's gone? Why not make your calling card some deep character; something that's a commodity, that will impact people in the future?

"During those three years of unemployment, I saw the fame vaporize. I watched my Christmas cards go from three hundred a year to twenty a year, just high school and close friends. The other people who thought I was worthy of being on their Christmas list when I had a show in New York—two years later I wasn't worth a twenty-cent stamp."

Matt wasn't bitter as he was telling me this story. In fact, with the perspective of time, it was very clear that he looked back on this experience as a gift.

"That period didn't just influence my career and my life," he said. "In many ways, it shaped my life from that point on. It was a very grounding, humbling experience. And some people, I think, might have then taken the success that came afterward and cast aside that other period and said, 'Look, things are great now. It's fantastic. The sky's the limit, and nothing can ever go wrong.'

"I hope that at the end of all this—when I'm fired or I slowly walk off into the sunset with my head held high—I hope that people say that he was a good guy, he was a good person."

—Matt Lauer

"I don't have that feeling. I never have had that feeling. I always am aware of the fact that I'm only as successful as this last show. We went off the air ten minutes ago, and I will be judged on that show. Not the show that was before it. Not the show that was before that. In live television, you're judged on the last program that hits the air. I know that the tastes of people in this country change. And more importantly, the tastes of executives in this business change. And so you're always at their whim. If you get too carried away with thinking who you think you are, you're going to all of a sudden wake up, walk around the corner, and be confronted with reality. I always prepare myself a little bit for the fact that this will come to an end one day, so that when it does, it's not that hard to stomach."

• • •

Part of not taking anything for granted is not assuming that you can skate by on what you've always done. No one knows this better than lifestyle guru **Frédéric Fekkai,** whose upscale salon and products are continually on the cutting edge.

"I want to always raise the bar. I want to make sure

that we have great services, great products,

great attitude, great style. To me, it's just

about raising the bar all the time.

You can only do better."

—Frédéric Fekkai

"Especially in my business, the lifespan of success is not greater than five years," Frédéric said. "And fifteen years later, here I am sitting with you. To me, the idea is to not get stale. To not get stuck. To always be thinking out of the box. To always create some idea, and not rely on what you've been successful for. You cannot be successful twice for the same reason. People get bored. You've done something once that surprised everybody. After that, you've got to surprise them in other things. So good, you're a hairdresser. What's next?"

• • •

Always remember who you were when you were first starting out, because you'll need to **maintain that beginner's determination**—the sparks that started the fire—to do whatever it takes to achieve lifelong career success.

End Notes

"In the early 1990s I had some setbacks to the tune of about $900 million. People thought I was done. It was a difficult time for the real estate market, among other things, but I had not been as focused as I should have been. I had started to believe the 'Midas touch' theory that people had used about my success. I learned that to lose your focus and your momentum can cause some big problems. My focus improved and momentum increased. It was a good lesson, and I became more successful than I had ever been."

—Donald Trump

"I know I'm successful, but I've never felt I've made it. I think once you feel like, 'Yeah, I've arrived,' it's over. You know what I mean? I can feel that for a minute, but two seconds later I'm going to say, 'Shit, I hope I write something great next.' It's always that constant thing that keeps you hungry, keeps you moving."**—Diane Warren**

"I think as success grows, confidence grows. But I think it's important to also keep your confidence in check, because it gets harder to become as successful as you've been, once people know that you're successful. Because you're always being gunned for, and they expect you to raise the bar."

—Bobby Flay

"The most important thing is to be honest with yourself. To not bullshit yourself. And not believe your own press release. Before you were successful, it wasn't so easy to be humble. But once you're successful, it's much easier to be humble, and it's very attractive."—**Diane von Furstenberg**

"At any job, you have the ability to think you're a big deal, and to lord your authority over other people. Which can kill you. It will destroy your humanity. It will make other people feel bad. And it will limit your potential."—**Bob Pittman**

"Don't assume that you're going to live for 150 years. You know, treat it well now. Treat it with care and preciousness now. It's not going to repeat itself."—**Jeff Lurie**

13

Take the Risk

Bobby Flay • Phil Lombardo • Mark Burnett • Norman Lear • Joy Behar • Jeff Lurie • Bob Pittman • Brooke Shields • Anna Quindlen • Tom Perkins • Matt Lauer • Joseph Abboud • Cathie Black • Bill O'Reilly • Senator Kay Bailey Hutchison • Rikki Klieman • Peter Cincotti

"If you can make one heap of all your winnings,
  And risk it on one turn of pitch-and-toss,
  And lose, and start again at your beginnings
  And never breathe a word about your loss . . ."

   —**Rudyard Kipling, "*If*"**

SOMETIMES when I'm backstage just before walking out to perform my one-man show, *Talk Show Confidential,* I think about what's going happen to me in the next eighty-five minutes: *"I'm going to be alone on the stage . . . I'm going to have to capture the attention of all these people and entertain them—make this worth their while—and it's all coming just from me."*

It's scary, sure, but the very fact that I have created the show in order to stretch and test myself is what continues to drive me. If you don't take risks, and risk failure, how are you going to evolve? How are you going to experience new things? Most of all, **How are you going to succeed beyond where you are if you only continue to do what you've always done?**

Taking a risk entails leaping into the unknown. The leap requires confidence and courage. You have to believe that you can and will do whatever it's going to take to meet the challenges, as the people in these stories did.

• • •

If there were ever a venture that involves risk, it's opening a restaurant in New York City. Approximately 80 percent of all restaurants close within five years. With only a 20 percent chance of success, it takes a lot of courage and belief in yourself to be able to say, "I'm going to do it anyway."

Bobby Flay opened his first restaurant, Mesa Grill, in 1991, and his second, Bolo, two years later. Both have thrived despite the odds. Then, in 2005, Bobby took a calculated risk, this time with much more at stake personally. He invested his own money in a new restaurant, Bar Americain.

"You feel the success more if you take a risk," Bobby said. "Let's say you're a rich man who wants to invest in my restaurant. And you say, 'Hey, Bobby, you're a talented cook. I want to open a restaurant with you. Here's $3 million. I'll give you a piece of the action; I'll put up all the money.' What's my risk? Nothing. My reward can be good. However, I feel it's not a good thing for the investor, or it's not a good thing for me. I have less to risk, so I can work that much less. Or concentrate that much less.

"There's a term in the restaurant business: 'goodwill money.' Which means, if I only have $20,000 to my name, and you have millions, I can put up $10,000 and that would probably mean more than your $3 million would to you. That's an important thing. If you're successful then, the reward is fantastic.

"If the restaurant failed, it would really hurt in a big way," Bobby admitted. "But I think that's what helps success. Putting up my own money assures my concentration."

"Although I knew deep down it was a risk, I also felt like it was something I wanted to do, and I did it with confidence. Because it's sort of betting on me."

—Bobby Flay

Though the restaurant is still in its infancy as of this writing, Bar Americain appears to be another star in Bobby Flay's glittering universe.

• • •

Today, **Phil Lombardo** owns several television stations and is the former joint board chairman of the National Association of Broadcasters. He didn't become influential, wealthy, or successful by accident. He did it by doing whatever he needed to do to learn and advance—even if that meant taking a risk others would not have dared.

Phil was working in the late 1960s as a program manager at a station in Cincinnati, Ohio. In the two years he was there, Phil led the station to number one in the ratings. Part of his understanding with Avco Broadcasting, which owned the station group, was that he wanted to move up and become a general manager of a television station.

"After doing all this great stuff for two years, a general manager's position opened in Indianapolis," he said. "I went in and said, 'I'd like that opportunity.' And I was told that I was too valuable doing what I was doing, and that they were going to go in a different direction. I walked back into my office and wrote a letter of resignation."

At the time, Phil was married with two small children. "You resigned without another job," I said. "That's a big risk."

"Yeah, I know," he agreed. "But I knew I was right. I knew I was not being treated with the same honesty that I was giving out. So I resigned. I went home and told Kim, my wife, 'I just quit.' She said, 'Why? It's a good job. You were doing great,' and I said, 'I don't want to be in a company that won't allow me to grow, and be further challenged. I'm ready to be a general manager. And I want to be a general manager.'"

"A lot of people walk up to the threshold, Bill.

But very few cross over."

—Phil Lombardo

So Phil Lombardo packed up the car and moved his entire family into his parents' tiny row house in Chicago. They lived crammed together with only one bathroom while Phil searched for a general manager's job. He literally pounded the pavement, setting up meetings, talking to as many people as he could. (By the way, from this story comes another Phil Lombardo pearl of wisdom regarding unemployment: "What you do is, you get up in the morning and you dress as though you're going to work. And you get out of the house, okay? Because if you stay there, eventually it will pull you down.")

Phil met a headhunter who specialized in the broadcasting business. The headhunter was so impressed with Phil that he offered him a partnership if he would go into the recruiting business with him. Phil offered to help any way he could, but said that what he really wanted was a television assignment. So he came into the headhunter's offices and worked without any pay, hoping that it would lead to the kind of job he was holding out for. Eventually, an opening came in for a general manager's job at a fledging ABC-TV affiliate in High Point, North Carolina.

Even though Phil's background didn't necessarily fit what they were looking for, there was no way he was going to let this opportunity go by. He did extensive research, calling all his friends in the business and getting as much information on the station as he could. He got the job, moved to High Point, and became a general manager.

• • •

Some people seem to have the appetite for risk hardwired into their DNA. **Mark Burnett,** the founding father of reality television, didn't decide out of the blue one day to introduce an entirely new format to American television. Long before then, early training as a paratrooper in a Special Forces unit cultivated Mark's innate appetite for risk and adventure. Throughout his career, he has demonstrated a "nothing ventured, nothing gained" attitude.

"What's the biggest risk you've taken along the way, and what did you learn from it?" I asked Mark.

"Moving to America," he immediately responded (Mark was born and raised in England). "You know, with nothing. Using all my money to rent a piece of fence on Venice Beach to sell T-shirts. Then leaving that, and trying a marketing business. Going down the road, looking into the possibility of how to buy a savings and loan to set up Spanish-language credit cards. Throwing that away and jumping into the very cool water of TV.

"The more you do, the riskier it gets, the more pressure you have on you. But you know, you have to keep going forward. One thing's for sure: There's no standing still. You know, you're either going backward or forward."

—Mark Burnett

Then *Eco-Challenge*—I mean, starting my own race, which had never been held before in America. And then *Survivor.* I mean, it's just nonstop."

• • •

Producer **Norman Lear** named his original production company Tokas-Adamn-Tokin, which is Yiddish for "Putting one's ass on the line." With a motto like that, it's no wonder Norman Lear turned down a three-picture deal with United Artists to do the pilot for the thrice-rejected *All in the Family.* After three decades in show business, Norman has developed real wisdom on the subject of risk:

"I remember telling my kids as they were growing up, 'You can lean into life or lean away. You can be cautious and careful, or you can just lean in. And if you lean in, you're going to get hurt a little more, but you won't miss out on anything.'"

• • •

In her late thirties, **Joy Behar** was living in Queens, New York, raising a child by herself. She went to comedy clubs at night to perform, earning $50 a set, and worked a bit on Lifetime Television. Her rent at the time was $275 a month ("Can you imagine? Even those days, that was cheap!" she quipped). When she landed a job on a television show called *Way Off Broadway,* her salary suddenly jumped to $6,000 a week.

"So I decide, 'We're moving,'" she said. "We moved to Manhattan. And I go from a rent of $275 to $1,750 a month. I was so panicked about it that I couldn't even write the numbers on the check. So I had a stamp made out of it, and every month, I would stamp it."

The show was suddenly canceled. But Joy still had to stamp that check every month.

"I wasn't gonna go backward," Joy remembered. "So one of the things I would say to a young person is take a risk. And you usually can fill it. But don't take such a risk that you end up on the street. That was a big risk that I took, but I had a certain amount of confidence that I could do it."

Joy took a risk that changed the landscape of her entire life, and in order to sustain the life she had established for herself and her child, she rose to the occasion and did whatever it took. She proves yet again that necessity can be the greatest motivator of all.

• • •

Jeff Lurie purchased the Philadelphia Eagles for $185 million— the most ever paid in the United States for a professional football team.

"A lot of people thought it was overvalued," Jeff said, calm and collected as ever. "I actually thought it was a very good deal at the time, because content, I thought, was king. If you can buy into a hit movie system—which is what the NFL is, with a great fan base and a great market for football—as distribution extended domestically and around the globe, the content holders' value should go up and up and up. So I felt I was able to use a certain strategic vision."

That unprecedented financial risk, seasoned with some luck, turned into a brilliant investment. Shortly after Jeff Lurie purchased the team, the explosion in digital media, cable television, and satellite raised the value of all the teams in the NFL.

"That could have happened ten years later," he admits. "Who knows. It was going to happen, but it happened right after I bought the team. It could have happened ten years later and we'd be sitting here saying, 'You know, it's been a decent investment. Kind of flat for the first seven or eight years, and now it's gotten better.' It just so happened that it started to explode right away. So I knew soon after that it was one hell of an investment."

You can play it safe and get what you've always gotten, or you can make a big leap and see what it yields.

• • •

From turning around a country radio station with sagging ratings to believing kids would watch music on television (MTV) to revitalizing Six Flags theme parks, throughout his career **Bob Pittman** has eagerly taken on challenges that are fraught with risk. His natural perseverance was enhanced by something he learned from his mentor:

"Expect and tolerate a lot of mistakes. They're a by-product of innovation."

—Bob Pittman

"Steve Ross, who really built Warner Communications into the first huge media and entertainment company, had a wonderful saying," Bob offered. "He built it starting with his father-in-law's funeral homes, into this mega-entertainment company. And Steve used to say, 'You know, at this company, you'll never be fired for making a mistake. At this company, you will be fired for not making a mistake.' Because mistakes are a by-product of innovation. The only way you don't make mistakes is by not trying anything new. If you're not trying something new, the business you're running will grow stale and fade away. Probably half the decisions you make are going to be wrong—or more. And you have to be prepared for it. You can't count your success by how many mistakes you avoid. You have to count on how much progress you've made.

"I think there are a lot of people who get petrified of the risk," he continued. "They think they have to be right all the time. I'm not right most of the time. But I have people who are not afraid to say, 'It's not working.' And I have to not be defensive. I have to say, 'You know, you're right. Sounded good, I guess it didn't work. Let's move on.'"

• • •

It's never easy to leave the cocoon of what's familiar. It's comfortable, safe, and reliable. But as we've seen, if you don't force yourself beyond your comfort zone, you can't grow. And if you don't grow, your career flatlines.

Actress **Brooke Shields** was managed by her mother until she was twenty-eight years old. She had had unprecedented success as a model and young actress, but in later years she found herself relegated to doing things like coffee commercials in France. The bills were getting paid, but Brooke was creatively unfulfilled. She knew she needed to hire a professional team to steer her career in a better direction—a necessary but emotionally difficult leap for her to make.

"Leaving my mom was huge, because I left something that was familiar," she said. "Whether it's good for you at that particular time or not, it's familiar. You know it. You know what to expect; you know how to deal with it. You know how to fight it. You know how to use it; you know how to do it. And then to all of a sudden act—I mean, I was older. I was twenty-eight. But it felt like a risk, because there were no guarantees in any of it."

After that, Brooke Shields's career underwent a resurrection. She starred in the successful sitcom, *Suddenly Susan,* which earned her a People's Choice Award, appeared on Broadway in revivals of *Cabaret, Wonderful Town,* and *Chicago,* and authored a best-selling book on postpartum depression. By daring to leave the familiar, Brooke Shields put herself squarely back on the map and is fulfilling her creative dreams.

• • •

The list of risks taken by all the successful people in this book is pretty remarkable, and it validates that risk is essential in anyone's path to success. There was **Anna Quindlen,** who quit her job at the *New York Times* when she became pregnant without knowing if they would hire her back (they did, in a greater capacity), and **Tom Perkins,** who invested his life savings in a new kind of laser that might not have taken off (it did, and made millions). **Matt Lauer** turned down offers to do lucrative infomercials even when he needed the money, not knowing for certain if a better opportunity would ever come along (something did: the *Today* show). **Joseph Abboud** left the security of Polo Ralph Lauren and struck out on his own, not knowing if his designs would afford him the same level of success (they did, exponentially). In nearly every business, stories of risk have become the stuff of legend.

Do you have what it takes to risk it all?

End Notes

> "I think as my career unfolded, I had, in addition to the ambition gene, the risk gene. I've always said I'm open to risk that's measured risk."—**Cathie Black**

> "My father was afraid to take a chance, and that didn't do well for him. He was a Depression kid, and he was afraid. And so he got hosed by the system. He played it safe, and in the end, he was disenchanted. So I said, 'Well, why would I want to do that? I'd rather take the chance.'"—**Bill O'Reilly**

> "You have to be willing to lose if you are ever going to achieve very much. Or you won't strive for anything bigger."
> —**Senator Kay Bailey Hutchison**

> "I think you have to really understand when you are ready to make a change. And then you can go into free fall. Then you can really be at risk. The only way you make fundamental change in your life, professionally or personally, is if you say, 'Okay, I'm tired of this pain. And even if I have to struggle for a while, the reward will be worth it.' Until you make that step, you can't succeed."—**Rikki Klieman**

> "A lot of it comes down to taking risks. Because I've found that a lot of times, you've just got to jump off the cliff and see what happens."—**Peter Cincotti**

14

Develop Excellent Everyday Practices

Sir Richard Branson • Donald Trump • Diane von Furstenberg • Bob Pittman • Bobbi Brown • Joe Torre • Brooke Shields • Phil Lombardo • Senator Kay Bailey Hutchison • Preston Bailey • Bobby Flay • Cathie Black • Maria Bartiromo • Dr. Judith Rodin • Dr. Mehmet Oz • Rikki Klieman • Joy Behar • Marco Maccioni • James Blake

WHEN IT COMES right down to it, work is a daily affair. Amidst all the goals, dreams, plans, it comes down to showing up every day and just *doing your work*. The big picture matters, sure, but it's the small practices you employ—things like delegating, organizing, following up, minding your manners, being ethical and honest—that make the difference between a good career and a truly remarkable one.

Here's some advice from those who have figured out the little things that really do matter:

Delegating and Collaborating

"I think I fortunately learned early on that my skills were limited, and that what I had to do was find people who had better skills than me in lots of different areas—not to try to do everything myself.

"**Collect the best people around you.** Almost attempt to see if you can't put yourself out of business by trying to find people who are better than you. Give people the chance to make mistakes, and don't jump down their throats if they do make a mistake."

—Sir Richard Branson

"I know what is required in each situation and what I am in charge of. That makes it clear, but I always keep in touch with the key people involved on every project or development. **I do not micromanage, but the responsibility is ultimately mine,** and I don't forget that. My name is on the product."

—Donald Trump

"Delegate everything, but not at the beginning. At the beginning, I did everything. But as you grow, I think that you want to **delegate everything that you don't have to do yourself**."

—Diane von Furstenberg

"In business, what you really have to do is trust other people. Delegate. And when I say delegate, I mean honestly give them the vote. At AOL we used to say if you delegate to somebody, you've given them the vote; you can't have the vote anymore. They get to decide. If you don't like the decisions they're making, and you can't persuade them to your point of view, you can fire them. But beyond that, you can't have somebody in the job and make their decisions for them.

"**You've got to trust people.** If someone's empowered to be the technologist, and they're going to build the next version of AOL, you've got to let them go do that. You can help them with the market research, but they've got to be in charge of it. As a leader, the way you can get broader is to have people you trust. Because then you don't have to know anything about technology, or sales, or programming. You just have to be able to give these people, all tied together, one cohesive plan. And a job like the ones I had for many years was managing the team, not managing their areas of expertise."—**Bob Pittman**

"I'm open-minded. I'm not the last word on everything. I pretty much know what I want, but there is some room. **I love when people challenge me.**"—**Bobbi Brown**

"I know I delegate a lot of authority to my coaches. **But if it's bad news, I always deliver it myself.** I don't give that to one of my coaches. I'm getting paid more than they are, and it's not for them to deliver that kind of message to anybody."

   —**Joe Torre**

"I'd rather delegate to someone smarter than myself, because then I benefit more. I'm not that egomaniacal that I think I can do it all. It's hard not to micromanage, when you've learned to do that your whole life. But I'm getting much, much better, because life is very short. And I'm realizing that I waste a lot of time trying to do other people's work."—**Brooke Shields**

Discipline and Organization

"If you're not disciplined, you're a scattered person. Every little thing is going to push you one way or the other. So it's important to have a discipline. Organizing yourself, that's discipline. I have seen very talented people who are totally undisciplined. And consequently, the level of responsibility that you give those people should be minimal. They can be their own worst enemies, because they're so distracted.

"It's attention to details, and most people hate details. **You have to discipline yourself to take care of the little details, so they don't turn into huge problems.** I had to force myself to take care of the details, and now it's just second nature. When you do that, you'll file away a lot of information that you can use at the appropriate time."

   —Phil Lombardo

"I am a list maker. I know I might forget, because I'm doing so many things. So **I write down the things I know I have to do**."

   —Senator Kay Bailey Hutchison

"Encourage it by writing things down. I mean, it sounds so simple, but I think note making is the greatest thing in the world. **If you tend not to be good with details, write things down as often as possible.** Absolutely."

   —Preston Bailey

"Every day, no matter who you are, you know that there are three things, or thirty things, that you were supposed to do that day. If you don't do them, you've got to do them eventually anyway. They never go away. So what I try to do is **attack exactly what I have in front of me, as soon as I can**. Phone calls that you don't want to make. Menus that for whatever reason I'm just not inspired that day to make happen. I force myself to make them happen."

   —Bobby Flay

"**Start every meeting with a 'What do we want to accomplish today?** Are we making decisions? How long is the meeting?' End on time—or early!"—**Cathie Black**

"I live by a deadline life. I'm on air a lot, so I have constant deadlines. And my columns are due on certain days. I won't think of something unless it's coming up the next day. I can't. **I have to prioritize.** I look at my life as deadlines, all the time."

   —**Maria Bartiromo**

"I believe in being really well-prepared. I never want a day to unfold without being well-briefed—either with materials the night before or early in the morning—for the meetings I'm going to have. Because there's always uncertainty that happens. And so, if you don't lock in the things that are certain—where you have control and can be prepared—then you can get totally floored by the unexpected things that happen. So for me, it's been a really good dialect to **nail down that which I can control and predict, in order to be totally flexible and adaptable when unexpected things happen.**"
   —**Dr. Judith Rodin**

"**Don't lose the forest for the trees.** Don't spend all your time doing the urgent but short-term tasks; take time to do the strategic planning. If you are running really hard, but in the wrong direction, you're just wasting time."—**Dr. Mehmet Oz**

Ethics and Manners

"**Your word is your bond.** It's as clichéd as that. The day you go in to negotiate a plea, or negotiate a deal—whatever it may be in your life—the day that you exaggerate, that you fib, that you shade the facts, that you spin, you lose your reputation for credibility. You will never be trusted again."—**Rikki Klieman**

"Pure ethics in business is critical. **Your reputation is everything.** Your reputation for your brand, your reputation for yourself. It's critical that you conduct your life in a manner in which, you know, if you wake up and read about it the next day, you're not going to feel really uncomfortable about it. In the end, you're only as good as your reputation. Quite a few businesses have messed up big-time."—**Sir Richard Branson**

"You have to **hold on to your true core values,** no matter how destructive the business you're in. Even if you work on Wall Street. Even if you're an Enron executive. If you hold on to your core values, you will succeed in spite of the things that go on around you. And you'll survive."—**Joy Behar**

"For me, in my life in general, the most important thing is honesty. I have never lied. I've taught my children never to lie. I will not accept lies. **Great honesty makes your life simple.**"

   —**Diane von Furstenberg**

"With manners, it all comes down to, basically, **respect:** the amount of respect that you demonstrate to someone, in any interaction. A customer coming through the door is a business dealing on its own, in itself. It's a contract between the innkeeper and the traveler, the visitor."—**Marco Maccioni**

"Walk down the hall and **talk to people** rather than send a chain of e-mails."—**Cathie Black**

"My parents always stressed **being a good person,** and it manifests on the court. I think it's part of the reason I've got a lot of fans. I try to treat the other player with respect. I try to treat the ball kids, the umpires, and the fans with respect. And I always try to carry that out, on and off the court, the way I know my parents would."—**James Blake**

"**Just be respectful of other people.** Whatever you do, don't cause anyone to lose their dignity. Don't scream and yell at people. Don't call them an idiot. When you're the boss, you can get away with that stuff, but *you can't do that*. That's a temptation to some people."—**Bob Pittman**

"A lot of people have said to me, 'I'm going to send this, I'm go-

The Art of the Thank-You

In the "old days"—back in the 1970s—when I'd give a party, I'd get a ton of thank-you notes within a week. In recent years, though, maybe just two or three notes appear in the mail, even after a gathering for as many as seventy-five people. Okay, maybe you're thinking the parties now suck. Wrong. They're better than ever; I now have a wife who makes sure of that. But it's just apparent that most people don't bother to write thank-you notes anymore. So when you do write one nowadays, you will really stand out.

It's really easy to develop the habit of sending a handwritten note as a follow-up to business encounters or social events. Get decent note paper and discipline yourself to write a couple of short, gracious lines within twenty-four hours of an occasion where you have been entertained or benefited from someone giving you their time. It will take you less than three minutes to write, address, and stamp it, but the results will last far longer.

ing to do that.' And you never hear from them again. If I say to someone, 'I'm going to do something,' I do it. I drive my assistant nuts. But I come home constantly with little things. I don't care if it's the guy at the gas station or the girl at the Verizon store that wants to be a makeup artist. Or whoever it is. I **follow up** on what I say."—**Bobbi Brown**

FOUR

The Challenges of Success

15

Confront Fear, Insecurity, and Other Inner Demons

Anna Quindlen • Dr. Judith Rodin • Jeff Lurie • Bob Pittman • Maria Bartiromo • Peter Cincotti • Bobby Flay • James Blake • Preston Bailey • Christie Hefner • Brooke Shields • Bill O'Reilly • David Rockwell • Bill Bratton • Frank Rich • Phil Lombardo • Diane von Furstenberg

WE ALL HAVE a little voice inside our heads that makes us doubt ourselves. It's the one that whispers, *"You're not good enough . . . You'll never make it . . . Who are **you** to think you have the answers?"* It can be insidious and horribly undermining, causing us to question ourselves on the deepest levels. Successful people don't usually talk about feeling insecure, because that's the antithesis of what they're supposed to put out there. But I think it's comforting to know that even the most successful among us feel unsure at times.

Interestingly, the people I interviewed generally fell into one of two camps: they either sought to quash the fear and forge ahead, or they welcomed it as a self-regulating device. Either way, none of them denied that it reared its ugly head from time to time. Reading about their coping mechanisms may give you some ideas of how you can deal with your own insecurities whenever they threaten to derail you. **Minimizing the obstacles one is bound to face in the pursuit of success begins with minimizing the obstacles within oneself.**

• • •

When I asked **Anna Quindlen** about the voice of negativity, she knew exactly what I was talking about.

"It's huge, that voice," she said, nodding vigorously. "It's the fraud factor. It's that feeling the someday someone's going to knock at the door and go, 'Okay. You've been doing a pretty good imitation of a serious person for a long time, but we know. We know you're not really that smart. We know you're not really that good. We know you don't really have it all together. And they're going to take you away to the fraud prison, and there you're going to molder for the rest of your life.'

"I think most of the bad decisions that are made in people's lives, as in their work, come out of fear."

—Anna Quindlen

"I think the easiest way to get over that is to realize everyone has it," Anna continued. "It's not that anyone doesn't have it. Some people do a better job than others of hiding it. You know, people who don't have it, I think, are often incomplete people, because they don't keep testing themselves against their own fears and insecurities. I think that's a good way to get to the next level, too. By saying, 'Well, you know, here's something I really can't do.' And then you say, 'I don't know, maybe I can do that.'

"I think also, you get over the hump at some crucial point," she continued. "I think I probably got over the hump when I was in my early forties. I think it was then I realized decisively that not only was I not a fraud, but there were an awful lot of people in positions of power and influence who were."

• • •

Dr. Judith Rodin, who is clinically trained in the inner workings of the human mind, confirmed Anna's thoughts on personal insecurity.

"I used to talk to Penn undergraduates about this a lot," Judith said. "Because they actually didn't believe that anyone else felt it. So the first thing I would tell them is to acknowledge that you're not the only one feeling it. That everyone in the room is probably feeling that insecurity. Each individual feels, 'Gosh, you know, I'm the only one who's feeling I'm dumb,' or 'I'm going to get found out,' or 'I'm not whatever.'"

Judith admits that even a high-achieving academic can feel that way sometimes. "I almost didn't go to graduate school, even though all my professors were telling me how terrific I was, because I kept saying to myself, in my own internal doubting mode, 'I'm not as good as they think I am. I'll never have an original idea. How could I get a Ph.D. when you need a truly original idea to do your dissertation,' and all of that.

"I will say, in all sincerity, that somewhere around the middle of my years at Yale, I was sitting in my office one day when I said to myself, 'I don't feel that way anymore.' And then I asked myself if it was because I'm so supremely confident or because I realize everybody else is dumb, too? No. It's because I came to recognize that other people have self-doubts. Self-doubts are part of the reality of being a human being. And secondly, my own successes had given me more confidence. So it's something you'll acquire as you grow."

• • •

Jeff Lurie seems to have made peace with the negative voices in his head. He accepts insecurity for what it is without trying to quell it, overcome it, or ignore it.

"I think the way I deal with it is to recognize that it's just a normal characteristic," Jeff said. "Everybody has some degree of insecurity. It's how you manage it. It's not trying to rebel against it. It's not trying to back out and overcompensate with a false sense of security. It's not about narcissism, where you take the insecurity and try to foster so much love toward yourself that you interfere with everyone else's lives. It's just part of being human."

• • •

You wouldn't know it from viewing **Bob Pittman**'s impressive media résumé, but he, too, is intimately familiar with that insecure voice. Like Anna Quindlen, he welcomes it.

"I don't move it aside," Bob said. "I think that voice is my friend. I'm an incredible self-doubter. Any decision I make, I worry whether I made the right decision. So I'm constantly revisiting decisions. When you figure about half the decisions you make are gonna be wrong anyway, it allows you to catch the wrong ones, fix them, try again. Keep trying until you get it right. I've had people on my team who stun the other team members because they are regular dissenters—usually to me and my ideas. But I always need a strong 'Doctor No.' Somebody who says, 'Can't do that. Nope. That won't work.' Because I think it's important to hear the negatives and to have a solution for their complaints.

"There's this wonderful story of President Kennedy and the space program," he continued. "He makes this big announcement, 'We're going to put a man on the moon by the end of the decade.' He had no plan, before the announcement, other than keep up with the Russians; beat the Russians. But what he did next was so brilliant. When people said, 'You can't put a man on the moon,' instead of saying, 'Yes, we can,' and then shutting off the debate, he said, 'Really? Why not?' And they said, 'Well, you don't have any rocket fuel to get there, you don't have a navigation system, blah, blah, blah.' And he made a list of it all.

"Then he asked, 'So, what you're saying is, as soon as we solve all these problems, then we can have a man on the moon?' In essence, the dissenters gave him the plan. And I think that little voice in my head is one of my dissenters."

It may be helpful not to dismiss that little voice in your head. Maybe it's actually vocalizing your next move.

$$\bullet \ \bullet \ \bullet$$

Maria Bartiromo, though polished and poised on television, freely admits that she has private moments when her confidence wavers—which she is able to use for her benefit.

"I think when you're feeling insecure, the first thing to do is to try to figure out what to learn from this experience," she offered. "Why are you feeling insecure? Who is it, or what is it, that's triggering this? And what can you learn from that person, or from this experience? It's not necessarily going to make you feel better. But in retrospect, when you look at the situation two weeks later, you'll say, 'You know what? I did learn something from that.' That's number one.

"Number two is, I think you always have to remember your successes. And I think you have to say to yourself, 'Look, this situation is kicking my butt, and I'm reacting wrongly to this. I'm doing the wrong thing here. But what about what I did last week?

Stage Fright

It might surprise you to know that even **Maria Bartiromo** gets nervous speaking in front of people. Even though she appears relaxed on television, she still gets rattled in front of a live audience. A coach once gave her some great advice: "Maria, you constantly forget something that you must remember every time you're up there. They asked you to do it, because they want you to do it. These are your people. They like you."

I speak in front of live crowds all the time, and my advice to myself and others is to remember that the audience isn't sitting there projecting negative thoughts at you. They're just waiting to hear something from you. That usually helps relax me.

I mean, that was huge, what I did last week.' It's really important to remember your successes."

• • •

Doubt inevitably accompanies any creative process. Musician **Peter Cincotti** hears the negativity as a small alarm bell signaling that his artistic efforts might have veered off course.

"Sometimes doubt can be a good thing. It can propel you to re-examine what you already think is good, and be the reason for making it even better," Peter explained. "Rewriting a song should always be an option. Sometimes you'll go back and be glad you did, and other times you might say, 'No, wait, this is perfect the way it is.' But I think the balance of doubt and self-assurance is important. If you have too much of one, the quality of what you produce might suffer."

• • •

Bobby Flay doesn't bother trying to pretend that he's confident about everything 100 percent of the time.

"I used to hide it," Bobby admits, when I asked him how he deals with insecurity. "That was the first thing I would think of doing. Hiding it from myself, hiding it from everybody else. Now I don't. Because I experimented with not hiding it, and it goes away a lot quicker."

"Can you give me a specific example?" I asked.

"Yeah, I'll give you sort of a general one," he said. "You know, pastry is not my thing. I'm a savory guy, right? But when we first opened Mesa Grill, I always thought that because I'm the chef, I was supposed to know every single thing. You should know as much as you can, but the thing that was my insecurity was that I didn't know a lot about pastry. I didn't know a lot about the science of it. Because that's really what it is. It's more of a science than a craft, like cooking is.

"I kept the fact that I didn't know a lot about pastry in for a while, and then a couple of years into it, I just sort of gave it up. I hired my pastry chef, and just said, 'Look, this is not my game. I don't know how this works. I can tell you what I like and what I don't like, but other than that, it's your thing.' I handed it off to somebody who really knew what they were doing."

It takes guts to openly admit that you don't know something— especially when you're the boss. But why waste valuable energy trying to bolster a false sense of confidence? Once Bobby Flay released himself from thinking he had to be perfect, he was able concentrate on what he enjoys and does best.

• • •

With thousands of people in the stands watching your every move with hawk-like attention, it seems only natural that a professional tennis player such as **James Blake** would experience pangs of self-doubt. How does he keep his cool in those moments?

"I try to deal with it by thinking of others," James said. "I try to realize, 'Okay, well, I'm not perfect,' and what I draw from that is that no one else is, either. And so there's no reason to worry too much about it. Because everyone has these insecurities. So if I'm insecure on the tennis court—if, you know, someone's attacking my backhand, or putting too much pressure on that—I say, 'Okay, well, let's find his weakness, and see if I can make him insecure on the court as well, and make him uncomfortable.'

> "I know everyone's dealing with insecurities. I
> don't think most people have any reason to point mine
> out, and I have no reason to point anyone else's out."
>
> **—James Blake**

"In terms of insecurities off the court, I just try to remember back to my high school days, when I was really insecure. I was still small, and I wore a back brace all through high school. What I draw on is the fact that when I was five foot three in high school and ninety pounds or something, wearing a back brace, I still managed to have some friends. You know? I had people who liked me for who I was. 'Cuz they sure as heck weren't liking me for anything special I was doing back then."

• • •

In spite of the fact that he has orchestrated some of the most high-profile events of recent years, **Preston Bailey** still secretly questions whether he has what it takes. In his mind's eye, he still sees the unsure young man who arrived from Panama years ago with no idea what he was doing. Rather than be hampered by his fear, Preston uses the negative energy as motivation.

"I'm still coming from a place that I'm gonna screw up, and that I'm not talented," he confessed. "And each time, that voice keeps me trying harder, because I think I'm gonna fuck it up."

As long as he keeps thinking he's going to get it wrong, it's likely Preston Bailey will continue to get things right. It may not be a formula that serves everyone, but it certainly works for him.

• • •

One of my favorite books of the 1970s was *How to Be Your Own Best Friend*, by Mildred Newman and Bernard Berkowitz. I've read it several times. The title itself is magical. Being able to support and lovingly advise yourself, especially when the going gets rough, is invaluable. Something **Christie Hefner** said when I asked her about how she copes with stress reminded me of the book and how we could all benefit from being as supportive of ourselves as we would be to our best friend.

"I think I've been fortunate in that I have a really wonderful circle of 'kitchen-cabinet' friends," Christie said. (I'm not surprised—I've known Christie personally for years and she is about as warm and true-blue as they come.) "If I'm doubting myself in something, these are confidants that I can reach out to, and I think that's helpful.

"But then I also think sometimes you just have to sort of give yourself the same advice you would give a friend," she added. "You know, we're often better at giving a friend advice than ourselves. But sometimes I find if you do that—if you sort of step out of yourself and say, 'Okay, what would you say if you were sitting with a friend?'—how would you try to help them through it?"

• • •

Brooke Shields confessed that her self-esteem wavers more often than she'd like. To counteract the negative spiral of thoughts, she trains herself to focus inward.

"When I start to look outside myself, and start to compare myself to other people, I start to weaken a little bit," Brooke said. "I start to think, 'Oh, maybe I should be doing that.' It's a very juvenile way of doing things, that sort of comparison. It's a vortex. If I start doing that, I have to pull myself back and just go into my own little world."

Brooke shared a story with me about her friendship with an acclaimed veteran actress who has enjoyed a long, distinguished career (Brooke did not want to reveal who it was, out of respect for the woman's privacy). This screen star clearly enjoyed Brooke's company and actively welcomed her into her social circle. Each time Brooke was in her presence, however, she spiraled down into that vortex of insecurity.

"I become tongue-tied whenever I'm around her," Brooke said. "The last time that I was around her I said to myself, 'Do not start being self-deprecating. You get around her and the first thing you do is defer, defer, defer. She's invited you over for dinner because she obviously likes your company. So let's just take it at that. You're not 'less than.' There are only five people at the whole dinner at her house. She must like you. Why don't you just assume that, going in?'"

On her way to the dinner party, Brooke swore that if she had anything negative to say about herself, she'd just keep quiet, even if it meant she wouldn't say anything all night. During the evening, someone asked the hostess if there was any other actress's career she envied. Brooke was shocked when her friend immediately revealed her own insecurity and said yes.

"She started saying things like, 'All the good roles are going to so-and-so, and she's doing this, and so on.' And I'm thinking to myself, 'This cannot be the truth. I mean this is *this woman*. I pray to God I'm as respected as she is!' You know? The mere fact that the question was posed flipped me out, and the fact that she had an answer. I mean, does it ever stop?

"It was a really personal moment," Brooke said. "Because I realized we all do it. It gave me confidence, in a way. I realized she's just like every other actress, who wants this and wants that, and is trying to always be better, and keep working. It was just amazing to me to see that happen. I realized that we're all in this, and no one's better than anyone else."

• • •

The most surprising answer I got to the insecurity question came from the hard-hitting television journalist **Bill O'Reilly**. Here's how he overcomes negative thinking:

"I use Eastern philosophy," Bill responded. "I use the Zen thing to overcome that. Because that's right. Everybody's got this little voice saying, you know, 'You're gonna screw up.' But whenever you have a negative thought—which is natural, by the way—then you replace it with a positive thought. That's what Eastern philosophy does. So on the air, if I said, you know, 'I'm gonna make a mistake,' then I say, 'No, I'm not. I'm not going to make a mistake. I'm good at what I do.' Negative thought, replaced by a positive thought, wipes out the negative thought almost 100 percent of the time."

• • •

David Rockwell is another who takes a philosophical approach to self-doubt:

"I. M. Pei got an award two years ago from the Cooper U [Cooper Union]—a lifetime achievement award," David said. "And in his acceptance speech, he said, 'If you live long enough, people will forget your mistakes.' And in architecture, you build your mistakes. So, I guess I've mastered inner doubt by just believing in the level of optimism you have when you're doing the work.

"I've never really given in to it. But that doesn't mean I don't acknowledge it," he qualified. "I think acknowledging inner doubt is helpful. For instance, when we did the Kodak Theatre for the

Academy Awards, that was a quantum leap into a world fraught with so much potential downside. So maybe that's how I deal with inner doubt . . . I take these quantum leaps, where the actual risk is so much greater than the inner doubt."

• • •

Backed by his faith in his abilities, chief of police **Bill Bratton** continually embraces new challenges. Yet even this rock-solid authority figure has moments of doubt.

"I'm not so confident that I'm not self-questioning," Bill said. "I'm continually questioning. I have my good days and bad days, like anybody. But I don't stay in a funk."

"How do you get out of it?" I asked.

"I work through it. You know, if I'm coming to work and I'm just . . . I come in, and just start plugging away. I have confidence by the end of the day I'll have worked my way through it."

I agree: momentum is an effective way to dispel a negative funk. **Just get moving and see what happens.**

• • •

At the time when I interviewed journalist **Frank Rich,** he was facing a book deadline. The deadline was tight, but that wasn't what was concerning him. Deep down, Frank wondered, as a lot of writers likely do, if he had anything new or worthwhile to say.

How does Frank Rich quiet those voices of doubt and motivate himself to get started?

"I talk myself up from it and say, 'Well, you know that once you get into the actual doing of it, you'll be stimulated by the intellectual and creative effort,' " he said. "And that's usually the case. It's always the anticipation. You know, in the Steve Sondheim show *Sunday in the Park with George* . . . the blank canvas. It's the great exciting thing, as well as the terrifying thing, filling it up. And I always identify with that, because as long as it is blank, it's terrifying. But also, it's an opportunity. So the moment you start to alight on it, and get caught up in the creative experience, a lot of this takes care of itself."

• • •

Television industry magnate **Phil Lombardo** takes an efficient approach to insecurity:

"I think everybody has self-doubt, at some point or another. But if you dwell on it, it will pull you down. So what you do is, you sort of brush it aside. You analyze it, and then you brush it aside. If you don't have self-doubt, you're not being critical of yourself, and you should always be critical of yourself. But you've got to analyze it and move on."

• • •

The unwavering **Diane von Furstenberg** has no time or patience for fear. She obliterates it from her psyche as soon as it dares show itself.

"It serves you every single day of your life not to be afraid. You should never be afraid. Fear is a handicap. So you deal with it. You think about it. You think, 'Why,' and whatever. But to not be afraid is a huge, huge plus."

• • •

Fear of success abounds. Unfortunately, many among us have the psychological need to hold on to negative thoughts and insecurity because they keep us safely parked in our comfort zone. But if you do not at least *try* to move beyond where you are comfortable, you will not grow. **Find a way to deal with insecurity or your immobilizing fears, and you will find a gold-plated opportunity for growth.**

16

Learn to Cope with Stress

Mark Burnett • Jeff Lurie • Craig Newmark • Dr. Mehmet Oz • Joseph Abboud • Senator Kay Bailey Hutchison • Brooke Shields • Frédéric Fekkai • Christie Hefner • Richard Johnson • Frank Rich • Renée Zellweger • Matt Lauer • Jim Cramer • Anna Quindlen • Bill Bratton • Jane Friedman • Tom Perkins • Maria Bartiromo • Bill O'Reilly • Donald Trump • Norman Lear

STRESS IS TRULY a subjective thing. One person's stressful situation—crowded sidewalks, honking horns, blaring fire engines—could be another person's exciting adrenaline rush. It's crucial to realize that, as you pursue success, you must find ways to manage stress, because too much of it will damage both your health and your career.

Dealing with stress has been an ongoing challenge in my life. I've been living in New York City for thirty years and the place is both an engine that creates stress and a laboratory for studying it. Almost any day you can watch seemingly normal and successful people explode into tense, raging, and sometimes almost berserk behavior right in front of you.

Here's an example: I was walking about twenty feet toward an open elevator in my apartment building when a frenzied woman inside the elevator screamed out at me, "I can't wait for you, I'm in a hurry!" The door closed in my face. It would have taken about three seconds for me to make it inside. She was acting like a stressed-out psycho, and the situation she created didn't do much to lower my pulse, either.

Would that I had the qualities of the Dalai Lama—you know be totally in the moment, enjoy delays, contemplate the beauty of the elevator door, et cetera. But I don't. I do, however, have a couple of personal strategies that I've devised to help stabilize myself when I feel the internal pressure mounting.

Years ago I took a course in hatha yoga. One of the things we were taught was deep diaphragm breathing. I learned to concentrate on slowly breathing in very deeply through the nose and then exhaling even more slowly through pursed lips. As I exhale, I pretend that I am blowing out the tension. Doing that breathing routine just three or four times calms me down and seems to lower my pulse.

When possible, I close my eyes and combine deep breathing with visualization. I picture myself under a thatch-roofed hut on the beach at one of my favorite places in the world, the Anse Chastanet Hotel in Saint Lucia. I breathe deeply as I imagine looking at the horizon, watching sailboats glide by. I see the water dappling in the sunshine and the birds flying in the clear blue sky. Other times, I use visualizations from my childhood. I am at the park, we are playing a game of stickball. My friend Steve is on the mound. The ball is coming at me. I watch it, I swing. Both of these little mental movies take me far away from what's bothering me—and I get to hit as many home runs as I want.

I think you'll find these insights about dealing with tension from several of our cast of characters helpful. Breathe deeply, slowly exhale, and read on.

• • •

Producer **Mark Burnett** is no stranger to stress. Producing five reality television shows at once means keeping a lot of balls in the air. You have to deal with all kinds of things—personalities, location crises, ego clashes, negotiations, last-minute changes—all of which can add up to a giant headache. Mark Burnett has adopted what I think is a terrific philosophy that enables him to take it all in stride.

"I don't worry about things I can't control," Mark said evenly. "The important thing to remember is that things continually go wrong—wrong being not exactly what you intended. But if you start off knowing that, and accepting that things won't exactly go correctly, you'll be far better positioned to roll with the punches a little bit, rather than get knocked down. You won't be the tree that breaks in the wind; you'll bend with the wind a little bit."

Mark Burnett aims to sidestep stress by keeping his focus on what is coming, not on what has already been. He channels his energy forward and doesn't worry about what happened yesterday, or even an hour ago. It's a very interesting approach.

"You know, I don't really know what stress means," Mark said. "It's just a word that's thrown around, right? But anxiety is a word I do understand. That means something to me. I will tend to more anxiety from putting things off than just doing them. In other words, anxiety is more about worrying what may happen, versus what has happened. When something has occurred and it's not the most positive situation—maybe it's even negative—it is what it is. It's done. You need to worry about the next thing."

• • •

The driving motivation behind **Jeff Lurie**'s success, as we've already seen, is his awareness that life is fleeting. His father's death when Jeff was young was a huge blow, yet it ultimately created within him a deep appreciation for life that enables him to stay even-keeled amidst crushing pressure.

"If you know you're only going to have thirty, forty, sixty, eighty, one hundred years, and you can't even be sure you're going to be healthy, or not paralyzed, or whatever it is, don't let stress beat you," Jeff advised. "You have to see how wonderful it is to be alive. Because most of our time on the planet is gonna be in a casket. That's how I see it, you know? We're going to just be lying in a casket, or scattered to the wind. We're in that tiny, less-than-one-percent of time that we're on this planet—we're in that now, whether it's ten years or one hundred years. Remembering that gives me a tremendous ability to be upbeat. It's a gift from my dad. It was unfortunate that it had to happen, but that's what happened."

The next time you feel like the walls are closing in on you, or your stomach is in knots because something didn't go as planned, remember Jeff Lurie's approach. I can personally attest that **switching to an attitude of gratitude almost always puts the world in perspective**.

• • •

Humor can be a terrific outlet. When I asked **Craig Newmark** what he does in pressured times, he said:

"I reflect on the absurdity of life. That helps a lot."

• • •

There is no question that exercise combats stress. It's been proven time and again in studies, but we don't need a clinician to tell us

Rise and Shine

On the list my son made called "The Wisdom of Bill Boggs as Told to Trevor Boggs," item number four is, "It's best to exercise in the morning." I heartily believe that exercise first thing in the morning gives you an edge on the entire day. Try it. If you can get yourself into a routine of doing some kind of aerobic activity as often and as early as possible, I think you'll find your stress level drastically reduced.

---

that we feel better—more grounded, more able to withstand the currents of daily life—if we're physically active.

It's no surprise that **Dr. Mehmet Oz**—a world-renowned cardiologist—is attuned to the mind-body connection. He plays tennis, basketball, does yoga—anything, he said, that allows him to clear his head by letting loose and not having to play by his usual rules.

"I feel that I have to channel all of the emotions, negative and positive, into one driving force that's productive," Mehmet said. "I think it's like a window looking out into the world: if it's crisp and clear, you can really make decisions as accurately as possible, and move in that direction correctly. If it's clouded because you're angry, frustrated, insecure, scared, then you don't have the perspective that you need. And you end up creating lots of friction, which just slows down the system."

• • •

Here are what a few other interviewees had to say about the link between their physical routine and stress reduction:

"I play squash three or four times a week. And I work out at the gym. I don't know if there's something chemical that happens, but I do believe that my attitude is better about problems. I work through issues better when I do that."—**Joseph Abboud**

"I stay in good shape physically. You know, I run and walk, and that is very helpful. My life is truly filled with stress. I've got two children; I've got really long hours. People pulling at you all the time, never having the time that you would like to do things. But I think physical exercise is the very best of all ways to keep some balance."—**Senator Kay Bailey Hutchison**

"I have to physically deplete myself. I take an exercise class. I run, or I take a spinning class. Something physical that gets me tired, so that my defenses are broken down. I have to just physically get myself so exhausted, and then I can just think more clearly."—**Brooke Shields**

"I play soccer almost every Saturday when I'm in the country, in upstate New York. We have a league, and it's very competitive. I play with all kinds of people, and I love that. I have to say sport helps me focus more. I'm much more alert to what's going on. When I don't do any sport, I feel that I'm not seeing clearly."

—**Frédéric Fekkai**

"I think it's important for your mental health to be fit. There are certain sports—scuba diving, skiing—where, because of the nature of the sport, you pretty much have to be in the moment, because it's dangerous not to be."—**Christie Hefner**

• • •

Mindless activity can be a great antidote for stress. Paradoxically, it can help you gain some much-needed perspective.

The *New York Post*'s **Richard Johnson** deals with stress on a daily basis. He has a limited number of hours each day to round up information, check facts, and write the stories for Page Six. Though he thrives on the excitement of a busy newsroom and adrenaline rush of a deadline, he still needs to unplug now and then.

"I was just thinking about this the other day," Richard said, laughing, when I asked him what he used as a source of renewal. "I like to go to the Knicks games. I like to do things like chopping wood. Raking leaves, stuff like that. I have no trouble spending a couple of hours doing mindless, menial labor."

Another deadline-driven writer, the *New York Times*'s **Frank Rich**, also swears by emptying his mind.

"Stress is hard," Frank agreed. "How do I handle it? I've gotten better about it as I've gotten older. Doing something mindless,

Music as Medicine

Music has been very meaningful to me as mood lifter. There are certain songs that I can play that can almost instantly bring me right into the frame of mind I need to be in. I listen to Frank Sinatra singing "Pennies from Heaven" or Frank and Sammy Davis Jr. singing "Me and My Shadow" to get myself centered before going out to do a show. Pink Floyd takes me back to the '60s, when I wasn't experiencing that much stress (or if I was, I don't remember it). I always associate The Doors with my halcyon days living in bucolic North Carolina.

Renée Zellweger expressed the essential quality of music beautifully:

"I love to be moved by something," she said. "Music, I can't live without it. I absolutely need it. I need it. It's food of a different sort. The ability that it has to make you feel something. I get so completely inspired by that."

you know? I mean, there's nothing I enjoy more than walking around New York listening to an iPod, as idiotic as that may sound."

"What do you listen to?" I asked.

"I listen to everything—I do like Broadway music, and what we call the Great American Songbook. But I also love jazz. And a certain amount of contemporary music. I have sons who are twenty-five and twenty-one, who really educate me. They say, 'Listen to Radiohead, or Kanye West, or whatever,' and I'm going to do it. I think the iPod is the greatest invention in the history of the world."

• • •

There were those I spoke with who took comfort in the familiar as a way to escape daily stress.

When stress starts to build, **Matt Lauer** turns to the most precious source of joy there is: his family.

"Viewers will often ask me, 'How stressful is being on the air?' They don't understand that that's not the most stressful time of the day. That's the payoff to all the work. The stress comes in getting that show ready to go on the air. Getting the right guest, and producing the right segments. Once the show goes off the air, I can spend three, four hours in the office dealing with deadlines and stories and scripts and phone calls.

"When I feel that building up, I get in the car and go home," Matt said. "Even if I then have to make a few phone calls later that afternoon to continue that process, the act of walking out the door—sometimes even the act of walking home, as every block passes, and I get more distance between me and Rockefeller Center—it starts to go out of my system. The moment the door opens, you've got a five-year-old and a two-and-a half-year-old and a wife sitting there. I have a really good ability to, at that moment, leave work behind."

• • •

Back when **Jim Cramer** was tearing up Wall Street, he'd come home at the end of the day and pour himself a drink to decompress. Then he got a little older and found a far better drug:

"I'd come home and throw myself into what my kids were up to. They're pure, you know?"

• • •

For **Anna Quindlen,** jumping into a predictable daily routine keeps anxiety at bay.

"That orderly life," as Anna explained it. "I mean, every single morning, I do this. Every single morning, I power walk for an hour. Every single morning, I talk to my best friend on the telephone. Every single morning, I get the same drink at Starbucks, and read the papers. And so the motor can't rev too much, because I'm only doing one thing at a time, and it's always the thing that I'm used to doing."

If you're a creature of habit, why not take a page from Anna Quindlen's playbook and **establish some comfort touchstones of your own**?

• • •

Some people do exactly the opposite of what you might expect them to do in tense situations. Rather than jumping in and responding aggressively, they take a moment, back off, and *slow down*.

LAPD chief of police **Bill Bratton** runs the third largest force in the country. He's pretty accustomed to nerve-racking emergencies.

"My press secretary in the Transit Police used to joke about this," Bill said, laughing. "He said you could tell how significant the crisis was in terms of how long it took the chief to stand up, walk out, get a cup of coffee, and come back. The more significant the crisis, the longer it took him to think about it. And I think as a leader, when faced with crises, I don't scream, yell, fly off the handle. If anything, I kind of just slow down. I'd be willing to bet that my heart rate probably slows down during that time. And I just start assembling. 'Okay, there it is. What do we do about it?'"

He continued: "I believe I approach most crises, most problems, from the perspective of not just how do we address it, but how do we get multiple benefits out of it? In other words, how do you take that negative and turn it into a positive? I'd like to think, because I'm not somebody who jumps up and down when someone comes in with bad news, that people aren't reluctant to bring the bad news in."

When things start skidding toward the edge, don't panic. Take a breath, a walk, whatever you need to get yourself steady before reacting.

• • •

HarperCollins's CEO, **Jane Friedman,** is another levelheaded leader. What does she do when the pressure builds, or when things go awry?

"I don't like yelling," Jane said. "I'm not a yeller. I have had people here who have yelled, and I've had to let them go. I think yelling is not the way to make things happen. Stress? Ha! I walk a lot around my office. I take deep breaths. I think that the best way to handle stress is to get up and walk.

"You know, there are days that it is overwhelming here," she confessed. "There are days when the phones don't stop ringing, when everybody needs to see me. When my schedule looks like a train schedule. When it just doesn't stop. I realize that it's very important for me to be even. I think if you ask people around here, they will say I have no moods. I'm very even-tempered. I can get annoyed, and I can curse, and I can do all the rest of it. I try not to curse, because I think it's not a good thing to be the boss and curse. But to relieve stress, I basically just work my way through it."

• • •

And then, of course, there are those who thrive on stress, like the unfailingly energetic **Tom Perkins:**

"I've been under a lot of stress for a long time," Tom said. "And I think I've learned to kind of enjoy that. I've never had an ulcer. It's just part of life. It's fun. It's like breathing for me."

"Well, as you said, stress successfully overcome is triumph," I reminded him.

"Is triumph!" he exclaimed, eyes twinkling. "You become a triumph junkie. You know, it's pretty powerful stuff."

End Notes

"It would be pretentious to say that we can handle stress. I get stressed once in a while. One thing that I do to help me deal is to sit down with people—advisers, a bunch of people around me who I like and are smart—and just bounce ideas and talk a few out."—**Frédéric Fekkai**

"How do I deal with stress? I get massages once every other week. When I go on vacation, I will go to a spa, and on hiking trips. I love hiking."—**Maria Bartiromo**

"I get a lot of sleep. I think that's important. Rest is a big stress buster. The people who can't sleep and are under high pressure turn to alcohol, and self-medication, which is a disaster. So I get a lot of rest. On the other hand, you have to carve out time for yourself to do what you think is fun. Watch the game, go to a movie, read a book that you like. You've got to be able to have enough stuff going on so that when you feel stressed, you have something to look forward to."—**Bill O'Reilly**

"It's easier to deal with as you get older, and you have more experiences to reinforce that there are no great consequences for whatever it might be that you're ruminating about."
—**Renée Zellweger**

"I don't usually feel stressed. I'm used to a busy schedule and it usually energizes me. I think people feel stressed when they aren't prepared for the problems that are bound to come up in the course of a business day. I expect problems, because that's the nature of the business. I think that's a big help in handling stress."—**Donald Trump**

"There's stress, and joyful stress. And having a good time. Stress that is consonant with that kind of hard work and everything is joyful stress. That's the stress I experienced. I was laughing through it all."—**Norman Lear**

17

Allow for Regrets, Failures, and Mistakes

Bob Pittman • Joe Torre • Sir Richard Branson • Dr. Judith Rodin • Mario Cuomo • Anna Quindlen • James Blake • Joseph Abboud • Dr. Mehmet Oz • Daniel Boulud • Preston Bailey • Cathie Black • Matt Lauer • Mark Burnett • Diane von Furstenberg • Norman Lear • Maria Bartiromo • Bill O'Reilly.

ONE OF THE MOST compelling things I learned in the process of writing this book was the value of failure. I knew risk was essential for career advancement. However, I didn't fully grasp that it is important to be willing to fail. We actually *need* failure in order to grow.

If you get nothing else from the following stories other than the validation that everyone makes mistakes, that's fine with me. It's an important thing to understand, because it stops us from beating ourselves up when we mess up. You're going to make mistakes—as **Bob Pittman** said, if you're not making mistakes, that means you're not trying new things. The question is not how to avoid failing, but how to come back stronger and incorporate the lessons learned from the experience.

• • •

Yankees' manager **Joe Torre** continually has to make split-second decisions. Who to put in the game, which plays to run, when to take out the pitcher . . . his choices during the course of a ball game can yield only one of two results: victory or defeat. If his call works, he's a hero. If it doesn't, he's lambasted by fans and a press corps the size of the one covering the White House.

Despite this pressure, Joe Torre manages to remain steady and placid. He doesn't get overly inflated by the highs, nor deflated by the lows. And he certainly doesn't beat himself up for making a mistake. In fact, in Joe's mind, there's no such thing as a mistake.

"I cannot allow myself the hills and valleys—or allow my players to get too high or too low. Because you need to maintain some kind of excellence that eliminates the real high and eliminates the real low. You have to stay level."

—Joe Torre

"I never look at a move as being the wrong move," Joe said. "I look at a move as a move you made that didn't work out. I mean, I could have bases loaded with the winning run at third base with one out. If you're going to pull the best hitter in baseball that's ever played the game, and put him on home plate, and you hit into a double play, all of a sudden, it's the 'wrong move.' No, it's not the wrong move. It just didn't work. So I try to gain perspective. When you're stressing about something, you're always saying to yourself, 'I wish I would have done this.' It's like, you know, 'I wish I'd bet on the horse that ran first, instead of the horse that ran second.' When you take all your information and you make your decision, that's the way it goes."

Joe Torre knows that everyone makes an error at one point or another. The telling question for him is what you do *after* the stadium lights fade.

"When you start looking at how you respond to negative things—how you pick yourself up off the floor—to me, that's the person I admire," Joe said. "Like when Mariano Rivera, in '97, in his first year as a closer, gave up a home run in the division series to Sandy Alomar that kept us from going on. What'd he do? He just came back to become the best closer that's ever been."

• • •

You must be willing to fail big-time if you want to operate on the level of **Sir Richard Branson**. A multibillionaire with a legion of successful companies to his name, he has made an indelible impression as one of the world's most dynamic and progressive entrepreneurs of his time.

Sir Richard and I met on a winter afternoon at the Hotel Gansevoort in downtown Manhattan. He was visibly exhausted, having just completed a seven-country tour visiting the thousands of employees who work for his various Virgin companies, but that didn't detract from his movie-star looks and famously dazzling smile.

Sir Richard is unfailingly resilient. There's not much that keeps this man down. He has a major taste for adventure and has made news several times with his extreme-sporting endeavors. He attempted to beat the record for crossing the Atlantic Ocean by boat in 1985; the boat nearly made it but sank less than 100 miles short of its destination. A similar fate met his attempt to circle the globe in a hot-air balloon, which, too, ended in a hasty rescue from the water. Yet Richard recounts these experiences with more glee than regret.

"I strangely wasn't feeling an enormous sense of disappointment," he recalled. "It really is, I think, in the trying where people get their satisfaction. Having a gold medal to say you're the quickest or the fastest or to say you've succeeded is not that important. It's the incredible experiences that you have planning adventures, and the participation of other comrades, and just doing things which man has never done before."

Sir Richard elaborated on his bounce-back mentality. "I'm not somebody who minds too much if I fail. Maybe I'm just fortunate, because we've got so many different things going that a failure is not as important. But I think I'm the sort of person who enjoys the thrill of trying to create. And then if it doesn't work out, as long as I've given it everything I could to make sure it was successful, I can pick myself up and move straight on to the next thing . . . I think that's important in life. Because whatever your dreams are, you are going to fail on occasions. There's no point in being too concerned about it for too long."

Sir Richard Branson's next big venture is to launch Virgin Galactic, which aims to fly passengers into space in 2008 at $100,000 a pop. A few hundred people have already signed up and paid in full. Whether his space odyssey is successful remains to be seen. Regardless, Sir Richard Branson will likely come out smiling and grateful for having had the chance to try.

• • •

Even when you do everything 100 percent correctly, sometimes things outside of your control can sabotage your efforts. There's nothing you could have done differently, and you're left frustrated and disappointed, trying to figure out how to make sense of it all.

Dr. Judith Rodin was a graduate student at Columbia University in 1968 when the historic student sit-ins occurred there. She had spent a year training laboratory animals and doing the research critical to getting authorized to start working on her dissertation. The animals were housed in the mathematics building on campus, which was one of the places barricaded by the students.

"I think you have to be willing to challenge yourself, to push yourself. To do things that maybe somebody else wouldn't do. To go places somebody else wouldn't go, both literally and metaphorically. That's an important part of really succeeding. If you're risk-averse, you may be safe. But you probably won't be brilliantly successful."

—Dr. Judith Rodin

"Several buildings were taken over," she remembered. "But ours was the only one that had living animals in the basement. And so we tried to negotiate with them to just let us go in and save our animals, and our research. They wouldn't because they had a stance, and they wanted to make a point. And so it was a real lesson—first of all, in wrestling with conflicting convictions, because I supported some of the things they stood for, even though I didn't support all of the ways they expressed it. But I needed to get my research done. The animals died, and I had to start over again.

"I really learned that you've got to work hard, but sometimes life intervenes," Judith continued. "And then you have to start over, and work harder. It was a really important lesson. Because up to that point, I was successful. You know, I worked hard, and I got good grades, and good things happened. I got into graduate school when I applied. But this was a lesson in perseverance that stayed with me.

"Now I'll use my psychology," she said, smiling. "You need to learn how to cope with failure. In some ways, the earlier you use that, the more potentially successful you will be. I've seen, in my lifetime, both as a psychologist and by watching people, the people who have too many successes don't learn how to fail. And there's a set of coping skills around learning how to fail. You pick yourself up. You know, that's why sports are good for some people, and other vehicles where people learn how to fail successfully."

• • •

I've observed that people continue to repeat patterns of behavior— self-destructiveness, carelessness, closed-mindedness, and so on—and the patterns tend to produce a series of similar failures. Nothing will change until an individual gains enough self-knowledge to see the pattern clearly and understand what they're doing. It then takes a concerted effort, sometimes very painful, to break those old bad habits. A series of seemingly coincidental failures can be an opportunity to look at ourselves more closely and break a negative cycle of actions.

Multiple lost elections made **Mario Cuomo** realize that he needed to reconsider an element of his political persona. Though today he is generally regarded by the public as a warm, engaging man, early in his campaigning career, he would unknowingly alienate potential voters.

"I lost twice before I won," he said, referring to his failed attempts to become mayor of New York City and lieutenant governor of New York State. "I learned that the skills that made me a competent lawyer—which I took for granted would also make me a competent politician—those skills were not sufficient," Mario said. "I had to add dimensions to my persona. I was not a chatty kind of guy, you know? I could have a conversation with you, but

I wasn't a guy who would go to parties and spend a lot of time socializing and trying to win friends. I was mostly a loner. Even as a young lawyer, I took cases against the mayor and against the governor, and got into *New York* magazine for beating [Mayor] Lindsay and [Governor] Rockefeller. I saved three people from the electric chair. But you know, I did it by myself."

"But you can't do that," he continued. "You have to grow in many dimensions. You have to get out there with the people. You have to be with them as much as possible. I learned from my defeats. I was talking at a level that I was accustomed to in the courtroom—not just the way you talk to a jury; that's the proper level for a politician. I was talking to them the way you talk to an appellate court, which is all very intellectualized. And you can't do that. You have to talk in a language they understand. As a lawyer, I can write a twenty-five-page brief and expect it's all going to be read, and so it takes me twenty-five pages to get the argument made. But in politics, you get past the first couple of sentences, you're finished."

> "Some people have a defeat, learn nothing.
>
> And that's a real tragedy."
>
> **—Mario Cuomo**

Mario Cuomo regrouped and learned better ways to communicate, and his distinguished career in politics—three terms as the governor of New York State—is the prize he has to show for it.

• • •

Just as Mario Cuomo became a better politician as a result of being defeated, **Anna Quindlen** became a better writer because of a botched opportunity when she was a neophyte reporter.

"The night that Nelson Rockefeller died, the city editor of the *New York Times* pulled me in to do the lead-off story for that night's paper," Anna said. "I had a little bit of a reputation as a wordsmith. And I think that he thought he wanted a more impressionistic, big-picture rendering, as opposed to your standard-issue, 'who, what, when, where, and why' story. We were under a really tight deadline. I was getting some fairly contradictory signals, and to be honest with you, I blew the story in the way that I wrote it, for a variety of reasons. Some were not my fault, but some of it was that I just wasn't up to the task. The crack rewrite man of my generation, a guy named Bob McFadden, took over and pulled the story together as I was sitting there pounding away. He did his usual impeccable job. The next morning, when I woke up and saw one edition with my byline, one edition with no byline, and one edition with McFadden's byline, I knew I was in trouble."

"In what sense?" I asked.

"I'd blown a really, *really* big story," she said. "It was a perfect opportunity to be marginalized the rest of my career. It became pretty clear to me that the perception was going to be that I was a dab hand with a phrase—you know, I could produce a metaphor or a simile, but I wasn't a real bedrock reporter. Over the space of about twenty-four hours, I decided that what I needed to do right away was get myself in a job in which I would basically churn out one 'who, what, where, when, and why' story after another, for a year or two."

The next morning, Anna went to see the city editor and asked him if she could cover City Hall. He said yes, and Anna worked in the City Hall bureau of the paper for two years. After that, she said, she'd written so many lead stories that nobody ever questioned again whether she could churn out a hard news story.

Those two years weren't fun, or glory-filled—in fact, Anna described them as "castor oil." But they were necessary for her growth as a writer. It took a big, public flop to make Anna Quindlen a great reporter.

• • •

James Blake, as you already know, has been with the same trusted coach, Brian Barker, since he was eleven years old. Yet when James was transitioning from the juniors to the pros, a lot of other coaches started swarming around, intimating that James should trade up to a "real pro coach." James was just insecure and vulnerable enough to allow those voices into his head.

"There were a lot of coaches giving me advice," he remembers. "At the beginning of my career, I didn't have success right away. So I thought, maybe all these guys have quick-fix answers, and this is how I should play. And I played a much more passive game than what Brian would have had me doing. I basically listened to too many people telling me things they didn't really know about. They might be good coaches, but unless you know a person's game, you can't be an effective coach, I don't think. So I was listening to people who didn't really know my game. That mistake cost me for maybe a year or two, where I wasn't playing the way I should be playing."

James won't make that mistake again. "There are still people who give me unsolicited advice," he said. "Whether it's an older coach, or an older player. And now I know much better to take it in one ear, and maybe I'll mention it to Brian, but it's not something I'm gonna take and run with. They might be great tennis minds, but they might not know exactly what I've been dealing with, or what I've been working on. You have to surround yourself with the people who are really going to help you."

• • •

Mistakes can be costly, as **Joseph Abboud** regrettably learned.

Boston was Joseph Abboud's original home, so when his private label flourished, he quickly set his sights on opening a store on Newberry Street, which is the Fifth Avenue—or Rodeo Drive—of Boston. It was, he said, like coming home for him, a real "local boy makes good" story.

But the story didn't have a happy ending. Joseph signed a long lease without doing enough research, and he quickly discovered that the street lacked sufficient parking. Customers couldn't get to the store, and if they couldn't get there, they certainly couldn't buy enough clothes to make the venture profitable.

"I learned that you don't make big financial investments strictly on emotion," Joseph said, flashes of regret still in his eyes. "I think you let your passions drive you to a certain point, but when you think about financial commitments, and you realize that a lot is riding on this . . . not just my money, but our company's health, and all that. So I think you have to sometimes step back. I mean, there's a very fine line between just being so passionate and driven. But sometimes you just have to step back and look at it."

Therein lies a basic business lesson: Trust your heart to lead you in the direction of your passion, but consult with your head before shelling out the money.

• • •

One particular memory of regret for **Dr. Mehmet Oz** set the marker for many of his future decisions.

"I haven't told anybody this," Mehmet confessed. "But when I was in college, I was given an opportunity. I was nominated to a position on a sports team. And I turned it down because, at the time, I didn't think I was the best candidate for it. I thought there were other people on the team who were better. Afterward, I had a large group of individuals approach me and say, you know, 'We nominated you. We wanted you. It was our belief that you were the best person to lead us, and you turned us down.'

"I've never turned down a leadership position since then," he said. "Even if I didn't think I was the best person. The fact that others thought that I could do it, or should do it, gives me confidence that at least I ought to give, in fairness to them, a shot at doing it."

"The things I regret most, the failures I regret most in life, are things I didn't do, not things I did. That's really been a guiding light for me."

—Dr. Mehmet Oz

Before you say no, it might be helpful to ask yourself, "Might I regret this one day?"

• • •

Certainly delegating is important, as we heard in a previous chapter. But when everything is on the line, it's usually wise to oversee the details yourself. That is *definitely* not the time to trust someone you've never worked with, as chef **Daniel Boulud** learned when he just barely escaped career ruin.

Around 1990, when Daniel was the executive chef at Le Cirque, the restaurant was asked to prepare sumptuous breakfast baskets for three planeloads of people. They were not just ordinary passengers—they were eight hundred celebrities and notable public figures being flown to Malcolm Forbes's birthday party in Morocco. Liz Taylor, Nancy Kissinger, Barbara Walters . . . the A-list of America, basically. The contents of the baskets had been planned for months and were calculated down to the most minute detail. Daniel and his staff worked until 3:00 AM the morning before the planes were scheduled to leave. The catering company that Sirio Maccioni (the owner of Le Cirque) and Daniel had hired to assist them with the logistics arranged for a refrigerated truck that would hold the baskets overnight. The driver was supposed to sleep in the truck in front of the restaurant and be ready to head out for the airport at 6:00 AM.

At 6:00, neither the driver nor the truck was there. Daniel and Sirio headed to the airport, assuming the driver had just gone ahead.

"Then it's 7:00 . . . 7:15 . . . 7:30, no truck," Daniel recalled. Although he and I were sitting in his skybox office—a glass-enclosed room above the kitchen of his four-star restaurant, Daniel, on Sixty-fifth Street in Manhattan—I could tell he was reliving the tense scene on the tarmac as though it were yesterday. "Eight, no truck. Everybody was fuming. All the biggest society and movie stars were coming in, and me and Sirio were going crazy. We were trying to call the police, the chief of police, a helicopter . . . I mean, we panicked, totally. It was a nightmare."

Turns out that the driver had gone home in the truck and had fallen asleep in his driveway. Someone reached him just in time, and the baskets made it onto the plane only twenty minutes before takeoff.

"That is one of my biggest failures in my life," Daniel said. "It's something where you work so hard to make sure you don't disappoint anybody—your customer—and yet . . . I hated that caterer for the rest of my life, for sure! If it's going to concern me and my organization, I learned to never depend on a third party to organize the logistics. That third party should never have been in the mix. That was my mistake."

• • •

In the glittery world of gala events, part of the illusion is that all is perfect. Yet event planner **Preston Bailey** knows that is far from the truth.

"One of the realities is that sometimes you're going to screw up, and there's nothing you can do about it," said Preston. "You have to understand that one time, sometimes at the party, something's going to go wrong. You're just going to have to make sure that if it goes wrong that you accept it, and not take it like it's the end of the world. Not take it so seriously."

Things do go wrong, like the time a large floral arrangement fell on a woman's head because the mechanism Preston and his employees built wasn't done properly.

"It seems a little bit simple, but it really is. Anything that you have screwed up, look at it. Analyze it. Not 'What should I have done?' but 'What could I have learned from it?"

—Preston Bailey

"What are you gonna do?" Preston said. "You learn that from there on, you have to do better mechanisms. Learning from your mistakes is a really big thing, I think, in any success."

• • •

Mistakes will happen. Of that you can be sure. The real test of whether you've got what it takes is what you do as a result. The key thing is to remember that whenever one door closes, another one opens. **No matter how big your mistake or colossal the failure, there is *always* something to be learned.**

End Notes

"I've always had a fairly simplistic view. You just have to pick up, get on with it, and try to learn from it. What could you have done differently? Did you read the tea leaves? Did you really give enough thought to it?"—**Cathie Black**

"There's a big difference between having a goal, and moving in that direction, and taking no prisoners and getting there at all costs. I didn't do that. But having a goal is a very healthy thing. Sometimes you reach it, and you're thrilled, and you should stop and thank your lucky stars. Sometimes you don't reach those goals. I had a lot along the way I didn't reach. But that was valuable, too. There was a lesson to be learned in falling short, as well."—**Matt Lauer**

"There are always situations that don't go exactly right. And you know, you've got to make up your mind how you're going to deal with it. Don't start crying about it. The truth is, no one else really cares. You like to think they do. And you like to go in there and tell them your hard-luck story. But the truth is, everyone's got their own hard-luck story. Don't make your problem my problem."—**Mark Burnett**

"That's another major, major lesson—you have to realize that sometimes the worst thing that happens to you can be the best thing, if you turn it around."—**Diane von Furstenberg**

"One of the big surprises in life, and in show business, is thinking you got something right and it fails. And sometimes it fails, and you think you still got it right. But sometimes it fails and, 'Oh, shit, how did I not see that?' "—**Norman Lear**

"I do think I have made mistakes in the past by taking things too quickly and lightly. In the rush of work, stuff comes at me. And you know, it's very important to think things out. To look at a project and deal with a person who you may be working with and give that person and that idea proper time and thought. I've learned that every idea and every person in your life deserves the time and the respect that you should be giving."—**Maria Bartiromo**

"If you fail, that's fine. It doesn't matter. At least you gave it your best shot. Failure is in the eye of the beholder. I say that anybody who's given it an honest shot is a success, because they'll always land somewhere, and do something."
—**Bill O'Reilly**

18
Overcome Adversity

Matt Lauer • Senator Kay Bailey Hutchison • Phil
Lombardo • James Blake • Bill O'Reilly • Jeff
Zucker • Brooke Shields • Christie Hefner • Dr.
Mehmet Oz • Bill Bratton • Bobbi Brown • Frank
Rich • Maria Bartiromo • Linda Huett • Marco
Maccioni • Rikki Klieman • Mark Burnett • Donald
Trump • Mario Cuomo • Norman Lear • Diane
Warren • Diane von Furstenberg • Joy Behar

AFTER A YEAR, the show I was helping to
produce in Philadelphia, *McLean and Company,* was doing really well. It had good ratings, and the show had found its groove. On December 23, the host, Bob McLean, was called upstairs to the management offices. We all assumed he was getting a year-end bonus, but when he came downstairs, normally ruddy-faced Bob McLean was ashen. We asked what happened, and he said forlornly, "I got fired."

Bob was shaking as he packed up his belongings in two paper bags. We walked him to the door; he had tears in his eyes. The whole thing was unbelievable. The management had relocated Bob from Toronto along with his entire family, which included two young children, and then they fired him for political reasons two days before Christmas. It was snowing, and as I watched him walk off into the storm with those brown bags in his hands, I turned to the executive producer and said, "What the hell kind of business are we getting ourselves into here?" Thankfully, Bob was able to return to Toronto and resume his career—much the wiser, I suspect.

Many of us have experienced episodes like this, and if we haven't, chances are we will in the course of our career. The hard times can hurt like hell, but those who have what it takes to survive have established inner resources to help them through.

Frank Sinatra once said something to me that has helped and guided me in my toughest times. Referring to the down point in his life when his throat had hemorrhaged, his marriage to Ava Gardner was on the rocks, he'd lost his recording contract with Columbia Records, and only handfuls of people were showing up to see him in clubs, he said, **"Sometimes you have to scrape bottom in life to understand how really wonderful life can be."**

You will face adversity at one point or another in your career. It helps to always remember, as Joe Torre quoted, "Tough times don't last. Tough people do."

• • •

Matt Lauer knows all too well the painful sting of adversity. Yet he also knows what can come of it when you emerge through the looking glass.

You've already heard Matt talk about the nadir of his career, when he was holed up in a tiny cabin wondering if he'd ever get back into the game at the same level again. Matt recalled his thinking from that time:

"I remember when I had this show *PM Magazine* in New York. I used to drive out to see my parents in Connecticut, and I'd drive back in on the Bruckner Expressway. I'd get to a point on the Bruckner and there is Manhattan in front of you in all its glory—that beautiful skyline. And I used to think, 'Wow, that is my viewing audience; this is a big deal.' What started to happen when I was unemployed was I used to find myself driving in to pitch myself for jobs and I'd look at that horizon again and I'd say, 'Has this skyline turned on me? Is there any chance I can get that viewing audience back?' Did I have a shot at getting back into the televisions that were in that skyline? I finally convinced myself that I did, and as luck would have it, I was given the chance."

I asked Matt how that down period affected him, both as a performer and as a person.

"I have much more empathy for the kinds of stories I deal with on a daily basis," he said. "I was never a silver-spoon kid—we weren't that kind of family—but I did have a rather charmed early career. My stepfather used to say to me, 'You're not a part of the workforce until you've been unemployed, till you've had to really search for a job. Then, you become an official part of the workforce when you get that next job.' I had never had that experience, and those three years of failure, underemployment, and unemployment did as much to shape who I am today as anything that happened in the twenty-five years prior to that. It made me, in some good ways and some bad ways. The good ways: I can empathize with people who are going through difficult times. I've been there; I know. It helps me completely identify with young people in this business who are struggling to get that break. In a bad way, I don't think I ever quite relax anymore and feel comfortable that they can't just take this away from me."

Sometimes the worst things that come at you are opportunities to grow. If you can interpret the pain as dues you are paying to get to the other side—be it freedom, happiness, a promotion, a greater sense of compassion, or whatever it is that we desire or require—that will help you have the guts to hang on.

• • •

Senator Kay Bailey Hutchison is one of the country's most powerful women. Early in her career, she faced some pretty intense discrimination that sharpened her brilliant political mind.

"I think facing adversity is probably the key to ultimate success. I have had a lot of adversity in my life, and I am much stronger for it. I think adversity shapes you maybe even more than success."

—Senator Kay Bailey Hutchison

"My biggest obstacle that I've ever faced was—I call it my 'first brick wall of life'—I graduated from law school when no Texas law firm hired women," she said. "I looked for a job for four months and never got a job offer. Ultimately, I decided to be creative, and look for another way to use my law degree. I interviewed to be a television news reporter in Houston, the NBC affiliate. And got a job. I was the first woman on television in Houston; it was that far back. But it turned out that the adversity and the significant disappointment that I had in going months without a job offer and seeing all of my friends from law school get job offers was a real shaping experience for me."

"How did that help steel your resolve?" I asked.

"What it did was show me that in my darkest hour, the light was so much brighter than it would have been if I had become a partner in a law firm. Because it was the television job that set me on a different course. It gave me immediate recognition in Houston, and I was asked to run for the legislature at the age of twenty-eight. I was elected to the state legislature at the age of twenty-nine, which never would have happened if I hadn't been a television news reporter as well as a lawyer. And so what it taught me is that **if you just keep on going, and you see through the hard times, you gain something that you would never have had that's better than you would have wanted**."

• • •

A fundamental component of **Phil Lombardo**'s success is that he does not allow himself to wallow when times are difficult. A macho Sicilian at the core, Phil looks adversity squarely in the eye and refuses to back down.

"Some people have a tendency to become overly self-indulgent," said Phil. "And that leads to self-centeredness. When that happens, it clouds their thinking, and I'm very careful to avoid that. That's a huge pitfall, and a lot of people step into it.

"I'll give you an example," Phil offered. "I had eye surgery two days ago—a cataract removed in my left eye. And it screwed up my vision terribly. I went yesterday for the follow-up, and I said, 'Why is my vision worse now than before?' They said, 'Well, it may take longer for you to adjust. Your brain is—your two eyes are fighting right now. They need to sort of balance themselves out.'

"Now, a lot of people would just say, 'Okay, I'm just gonna sort of chill out. And not stay with my normal pattern of life.' Well, last night I went to a black-tie affair at the Waldorf. Today I'm doing this interview with you. Okay? I have a meeting later this afternoon with my national sales rep. I have a dinner to-night. And basically, I won't allow myself to become self-indulgent. Because if you do, you begin to wallow in your own pity for yourself; you get so self-centered that you forget that maybe this is just a transitory period. So just move on. **Just keep moving**."

• • •

A broken neck, the death of his father, and a painful virus that paralyzed the left side of his face, all within one year—that's a lot for one mere mortal to overcome. But that's what separates athletic greats like **James Blake** from the rest of the pack.

"The goal for me, really, is when I'm done playing tennis, I want to know that I did the best I could. If you have that in your mind each day when you go out there, you have the right attitude, and setbacks don't get you down as much."

—James Blake

James was able to come back only after he accepted the fact that he might never be able to do so. It was the letting go that enabled him to rebound.

"I tried to draw on the fact that I had done the best I could," James said. "Some things are out of your control. I wish I was able to control whether or not I got shingles, but I couldn't. I guess that was just the way my body dealt with the stress of losing my father. There was nothing else I could have done, preparation-wise, to change that. So I have to just live with that. I'd had some success up to that point, so I could just draw on the fact that I had done more athletically than I had ever dreamed. What I was also drawing on for that six months that I was home was my friends being around. I was trying to find out if I'd be happy without tennis, and without what I was doing . . . if I could settle into a different lifestyle and still find a way to be happy. And I think I did."

A Zen Perspective

Bill O'Reilly, who turns to Zen philosophy in negative times, offered this sage advice:

"Life balances out, number one. You've got to have a philosophical view. It's going back to the Eastern philosophy thing. You replace a negative thought with a positive. If you can discipline yourself to do that, you're not going to need a psychiatrist, and you're not going to need therapy. And you're not going to need a bunch of people telling you how great you are. You'll be able to do it yourself, if you can master that. It's not that hard, either.

"The other thing is that if you can basically say to yourself, 'This is a bad period I'm going through.' Because everybody goes through bad periods, all right? But it will be followed by a good period. Because that's just the way life is. Life balances out. There are some people who get paralyzed, and who die young, and who are tragic figures. We don't know why that happens. But 90 percent of human beings on this planet will get opportunities, and the good will at least have parity with the bad. That's just the way it works. You've got to have enough belief in that system to be able to ride out the bad and say, 'It's going to pass. And then I'm going to get good things in my life.' If you can do that, you don't start to despair. The worst thing you can do is despair, because then you give up. And then the bad guys win."

"What would you say to somebody who's facing a difficult time like that, and who may have to let go of a dream?" I asked.

"For me, it was finding what else is important in your life. If you're letting go of one dream, that's a very difficult time for anyone, to let go of something they've dreamed of since they were a kid. But I think it's an acceptance of what reality is giving you. Because there are times that things are out of your control, and once you

Dealing with Criticism

"I have an incredibly thick skin. I think you have to be immune to it. I think one of the reasons I've had some degree of success is that I've been able to not get too wrapped up in what people say about me, either positively or negatively. That makes it a lot easier, when they say negative things, to be able to ignore them."
—**Jeff Zucker**

"The only thing that I take away from it is, 'Well, there must be something that I'm doing right, if I'm causing that much vehemence.' Because if there's anything negative to say about my book, it must have hit a chord, you know?"
—**Brooke Shields**

"I think it can serve the purpose of motivating you more. Like, you know, prove them wrong."—**Christie Hefner**

"You always have to guard against criticism that's jealousy, versus criticism that's valid. And never confuse them. If it's jealous criticism, that's life in the big city. If it's valid criticism, don't write it off. It is useful, and the fact that they took the time to criticize you means they care what you say."
—**Dr. Mehmet Oz**

"It's part of the acceptance that if you want to be in the limelight, well, sometimes you're going to pay the penalty of the limelight. Very seldom do I pick up the phone and yell and scream at editors; it's the old adage, there's nothing older than yesterday's newspaper."—**Bill Bratton**

"A lot of times, you get hurt. But if you're really smart, you take the criticism and you do something with it. Because a lot of times they're right. Other times, if you don't agree with it, you just have to keep doing what you really believe in."—**Bobbi Brown**

"You learn to tune it out, or you would absolutely go out of your mind. I learned very quickly—it's true as a drama critic, and it's true as a columnist—that way lies madness. Once you start thinking about how people are going to react, then you fudge everything. You have to be true to yourself. You can't pull your punches. Because then what the hell are you doing? Why are you even an opinion columnist if you don't have an opinion?"—**Frank Rich**

"It's hard not to get caught up in what people are writing about you, but it's so important to pull yourself back. I don't know who it was who told me that—you know, don't believe the good stuff, then you won't be upset when you hear the bad stuff. 'Cuz it's coming."
—**Maria Bartiromo**

"If you want to be loved or liked, it can get in the way. I think if you can ignore all of that, it doesn't matter if people love you or like you. If you're really working hard and being collaborative and being supportive of the whole enterprise, not just your bit of it . . . they will either admire you or they'll like you or not like you—but they will respect to some degree what you are giving."—**Linda Huett**

"Check your ego at the door. Be prepared to be praised, as well as insulted to the highest degree. And neither should define what you are. You're somewhere that you know—in between. But when everyone starts patting you on your back and telling you how good you are, understand it, you know, because the next person who's coming in has the knife, you know? And you should never, never let it become something personal, and let it sink in under your skin."
—**Marco Maccioni**

accept that, I think it makes a big difference in your healing process and in your recognition of the problem. You're going to find a better way to deal with it, I think, and be happier in that time.

"Some people have, at times, criticized me for having other things in my life outside of tennis," James added. "They might say it's almost like a softer side of someone; they want you to be a robot that only cares about tennis. But I think it's helped me on the court. It's helped me be calmer. And when you're calm, and you don't have the live-or-die attitude with every single point, being a little more relaxed actually helps your focus on the court. That's not to say I don't fight hard, because I do. I work hard, and I want to win every single point. Just because I have other things in my life doesn't mean it takes away from the tennis."

• • •

As time passed in my career and I traversed through other TV stations and networks, I came to learn a disheartening lesson: **The people in the office are not your friends.** They are acquaintances. They may seem like friends—you might travel with them, party with them, share confidences, laugh, and cry with them. But they are not your friends. If you are lucky, you have a handful of true friends in life. Love them; they will be with you through thick and thin. They will never sacrifice their relationship with you to advance their careers.

Sometimes those "friendly" people in the office can be secret agents of adversity as they covertly try to hold you back. When I shared this personal theory with **Rikki Klieman,** she nodded emphatically in agreement. Here's how she put it:

"Work is work. Go do your job. You want to have drinks with people after work, or you want to have lunch at work, fine and dandy. But I do think that there is a danger in familiarity at work. I really think there is. I think that when you least expect it, something you have said over a lunch, over a drink, in a candid moment, may come back to haunt you later on.

"If you are going to have a friend at work, which I think is valuable, you have to understand what the limits of that friendship are," Rikki continued. "Or you have to take that friendship and make sure that it's sacrosanct. I think backstabbing exists because somebody gets a promotion that you think you should have gotten. Somebody gets a raise. Somebody gets a corner office. I mean, it goes on probably in every profession in life."

I'm telling you this not to scare you, but to remind you that you always need to be on your toes in the workplace. I can't tell you how many times I've heard people express shock and outrage that a supposed "friend" at work had behaved in a cunning and hurtful way. Treasure your few true friends; count the others as simply co-workers.

• • •

When I asked the participants in this book how they have dealt with the backstabbing nature of the business world, I got one of two responses: either they didn't deign to acknowledge the bad be-havior, or they waited patiently for the right moment to get even.

Producer **Mark Burnett** adheres to the first line of thinking."It happens to everybody," he said matter-of-factly. "I don't let myself think about it. I don't really have a revenge kind of motive in me. I think it would hurt my energy. So I don't spend any time getting even with people. No time."

Phil Lombardo takes the opposite approach. He said, "It's gonna happen. Don't dwell on it. Don't make a big deal out of it. Just remember who's doing it, and don't give them a second chance. Okay?

"There's a phrase that I use from my Sicilian ancestry that basically says, you know, don't get mad, get even. When I find that somebody has deceived me, number one, I don't trust them a second time going forward. But number two, if they have done something despicable, there will come a time . . . there will be payback. That payback happens because a person like that cre-ates situations whereby they're going to put themselves in a very vulnerable position, and nobody's going to put out a hand to help them. They're gonna let him fall, because that's what that person was trying to do—create an environment so other people would fail."

Donald Trump sides with Phil Lombardo on the subject of getting even with those who have double-crossed him, to an even greater degree. "I go after them three times harder than they went after me—because betrayal doesn't deserve anything better than that. Once it becomes clear to me, it's a done deal."

• • •

Norman Lear has experienced many ups and downs throughout his long life in show business. He's learned a thing or two about the nature of adversity:

"Expecting it, I guess, is a factor," he said. Then he laughed. "I don't know how long ago it occurred to me that **if life doesn't provide that adversity, you will yourself**."

"How so?" I asked.

"You'll create the mischief, you know? We're all capable of creating our own mischief. To the extent that there's a creator, he, she, it, said, 'Wait a minute. I'm not gonna make it so easy for these people.'"

Well put, Norman.

End Notes

"I think for someone like me, adversity is almost as important as encouragement. Adversity is just something to push against."—**Diane Warren**

"When you're facing a failure, or a problem, or whatever, face it. Face it. Deal with it. And deal with it yourself."
—**Diane von Furstenberg**

"I always try to say, 'What is the reality of the situation?' "
—**Joy Behar**

19

Resist Ruinous Temptations

Clive Davis • Diane Warren • James Blake • Bill O'Reilly • Maria Bartiromo • Richard Johnson • Craig Newmark • Joseph Abboud • Anna Quindlen • Dr. Mehmet Oz • Mario Cuomo • Donald Trump • Christie Hefner • Peter Cincotti • Sir Richard Branson • Jim Cramer • Bob Pittman • Preston Bailey

WITH ALL SUCCESS comes the potential for excess. Spending too much money, drinking, philandering . . . you know the stories. We've seen ruinous temptations take down the career of more than one famous person. The VH-1 documentaries about rock stars who hit it big and then get sucked down into the vortex of money, ego, and vices define the stereotype of success and excess. I asked people how they dealt with the lure of certain temptations along the way, and heard some *very* interesting answers. . . .

• • •

Many turned a blind eye to temptation because they knew all too well the price they would have to pay. Their work meant more to them than any empty high.

Clive Davis has lived his entire career at the epicenter of sex, drugs, and rock 'n' roll, yet he was never even tempted. He said matter-of-factly, "What I've been impassioned by and enveloped in precluded excess. Because you can't combine the two. I would never be involved in anything that would detract from the mission. It's only fun if you're winning. It's only fun if you're getting good report cards. It's a horrible business to be in if the report cards are not good."

Diane Warren is another music industry veteran who escaped the clichéd trappings of that industry through her commitment to excelling. "I never even had the desire," she said. "It's weird. Like, even when I was eighteen, and my friends were going out meeting boys and staying out all night. You know what? I wanted to work. I didn't want to stay out all night and party. I didn't want to drink. I wanted to work."

James Blake has watched other professional tennis players around him reach a celebrity-status pinnacle and then lose their edge because suddenly they're offered all kinds of distractions—expensive toys, invitations to the hot new clubs, star-studded parties, and more. "I think when you first get those temptations, you maybe buy into them a little bit, or you give in to them, and then if you drop a little bit, you realize, 'Okay, those temptations aren't worth sacrificing any of my success. For me, the temptations now are there. But I know that it's just something I don't want to do. I don't want to give in to any of that, because I want to see how well I can do. I know if I give in to too many of the temptations, I'm going to end up at the end of my career saying, 'Man, I could have done better. I should have been able to resist all those things.'"

Bill O'Reilly said, "Never was a real problem for me. I'm not a big materialist, number one. I don't like a lot of stuff. So I didn't have that to deal with. Drugs and alcohol never interested me on any level, because I saw what they did to my friends. And nobody who was involved in substance abuse to any extent could compete with me on the athletic field or in the television industry. They just can't."

Maria Bartiromo knows the camera is none too forgiving. That alone is motivation for her to resist all kinds of temptations. "When I'm on camera, I have to look good, and so there is a lot of discipline in eating perfectly, exercising every day, not drinking," she said. "For me, that's the discipline. I find the other stuff easy. But keeping to a perfect diet is not so easy.

"It's a slippery slope," Maria continued. "I think that it's very easy to go out to a black-tie affair and have a glass of wine every night. You cannot do it, though. Then you go to restaurants, and people see you and send over desserts, cakes, and bits . . . and you just can't do it."

• • •

Then there's the age thing—you get a little older, and all of a sudden, it's not so easy to stay out until all hours and partake of all the exciting treats success affords you. I've always been an appetitive person—I love fine restaurants, a good bottle of wine, fun parties—all of it. But I found the important thing is to strike a balance between that and clean living, to have the energy I need each day.

If anyone can understand the lure of New York nightlife, it's gossip columnist **Richard Johnson**. If information is currency, Richard is definitely one of the richest men I know. Staying that connected to the pulse, though, often means being out and about around town. He laughed knowingly when I told him my theory about needing to scale things back as the years pass.

"Yeah, I definitely used to go out more," Richard agreed. "I used to stay out later, but I think I've sort of gotten over the hump. You know, it's sort of like when guys are learning how to drive: if they can survive until they're twenty-one, twenty-two, they'll start slowing down. I think that basically it's just, as you get older, it becomes less interesting."

Richard paused and then gave a short laugh. "And I guess maybe it's just too painful to wake up in the morning after three hours of sleep."

• • •

One of **Craig Newmark**'s favorite quotes is, "I can resist anything but temptation." Which is ironic, since he isn't tempted by a lot.

"I don't want much," Craig admitted. "And so, you know, if I don't want much, then there's not much that can nail me.

"You know," he observed with a shrug. **"How many things do you really need?"**

An excellent point, Craig.

• • •

The people we love can be our best protection from dangerous vices. Knowing that his family is home waiting for him has been all the motivation **Joseph Abboud** needs to bypass questionable temptations.

"I live out here in Westchester, and when I'm in the city, I don't stay there a lot," he said. "I come back home. I want to see my kids, either one side of the day or the other. I believe family helps protect against a lot of things they're going to face, so I've never been a real party person."

The same holds true for **Anna Quindlen**. "I wasn't really successful until I had three little kids, who had become completely the center of my world," she said. "And that really grounds you. Because a lot of those excesses have to do with being out there in the world. And I just didn't have enough free time to be out there in the world, you know?"

Anna continued: "And also, there's something about going to a college to give a commencement speech, or some black-tie dinner. And everyone saying, 'Oh, I love your work; I'm such a big fan; you're so wonderful.' And then you come home and somebody goes, 'We have no food in the fridge.' It puts everything in perspective."

• • •

Then there's conscience to keep one on the straight and narrow. **Dr. Mehmet Oz** lives right because he simply doesn't want to have to deal with the negative emotional repercussions of not doing so.

"Alcohol, substance abuse . . . for me, it's a little bit of an issue of perspective," he explained. "I look at the people who have trusted me. Not just patients who trust their lives to me, but family, co-workers, and the like. And I think of how I would be letting them down, if I did any of those things. We're all human—we have those temptations, and they're continuous. But the biggest thing for me is a very selfish motivation: My life is much simpler if I don't choose them. I don't have to remember who I lied to. I don't have to keep two different books, juggle a wife and a mistress. You know, all of those things go away.

"If you're going to be successful, you can't have two minds on a topic," he elaborated. "If you're going to be laser-focused, you can't be thinking, 'Am I focusing on the right thing today?' I don't carry any baggage. Nothing takes away from where I'm going, because I don't have any friction-building issues in the baggage that I'm carrying."

• • •

I tell my son that the single biggest thing a person stands to lose by becoming even slightly dependent on alcohol, drugs, gambling, or any other numbing pursuit is the ability to have a natural high.

The gifts you have to offer the world—all your talent, drive, determination, passion—are sadly diminished if they are clouded over. Life is meant to be enjoyed, of course, but as the age-old maxim says, **"Everything in moderation."**

End Notes

"Temptation is everywhere. You can eat too much. Drink too much. And your instinct to change affection—a beautiful gift that God gives men and women, but very, very easy to get swept away by. So you have to be aware that you're going to face these temptations constantly. And you have to think in terms of what it's going to cost you. . . . You have to think about what it's going to mean if you take that extra drink, get a little drunk. You have to go home, and the kids will see you. Or you're going to make a fool of yourself, and you didn't know your best client is sitting in the same restaurant. You have to always consider the possibility that you're going to get caught, and what will that mean to you, to your family, to get caught?"**—Mario Cuomo**

"[I don't drink alcohol, so] I don't have impaired speech or make mistakes of judgment due to inebriation, and I don't have hangovers. I'm always ready for the next morning, seven days a week. That can save a lot of time in the long run, so that might have added to my success."**—Donald Trump**

"I never tried cocaine, for a very simple reason. It seemed to me, at a time when a lot of people were dabbling in it, that one of two things would be likely: Either it wouldn't be a good experience, in which case not trying it was the right choice. Or it would be a really seductive experience, in which case I would also regret trying it. So I just never tried it."
—Christie Hefner

"In this day and age, temptation is everywhere and you gotta be living in a cave not to feel it. But there's a lot I want to accomplish and that remains my top priority."
—Peter Cincotti

"I get enormous satisfaction from what I do. We've got some incredibly exciting things going on, whether it's trying to work with alternative energy sources to petrol or trying to take people into space with Virgin Galactic. You know, they are, perhaps, my kind of drugs."
—Sir Richard Branson

"I would tell people that if you're gonna drink, get it over with in your twenties, because you're just never gonna be any good if you're drinking a lot. You just can't do it."
—Jim Cramer

"I think the key is, Don't lose your way. If you don't have a path, you're just hopping through a series of doing things,

and you might hop into doing some terrible things. But if you have your own path, you're not going to be distracted."
—**Bob Pittman**

"Fame is very addicting. I've had some exposure. I've been on *Oprah,* whatever, the different TV programs. I noticed a desire of wanting more of that. When I'm at the airport and someone says, 'Oh, my God, you're Preston Bailey,' it makes my day. So, you know, the desire is there. I'm not going to deny that. I try to keep it in check, though."
—**Preston Bailey**

20

Keep Your Life in Balance

Cathie Black • Bobbi Brown • David Rockwell • Anna Quindlen • Matt Lauer • Maria Bartiromo • Dr. Mehmet Oz • Phil Lombardo • Joy Behar • Jane Friedman • Dr. Judith Rodin

L IFE KEEPS RUNNING in cycles. There are going to be down days, and there are going to be up days. There will be times that demand everything you've got just to get through them, and times when fortune seems to be smiling on you. By understanding that, you can keep yourself anchored squarely in the center. Swami Satchidananda once said to me that you swing high in one direction, and then high in the other direction, like a pendulum, so that you can live comfortably in the middle.

You're going to live only one life. If you're enjoying what you are doing, you won't mind working really hard and putting in a lot of hours. But if you're logging so many hours that you're out of balance, things can start to go haywire. I frequently have to escape the intensity and magnetic force of New York City. For me, going back to the house where I grew up in Philadelphia helps me find the balance I need. When I return to New York, I feel the energy there in a different way. If I stayed subsumed in the city's powerful vibrations every single day, I'd be out of whack.

I believe that family has got to be, without question, more than 50 percent of your life. Because in the end, what matters is the real stuff in life that we cling to: The people who love you and who are loved by you in return. Your friends. The places and experiences that bring you joy, whether it's listening to music, being in the mountains, playing soccer with your children, whatever. Make sure you have things that can quietly offset the intensity of your work life, and tend to those with equal zeal.

Some participants shared wonderful insights about maintaining life in balance, and what they do to prevent themselves from veering off track. Heed what they say, because as **Cathie Black** so wisely reminded me, no one on his deathbed ever said, "I wish I'd spent more time at the office."

• • •

Bobbi Brown seems to have found just the right formula for herself.

"I think I learned early on how to be happy in my life," Bobbi said. "It was really stressful in the beginning, commuting back and forth, having a young child, and having a husband that went to law school. My husband really taught me to not get caught up in the minutiae. In all the little meetings that I think are a complete waste of time that you have to do when you're in a corporation. I'd go to those meetings, but I figured out how to work from home a couple of days. And those couple of days I worked from home, I would see my trainer, I would do what I needed to do at my kids' school. I'd do the grocery shopping. I'd be walking through the grocery aisle talking on the phone.

"I work seven days a week," she explained. "People who have their own businesses do that. But it's really important for me to time-balance. And I get my best ideas when I'm not in the office.

I get clarity on all the junk that's happening here, you know, when I'm away. When I sit in the office, do you think I get anything done? I don't."

At the end of our interview, Bobbi said something that I think is a fundamental truth:

"A lot of people forget that **the most important thing in life is being happy**. More than success. I know so many successful people who aren't happy. And I know so many people who are not successful who are happy. If you think about it, what would you rather be? So somehow, you've just got to find out what makes you happy."

• • •

David Rockwell neutralizes the intensity of his work life by disengaging from his everyday sensory associations.

"You need to change sceneries," David explained. "Part of relaxing and de-stressing is getting out of the place where you are. Going up to New Paltz on the weekends, mountain biking, hiking. Trees, not buildings. You know, a literal disconnect."

Where or what is *your* personal refuge?

• • •

Anna Quindlen managed to pare down her life to the essentials.

"I have a little sign on a Post-it note right over my computer that says, 'Say no.' I had to put the sign up, because I was bad at that."

—Anna Quindlen

"I say no to most social invitations," Anna said. "I say no to most speaking engagements. For a long time, until very recently,

I said no to every single thing on weekends. We had a zone of absolute purity from Friday afternoon to Monday morning, where all the five of us did was hang out together. And that was inviolate. So it sort of got pared down to the kids and the work, with a few detours along the way for a speech here or a dinner there. And what it's meant is that we haven't had as much face time with friends over the last twenty years as I would normally like to have. But, you know, you find other ways to keep close to people. It just seemed to me that **family came first**."

• • •

Matt Lauer, too, is vigilant about how he allocates his time.

"If the pie graph shows that work has become 80 percent of my focus, that's a very unhealthy situation for me," he said. "It almost needs to be 70/30—30 percent work, the rest family, friends, interests, physical fitness. And over the years, I've become much better at changing those priorities. Before I was married and had kids, I was very much career-focused. I was on that path up, and I was trying to get to that next level. So I focused a lot on it. Then I got married and had kids, and over a period of time—it didn't happen overnight—I reversed those numbers. What keeps me going, and what's allowed me to do ten years of this without burning out in this schedule, I think, is that I don't let it run my life. This is very important to me—I don't define myself by what happens from seven to nine in the morning. I define myself by what happens from nine until seven the next morning."

"So does that mean that along the way you've had to say, 'No, wait, Mr. Executive Producer, I don't want to do all of that,' in order to maintain the balance?" I asked.

"You have to choose when to say that, there's no question," Matt replied. "I mean, there are times when the job dictates that you are there. It dictates when you jump on a plane and fly off to some godforsaken place to get a story. You have to be willing in this job, for competitive reasons, to get up and do that. But you choose your battles. If it won't make that much of a difference if I don't jump on a plane, those are the times where I've learned to say, 'No, family first.'"

It can be a little tricky striking the balance between "doing whatever it takes"—which, as we've seen, is necessary for success—and saying no. In some ways, how far along you are in your career determines where you fall in that continuum. Matt admitted that flipping the ratio of work and family life came a little later, once he had achieved a certain amount of success.

• • •

Between her two television shows, biweekly and monthly columns, contributions to the *Today* show, and frequent industry functions, **Maria Bartiromo**'s work life is so hectic that she has to actually schedule private time for herself.

"I put it in my calendar, 'Seven, stay home, rest. Take bath.' I'll go to my calendar and randomly put that in on different days. 'Stay home. Cook dinner.' I will put this stuff in my calendar so that my assistant knows it's off limits. I can't do a business dinner that night. I have to go home."

Very smart idea. **We schedule everything else; why not schedule personal time to unwind?**

• • •

It is very common for surgeons to burn the candle at both ends. But **Dr. Mehmet Oz** views personal rejuvenation as a requirement.

"The biggest problem we have in medicine is that you don't heal the healer," Mehmet said. "When you take care of somebody, you give him a little bit of your chi—your life energy. You have to regenerate that. If your life energy's on low, you can't give any of it away. Or if you do, you make yourself sick. You know, we're harsh on ourselves. We expect a lot from ourselves. But if you don't reinstill in yourself some of that joy in life, then you start sinking."

He continued: "Folks have the ability to regenerate themselves. For me, having harmony at home is an absolute essential element of being in balance, of reinstilling my own life. Because if I'm not playing with the kids and having them, in a very innocent way, really charge me, I'm not here for you tomorrow as doctor-patient."

If you're not good to yourself, how can you expect to be of service to anyone else?

• • •

There's a wonderful song written by Burt Bacharach and Hal David called "The Balance of Nature." It's all about how nature balances itself out, which is obviously a metaphor for life. Spring follows winter, sunshine tempers the rain, laughter hopefully follows tears. We need to strike a similar balance between the driven parts of our lives and the quieter times if we hope to enjoy the fruits of our considerable labors. After all, isn't that what it's all about?

End Notes

"It's very important to keep a life in balance. I always find it disheartening when people devote so much of their life to one thing and allow the other parts of their life to suffer. If you are capable and determined to have a successful career, successful marriage, successful friendships—if you're organized, you can do it all. If you're not organized, you're gonna pull from one, and that part will suffer."

—Phil Lombardo

"There are certain things I wouldn't do in my career. I wouldn't move to Los Angeles. I really could not stand LA. My life is worth more to me than my career, ultimately."**—Joy Behar**

"If you ask my children, they will say, 'Somehow, our mother was the soccer mom. She came to the cello concerts. She was always there for our friends. Our house was always open.' Now, part of that is that I had the most fantastic woman who came to work for me for three months, and she stayed twenty-six years. That was a great help. She was the constant. But my children always came first. When they were very young—I wasn't always in this position, so I wasn't always out every night—if I had something to do, I used to try to come home and see them, and then go out. And I never, ever did anything from Friday night until Monday morning."

—Jane Friedman

"My husband and I have been a team, together, and I think that's how you balance it. I've always wanted a life outside of my business life. I mean, my business life is very entwined with my personal life. But you know, we enjoy travel. We enjoy people. We enjoy parties. We enjoy people with our kids. We do the soccer stuff. We've done all of that."**—Cathie Black**

"I used to think you could have it all. Now I think, over the years I've learned you can, but you can't have it all simultaneously. Maybe you need to have it all sequentially. And so, there are periods when I'm much more absorbed at work, and don't feel as balanced in my home life. Then I try to err a little on the other side, to pay back."—**Dr. Judith Rodin**

FIVE

Advice For Success

21

Know When to Reassess

Jim Cramer • Richard Johnson • Rikki Klieman • Bobby Flay • Sirio Maccioni

I REALLY BELIEVE no job is worth doing if it isn't fun. I not only believe that, I live by it. I remember sitting on the beach early one morning in Ocean City, New Jersey, just about the time I was turning fifty. I had read a line in a magazine somewhere that said, "Nothing is more precious than this day," and that got me thinking. I realized that my life was going by like a fast train in the night, and I had to make sure I enjoyed every day as best I could.

Within a relatively short period of time after that, I ended a lucrative executive-producing job that I knew in my heart was not well suited for me. I found my way back onto television at WNBC-TV and took the vocal training that enabled me to be ready to sing on stage at cabaret shows, which was an unfulfilled desire of mine.

There will probably be times during the course of your career when you will need to stop and reassess. If the work you are doing is more draining than interesting, if you are getting stonewalled, if you feel burned out, or even if you come to a painful realization that you aren't cut out for that job, there is absolutely nothing wrong with doing an about-face and embracing the challenge of reinventing yourself.

• • •

By the year 2000, **Jim Cramer** was at the pinnacle of his game. By Wall Street standards, he was the ultimate success story. But you don't bring in the kind of money Cramer was without something being sacrificed. It's a trade-off. He was running at maximum speed all day, every day, and his home life and well-being suffered. Not surprisingly, he burned out.

By the age of forty-three, Jim's obsessiveness was at full throttle. He was doing upward of four hundred trades per day, nailing a great percentage of them. But the pace was taking a serious toll. His strength had always been his ferocious energy and ability to consume and remember vast amounts of information, so when his ability started to wane even a little, Jim panicked. "In 1998, I lost a step," he recalled. "That's when I realized, 'Oh, my God. I'm not as good as I was.'"

To compensate, Jim started getting up earlier and earlier. "My experience, I always felt, should have made up for my youth," he said, shaking his head. "But it's a young person's game. And I thought about this. There was this guy I saw on *60 Minutes*. He started taking steroids and drugs because he was losing respect. I always felt I was losing respect every year. So every year, I set the alarm earlier. And then there was just no more time left. There was no more time left."

Beyond the time crunch, Jim also started to lose his sense of why he was driving himself so hard. "Initially I had a sense that I was on a mission. And then I felt the mission getting smaller and smaller as I did the job, and it drove me nuts. I used to sit there at my desk, with all these screens around me. In my third to last year, and my second to last year, and then my last year, saying, 'All I do is this. This is really the sum total of me. I just make a little money at it. But there's got to be something bigger, more interesting, more helpful.'"

Jim admits his self-worth was, rightly or not, tied up in his performance. "The money-management ethos goes, 'If you're not the number one guy, you're just not any good. And if your lowest quarter wasn't any good, you're not any good.' And I actually— much to many other people's chagrin—believed that. I had to get out of the business because I believed that. Finally, I had the best year that I knew of, and I quit. I had to go. I had my year where I knocked the lights out. And I know I had to go, because I can never do it again."

It is the rare class act who actually knows when it is time to exit gracefully. So few have gotten this right, in my opinion. Rocky Marciano retired undefeated. Jim Brown walked off the football field at his peak. Jerry Seinfeld ended his groundbreaking sitcom while he was still number one in the ratings. And Jim Cramer walked into his office shortly after Thanksgiving in 2000 and said, "I don't know what this is gonna be like for me, but I'm outta here.

"A lot of people thought it would kill me," he said, chuckling. "That I would never . . . that that was it. That my persona was that of a hedge-fund manager, and I couldn't be anything else. That was a huge risk that I took. Because I was worried that I'd die."

Jim Cramer didn't die. He reinvented himself as a television personality, and today, he's a far happier man for having done so.

• • •

Long before **Richard Johnson** became New York's gossip king, he came very close to following a career track that was proving financially successful but was miles away from his intended goal of making something of himself in the Big Apple.

Believe it or not, Richard was a carpenter in the Catskill Mountains in upstate New York. He started doing odd jobs and quickly built a reputation as a talented carpenter and contractor. People started coming to him for bigger and bigger jobs, and when he was presented with blueprints for a whole building, he abruptly recognized it was time to make a change.

"It was big," he remembered. "They were treating me like a professional, and it frightened me, because I realized that it was becoming a career. I'd be stuck being a carpenter for the rest of my life. I realized, 'I've got to get out of here, before this gets too cushy.'"

Richard passed on the lucrative project and headed to New York City, where he finished college and started his journalism career as an intern at a small paper called the *Chelsea Clinton News.* Before he'd even finished college, he was made editor-in-chief of that publication. He later made his move to the *New York Post,* and within a short time, his reign at Page Six began.

As Richard's story shows, it can be easy to get lured into work where you're comfortable, doing well, and making money. But if it isn't necessarily your path of choice, it's crucial to **pause and get yourself onto the right track** so you can flourish in a career of your own intention.

• • •

Rikki Klieman wanted to be an actress ever since she was a little girl. She appeared in local roles when she was young, including playing Peter Pan on stage at the age of twelve, and later went to Northwestern University to study theater. Rikki knew she had a good degree of talent, but then a surprising realization changed the course of her entire life.

"I remember going to an audition at Northwestern in my soph-omore year, for *A Man for All Seasons,*" Rikki said. "And a young woman freshman named Shelley Long happened to come in. And she read for the same part I did, which was the daughter, I think, of Sir Thomas More. I remember sitting in the audience waiting to read, thinking, 'I can't do this nearly as well as she just did.' I wasn't jealous of her. I was admiring of her. But I had a moment where I said, 'I'm not that good.'

"It was a very strange moment," Rikki continued. "I mean, it physically left me queasy. What am I, nineteen at that point? And I'm saying, 'I've wanted to be a performer since I'm four.'"

That jolt didn't quite deter Rikki—yet.

"I went to New York after college and continued in the theatrical world. I went to an open call for the movie *The Godfather*. I got off an elevator in a big building, and there were two hundred of me. We were all five foot two to five foot ten, Mediterranean types. I had to go in the line, and wait until I made it through the line. Going there, I thought, 'This is my big break.' I was going to be Apollonia, Michael Corleone's love interest who gets blown up in the fire in Sicily. I was perfect. I had long black hair you could sit on. But when I saw that there were a couple of hundred of me, I started to listen to the conversations on line. Everyone was saying, 'Oh, I've played Ophelia; I was in *Hair* on Broadway; I was in yada yada yada.' And I realized, as the line snaked around to get in the door, that all these people were out of work. Every one.

"I went inside to do my little reading," Rikki continued. "And all they really wanted to do is look at you, you know? I don't even know if I read a line. And I said as I exited that audition, 'I could be doing this for the next twenty years, the same thing.' Not only was I not going to be the best, I didn't know if I was going to get work.

"So I took myself home to my apartment, and I said, 'I've got to get out of here. I've got to really figure out what to do with my life.' I was twenty-four. I had wanted to be an actress for twenty years. That's a major life crisis at twenty-four. Oh, my God, every thing I've ever wanted . . . everything I've ever directed myself toward . . . I can't do this. Because I'm going to be waiting tables and being a temporary secretary until I'm sixty-four, trying to get my break. I am not doing this."

Realizing that acting was not her route to success or to the financial security she knew she needed was very painful for Rikki. Up until then, she'd been convinced this was her path. Now her world as she knew it had to be completely redefined.

"How did you sort it out?" I asked.

"I went to see a professor of mine from Northwestern, with whom I had done a lot of work in the debate/communication world," she said. "I told him the stories. He said, 'You know, you took this course with me on the First Amendment. You did very well. Why don't you think about going to law school?' and I said, 'Professor, girls don't go to law school.'"

"You really said that?"

"I did," she said, nodding. "And he answered, 'No, but women do.' And it's one of the moments that changed my life."

That's how Rikki realized that she could do something else that she had never even considered. She took the LSAT, went to law school, and eventually became one of the country's leading trial attorneys (which, she notes, is another form of performance). Eventually, she was discovered by Steve Brill of Court TV and offered a job combining her two passions.

It takes real courage to admit that something in which you've invested time and energy isn't going to work out. If you find yourself in this position, **trust your instincts**—you likely know deep down when it's time to let go and pursue something else that will take you where you really want to go.

• • •

Sometimes what we think is a good idea at the outset turns out not to be. Then we're faced with a choice: follow through no matter what, or cut our losses and move on.

With the success of Mesa Grill under his belt, **Bobby Flay** opened another restaurant called Mesa City. It was a downscale version of Mesa Grill, opened with hopes that thirty more could be rolled out across the country.

"We had it for about a year and a half," Bobby said. "But I hated it. I hated it, because it wasn't really about food. It was more about business. We sort of dumbed down the food from Mesa Grill, and all the customers were saying, 'We want Mesa Grill.' I was like, 'This is not Mesa Grill. It's Mesa City. It's another concept; it's less expensive.'"

The restaurant was making money, but Bobby despised going there. "I would say it was somewhere between a failure and a sense of, 'I don't want to do this anymore.' I sold the restaurant on a street corner one day. Literally."

He really did. On the street one day, Bobby ran into Steve Shields, the person who had owned the original space. Steve mentioned they were looking for a new space. Bobby sold him Mesa City on the spot.

The press screamed failure, but more than anything else, Bobby was relieved to be rid of the place. He could have hung on, but why do that? Remember, **No job is worth doing if it isn't fun**.

• • •

As best as you can, try to avoid getting caught on the slippery slope of momentum taking you in the wrong direction—even if the money and perks are good. Le Cirque's dedicated owner, **Sirio Maccioni**, rightly said that **if you're not giving something 100 percent, you're just wasting your time**. Don't kid yourself. If you know you're not giving your work your all and you're not having the fun you should be having, it's time to look around and make that next quantum leap.

22

Use What You've Got

Joseph Abboud • Preston Bailey • Maria Bartiromo • Joy Behar • Cathie Black • James Blake • Sir Richard Branson • Bobbi Brown • Peter Cincotti • Jim Cramer • Mario Cuomo • Christie Hefner • Senator Kay Bailey Hutchison • Richard Johnson • Matt Lauer • Phil Lombardo • Jeff Lurie • Sirio Maccioni • Craig Newmark • Bill O'Reilly • Dr. Mehmet Oz • Tom Perkins • Anna Quindlen • Diane von Furstenberg • Renée Zellweger

THE QUESTION that seemed to be the most difficult and, in some ways, uncomfortable for people to answer was this: "How do you think your looks—your personal appearance—have helped or hindered you in your career?" The responses varied from interesting to poignant to funny.

"I think we're all insecure about our looks one way or another. You know, I'm certainly no movie star, but I always figured presentation was important. Back in high school I had my little zone. You know, I wasn't the most athletic, I wasn't the best looking, but I was the best dressed. I wanted to be more attractive. I think fashion, in a certain way, can make people more appealing."

—Joseph Abboud

"I hope it helped. I think it helped. Being a tall black man, I think certain people are intimidated by it a little bit. Certain people respond to it in a positive way. Men tend to be weird about it, considering they don't know where I'm coming from. The husbands—it's a harder sell for me."

—Preston Bailey

"I think it's been a positive. And I'm not afraid of that. On the one hand, maybe important people would rather have lunch with me than another guy in a suit and tie. So, having said that, I think particularly in business news, you cannot fool your viewer, and you cannot fool your source. Because in many cases, they're smarter than you. And so if you don't know your stuff, and you don't understand the content, you won't last. So, sure, looks can definitely be helpful. But there's a point where you're going to stay, or not. And that's it."

—Maria Bartiromo

"I think that if you talk to all comedians, they're not necessarily unloved. I don't think that's true. We all have something that was off. Either the nose, you're fat, your hair. Always something about you that is not Cheryl Tiegs. I have a funny sort of croaky expression on my face. My voice is wacky."

—Joy Behar

"I would say that it is just part of my confidence. But it's not what I've ever sold myself on. There are very sexy women, in provocative clothing; that's just never been my shtick. You know, some of them have been very successful. But I always wanted to be viewed as a professional. Now I'm in a much more glamorous industry, so I can go out at night looking great, with makeup, done in a fabulous designer outfit, but it's not my calling card, if you know what I mean."

—Cathie Black

"I think possibly coming out of college, looks might have helped with my contracts, with people possibly seeing an upside of being marketable. Tennis players are very visible—football you've got a helmet on, hockey you've got a helmet on, baseball you wear a cap—so people end up relating to you. Throughout a whole match—it could be four hours—they see you a lot. So I think Nike realized that I was someone who, if I had success on the court, could be marketable. But as you improve and start putting up results, I don't think it makes much of a difference."

—James Blake

"I think maybe smiles help more than pure looks. I enjoy life a lot. I smile a lot. And I think that, perhaps, has helped."

—Sir Richard Branson

"That's a hard question to answer. Hmm. How do you say this? I've always felt good about my looks. My classic, simple style, I think, definitely works well with my brand. And my brand is me."

—Bobbi Brown

"Looks are subjective. Sometimes they work for you and sometimes they don't. So far, I think my look is working for me, but in the music industry today, there seems to be so much emphasis on looks. To me, music and looks have nothing to do with each other."

—Peter Cincotti

"Until now, they've hindered. Because I'm not, you know, a handsome anchorman. But now, I look like the guy that I should be. I'm like this kind of, you know, brainy, enthusiastic fan. That's what he looks like. At the hedge fund, it didn't matter. I was just in the office. But this job, I look like this guy. I mean, this is what you want this guy to look like. I think that if I were a pretty boy, it would hurt me."

—Jim Cramer

"My looks helped me by winning me sympathy. I'm serious. I was governor for twelve years, and I had to do it with this face. There's something about not being a dazzling good-looking person that puts some people at ease. You know? I can't tell you how many times I got offers of eye operations to get rid of the bags under my eyes.

"And there were times when looks were not helpful. You hear this, and you don't like hearing it. Almost always, you turn somebody off. There's something about you. You get up there, you look like a big guy, you've got big hands, you look very ethnic . . . and somebody says, 'I don't like this guy. He looks like a tough guy.'

"I remember my mother watching Jacob Javits, who was one of my favorite politicians. She saw him, and his eyes were always moving. And I said to her in Italian, 'You know, this man's very good.' And she said, 'No, I wouldn't vote for him.' I asked why, and she said, 'Look, the eyes.' So they see something in it."

—Mario Cuomo

"Whether we like it or not, ours is a society in which people tend to extend themselves more toward people who are more attractive than less attractive. There's been plenty of research done that shows that from the job interview to getting help in a store, it's harder for people who are overweight. And I'm sure that was amplified somewhat by the fact that Playboy is a company that celebrates beauty. So having an attractive woman running the company was very interesting to people. I think it made me a more appealing spokesperson for the company."

—Christie Hefner

"I think it was when I ran for Congress—which was a race I lost—that there was an article about my candidacy, which was a very unusual one at the time, because women weren't running for Congress very much. And it described me as "passably pretty." And I thought, you know, sometimes my looks have hurt, because they have tended to make it harder for me to establish my credibility."

—Senator Kay Bailey Hutchison

"Oh, I'm sure they've helped. I think for a gossip columnist, it's very important to get invited places. And I think people generally would prefer to have pretty people at their parties."

—Richard Johnson

"When you refer to 'your looks,' I don't embrace it as 'good looks.' I look at is as, just, your looks.

"Early on, I don't think they hurt me, I don't think they helped me. I think it was a neutral factor. During that period of time where I was losing a lot of jobs, I think it was very much a double-edged sword. At that time, I had very much of a slicked-back hairstyle-of-the-decade look. And what I used to hear was that people would like me when they met me—the executives—and they'd hire me. And then all of a sudden the ratings wouldn't be good. I've heard more times than I can tell you that the research would come back that I was too slick—that my suits were a little too nice, my hair was too coiffed. They even said that I came off as too young and slick. So I think at that particular time, my looks hurt me.

"And then in some weird ways, one aspect of my looks was a good thing in my career, not that long ago. When I started to lose my hair, and I embraced it and cut my hair off, I had no idea it would become the thing it did. I can't tell you the number of guys who came up to me on the street and said, 'Hey, thanks. Look at this.' And they'd point to their head and they'd have that short cut. They'd go, 'I was losing it, and I was doing everything to hide it. Thanks for making it okay.' So I think that helped me. It made me a little more reachable to some people."

—Matt Lauer

"I think they've helped. Take advantage of your assets. You know, your personality is an asset, your appearance is an asset, but a lot of people squander that . . . sometimes the people who are the most attractive are the laziest, because they are trying to get by on their attractiveness. And they squander it, and that's a shame. Because when you've got the combination of a good mind and a good appearance, then you've got two assets working for you."

—Phil Lombardo

"I don't know, I don't know. I do know that I was always able to buy beer in college 'cuz I had gray hair early. So that made me popular with my peers. But besides that—oh, God, I have no idea."

—Jeff Lurie

"In the beginning they helped. Now they hurt."

—Sirio Maccioni

"I really don't know. I mean, apparently, ever since Jason Alexander, four or five years ago, made *People* magazine's Sexiest Man Alive, I've been able to take big advantage of that. But that's about it."

—Craig Newmark

"It's important on television to be presentable. You don't have to be gorgeous. You have to be presentable. And you've got to keep yourself in shape. People want to see people who they can emulate in some way."

—Bill O'Reilly

"There's no question that physical appearances have their bearing. The first impression is a valuable one. But it's a very short-lived one. Physical attractiveness helps, but there are plenty of people in the media who are not that attractive or beautiful on the inside, and that comes through after a while."

—Dr. Mehmet Oz

"Well, I think you'd like to say it hasn't made any difference at all. But I don't think that's true. Up until recent years, I've always been taller than most people. Reasonably presentable, I guess. My father taught me to dress well—carefully, neat and clean, and all those things. And I think it helps. I don't think there's any doubt about it. I think we're all susceptible to that."

—Tom Perkins

"I think my looks have had virtually no effect at all on my career, except to the extent that I think I look like a generic woman of a certain sort. And that means that for a lot of people, I've been relatable to in a way that worked. You know, no one looks at me and thinks, 'God, if I were that thin and blond, I could write a best-selling novel, too.' There's a sense that people identify with me, that I think has been useful for readers of my work. But you know, on balance, no big up, no big down."

—Anna Quindlen

"Since I'm in fashion, the fact that I could wear my clothes, and I have good legs, helps. As a designer, one of the things that I always say is, 'Feel like a woman.' So, I think it's very important, if you are a woman, to take advantage of the asset that it offers. And I highly recommend it."

—Diane von Furstenberg

"I think that I'm exactly what I needed to be in order to do what I need to do in this life. That's what I think. I think if I were just a little bit more of anything, I would have failed miserably at a lot of things."

—Renée Zellweger

23

Industry Advice from the Pros

Joseph Abboud • Preston Bailey • Maria Bartiromo • Joy Behar • James Blake • Daniel Boulud • Sir Richard Branson • Bobbi Brown • Jim Cramer • Clive Davis • Bobby Flay • Jane Friedman • Matt Lauer • Phil Lombardo • Marco Maccioni • Craig Newmark • Bill O'Reilly • Tom Perkins • Bob Pittman • Frank Rich • David Rockwell • Brooke Shields • Joe Torre • Donald Trump • Diane Warren • Renée Zellweger • Jeff Zucker

T HE FINAL QUESTION I asked at each of the interviews was, "What do you say to someone who wants to make it in your specific field?" All of the answers are rich in insight, no matter what your goals might be.

• • •

"If you're going to be creating a fashion business, you absolutely have to have a point of view. But you also have to have something I teach in class, called a point of difference. If you wanted to launch a men's clothing collection, you can't say, 'I want to be another Ralph Lauren. I want to be another Giorgio Armani.' You have to have something to say. And that's the POD factor: the point of difference. You've got to come into the market with something that doesn't exist. But you also have to do it intellectually. You have to be commercial, you have to say, 'Well, can it work?' It's not just art for art's sake."—**Joseph Abboud, clothing designer**

"It sounds so simple and basic, but get into your client's head. You have to. Be aware of the finances. People hesitate to talk about finances. But because it's an entertaining business, usually after the party's over, the client forgets about it. Make sure the finances are clear.

"And do your best. This is not like the theater. It's a one-shot deal, and you've got to get it right. Be prepared that something's going to screw up, and plan how to back it up."—**Preston Bailey, event planner**

"Don't go into a profession for the money. I didn't go into journalism for the money. Nobody goes into journalism for the money. You go because you love it, and that's what I did. I love it. You must love what you do.

"I also think, equally important, is do the right thing. Because your reputation will always follow you. Don't *try* to do the right thing. Just do it. We all know in our hearts, when we're faced with a situation, this is the right thing, this is not the right thing. Do the right thing."—**Maria Bartiromo, television journalist**

"Number one, be yourself. Number two, show up. Just go to as many things as you can. Number three, work hard.

"One of the things about being a stand-up is that you have to work hard. There were times when I would do six sets in one night.

I'd go from the Improv to Greene Street, to Catch a Rising Star, to Folk City—I would do six sets in one night. Every time I would get up on stage, I would learn something, and I would add to the material."—**Joy Behar, comedienne and talk show co-host**

"If you're up high in juniors and in college, I think when you do make that transition to the pros, you've got to put all the rest of that behind you and not think about any results you had in juniors or college. Because that means nothing to any of the pros out there. It doesn't guarantee success. If anything, I think more people who have done really well in juniors haven't had as much success in the pros because they get ahead of themselves. A lot of their time and energy was spent worrying about wins when they were young, as opposed to improving. No matter how many wins you have when you're young, they don't carry over to the pros. So you've got to manage to figure out ways to improve. If you come on tour, no matter how good you were in juniors, it's not gonna be good enough for the pros right away. You've got to kind of pay your dues, and understand that it's really about improvement at that age, when you're making that transition. The guys are too good to just beat them with a reputation, or beat them with your name."—**James Blake, professional tennis player**

"The most successful chef is the one who has his mind open totally to what's happening in the industry. Also, travel is so important to a chef, so he can observe, experience, and learn from every cuisine. But he has to choose one, where he's going to excel."

—**Daniel Boulud, chef and restaurateur**

"Follow your passion—your hobby, maybe. There's no point in being an entrepreneur just for being an entrepreneur's sake.

"Try to protect the downside. For instance, when we set up

Virgin Atlantic, I had a record company. And I did a deal with Boeing so that I could hand the plane back at the end of the first twelve months if it didn't work out. So it wasn't going to bring the whole Virgin name down; I protected the bounce-back.

"Small is beautiful. If your company starts growing too large, break it in two. And if it starts growing large again, break it in four. Lots of small groups of people, I think, are much better. People always much prefer working for small companies than big companies.

"And be born under a lucky star. You're gonna need a bit of luck."—**Sir Richard Branson, entrepreneur**

"Well, certainly, you have to be nice. That's the first thing. Because people don't forget. You've got to be kind.

"You have to be talented. And if you're not talented, you'd better be a sponge. You'd better assist as many people as you can, and try to learn. That is probably the number one lesson. I never stop learning. I still learn from my artists. I learn all the time.

"Don't complain, and just do as much as you can, and as much for free. And just never give up. You have to keep going. You will totally make it, whatever it is. You might not have a *Vogue* cover, but you'll make it in some way.

"Drink a lot of water. Eat really healthy. And just go for it."

—**Bobbi Brown, makeup artist**

"I would tell people that they must be willing to put their neck on the line and say up or down. So many people I would deal with say, 'Well, on the one hand; on the other . . .'' I want direction in place. I want someone who's got the conviction of his views. I want someone who can cut losses very quickly, recognize when he's wrong and then admit it. Apologize, and not have any second-guessing. You need all that to be good in this business."—**Jim Cramer, television journalist and stock analyst**

"You've got to love music, because it's all-consuming. You can't do it unless you're committed to it as a passion. You're going to be spending X-hours a week in work. You can only consider music if you just can't get enough of it."—**Clive Davis, music industry executive**

"You have to know your subject matter. A lot of times they'll bring in hosts to do things that have nothing to do with the subject matter, and you can tell that that person is just being a host. Knowledge is such an important part of the power of this. I can pick up a lemon and talk to you about it for forty-five minutes. I really could. If somebody's just a host, after 'It's tart and yellow,' it's gonna get tough. Know your subject—that comfort level is really important."—**Bobby Flay, chef and television personality**

"I think that the most important thing for everybody is focus. The most important thing about a career, going up the ladder, is make sure you don't lose focus. You know, don't go out of scope. Figure out what it is that you want, and go directly toward that. And do everything you can to make it happen.

"If you want to be an editor, read other people's books. Share your thoughts on their books. Have community. Make friends. Make sure that you compliment people; they'll compliment you. It's a whole mechanism that I think is very important to one's future."—**Jane Friedman, publisher**

"This particular industry is one that forces you to develop a thick skin. If you're knocking on doors, or you're getting some jobs that are not leading in the right direction, and you're getting panned every once in a while and knocked back a couple of steps, you have to decide early on whether this is something you can tolerate for the long haul. Because it's not going to be eliminated from the business. Even today, people take shots at me. So, develop a thick skin or get out of this particular business."—**Matt Lauer, television host**

"You're going to get your better opportunities in a smaller market. If you think you come out of college and move to New York, and you're gonna be King of New York, it just isn't gonna happen. So I always went down in market size in order to move up. And I would take pay cuts. As long as I had the opportunity, it didn't make any difference."—**Phil Lombardo, television station owner and general manager**

"How to make it in the restaurant business? All right. Have a complete and total passion. Make the restaurant a complete and total partner. The restaurant business is a social partner in its own. So, you're gonna have a wife and a husband. And in between, there's something called a restaurant. You have to do it at 100 percent."

   —**Marco Maccioni, restaurateur**

"Read *Dilbert*. It's exaggerated, but it's fundamentally true."

   —**Craig Newmark, founder of Craigslist.com**

"In any kind of field—it doesn't have to be broadcasting—you've got to be prepared to have your feelings hurt. Most kids, as soon as somebody hurts their feelings, they fall apart. You've got to develop a shell if you're going into a competitive field."—**Bill O'Reilly, television journalist**

"I think to go into venture capital now and attempt to do what we did back in 1972 is impossible. I think people like ourselves have just made it too difficult. We have too big a network, too many contacts. So I think these days, to go into venture capital, you almost have to work for a firm like ours, and work your way into the business. And maybe later, you can branch out."—**Tom Perkins, venture capitalist**

"I think one of the big mistakes is when people put a lot of emphasis on networking. I always say, 'Why are you networking?' What's it going to do for you? You're going to expose yourself to a lot of people before you're ready to. What you really want them to notice is your accomplishments, not your networking. If you meet somebody too early, they're always going to think of you as a kid, even if later you've accomplished great things. Wait until you've accomplished something. Then they meet you and they're interested in you—you have something to say and you have a real reason to network."—**Bob Pittman, media executive**

"I tell kids I meet who are talented, practice. Just keep doing it. Wherever you can write something, do it. It doesn't matter where it's published, or even *if* it's published. Just keep writing. It's like anything else. It's like sports, it's like music, it's like acting. It's like giving speeches and becoming a politician. Practice may not make perfect, but it helps."—**Frank Rich, newspaper columnist**

"Really pay attention to what you're passionate about, and don't get that beaten out of you by people telling you what you should be passionate about. Grab any opportunity, no matter how small, to start to exercise your craft and your art. And find the opportunity to engage, and make some mistakes, and take some risks and do the work. Don't get seduced by the fact that architecture is the work of an auteur. Architecture is a teamwork endeavor, and figuring out how to collaborate is critically important."—**David Rockwell, architect**

"Don't give up easily. That's the first thing. You know, if you give up, you go into the ether, in anything. I think that you have to find a reason why you want to fight to achieve whatever it is you want to achieve. Then find the people in your field who you think are the best, and find out why. How. Find out what they did. Learn as much as you possibly can about whatever it is you want to do. Try to watch the best."—**Brooke Shields, actress**

"Basically, commit yourself to what you're doing. Commit to each other. People don't do this for me. They do it for their teammates. And they don't have to like their teammates. But I'd like to believe everybody in this game is in this game because they want to win."—**Joe Torre, professional baseball team manager**

"1. You have to love what you're doing and have a passion for it.
"2. Know everything you can about what you're doing.
"3. Be tenacious.
"4. Learn to negotiate.
"5. Be a visionary."

> —**Donald Trump, real estate mogul and television personality**

"You have to have talent, but after that, you have to work harder than everybody else, because everything's competitive. You have to know how to make the most of the talent you have."—**Diane Warren, songwriter**

"Be certain it's the *doing* that interests you, because that's all there is. Make sure it's the work itself that interests you—that it's not your perception of what it is that you might get as a result. You're going to be perpetually disappointed if going and having a really great audition isn't good enough for you. Because you could have twenty years of that. And if it's satisfying to you—if you're happy with the doing—you'll never fail. Never."—**Renée Zellweger, actress**

"Love what you're doing. Work hard. Be confident. Don't do it for the glamour of show business. And did I say, have fun?"

—Jeff Zucker, television executive

• • •

My mission in creating this book was to do work that would be valuable to you, my reader. I did my best to use my skills as an interviewer to extract insights, experiences, and wisdom from these leaders in their field to benefit you. If only one sentence, thought, or story you've read here takes root and makes your life and your career more fulfilling, I've achieved my goal.

Thank you for reading my book. Good luck, and remember my dad's commandment, "You're only going to get out of it what you put into it." And let me add one of my own: Do everything you can to make the most of each day, because that day will never return to you.

Have fun,
Bill

Acknowledgments

Many people deserve a round of applause for their direct help, assistance, and encouragement with this book.

First, a standing ovation to Debra Goldstein for her assistance in both the writing and the organization of the book. Her sunny disposition and unfailing optimism fit the project, and her will to prevail—which was evidenced when a tornado struck her house in New Jersey a few days before our deadline—rivals the resolve displayed by any of those interviewed here.

And while I'm on my feet, a big hand to Leslie Bennetts, who helped me get the project on track at the beginning.

As the book took shape, I also benefited enormously from the advice and conceptual acumen of my editor at Collins, Toni Sciarra, and my agent, David Kuhn, at Kuhn Projects.

J. T. Parson did a brilliant job typing transcripts from hours and hours of my audio tape interviews, and her help in countless other ways makes this book possible. My son Trevor's input about interview subjects and the tone of the book was valuable from start to finish.

My appreciation goes to Harry Higgins, Susan Magrino, Lois Smith, Ann Wooster, Dr. Jonathan LaPook, and Adam Leibner for helping me contact interview subjects. Also, gratitude to The Friars Club of New York for support all along the way. Peter Martin, owner of New York's Triad Theater, contributed by providing an open-ended run for my Off-Broadway show, *Talk Show Confidential*. Over the years, many in the Triad audience who have seen the show said, "you should write a book about this." Well, here it is.

In large and small ways, the encouragement and guidance of these people aided this effort—Steve and Sherry Dershimer, Harvey Lapp, Joe D'Antony, Richard Baker, Jim Korris, Andy Regal, John Lack, Joe Amiel, Diana Lewis, Dr. Robert Levine, Craig Neier, Jeffrey Moss and Rich Gore.

Thank you to Joe Tessitore, group president of Collins, for his enthusiasm for the book, and all of his help since I first sketched out my idea for the project over lunch. I appreciate the talent, hard work, and innovative ideas that have helped me from the rest of the team at HarperCollins as well.

Of course, I am enormously grateful to all of those whom I interviewed. I thank them for sitting down with me, sometimes in the middle of very busy days, to focus on their lives and tell me their stories.

Finally, a kiss to my loving wife Carol, whose encouragement, support, guidance, and ideas both steadied and inspired me every step of the way.

Index